KUTCHINSKY'S EGG

KUTCHINSKY'S EGG

A FAMILY STORY OF LOVE, LOSS AND OBSESSION

SERENA KUTCHINSKY

GALLERY BOOKS UK

London · New York · Amsterdam/Antwerp · Sydney/Melbourne · Toronto · New Delhi

First published in Great Britain by Gallery Books,
an imprint of Simon & Schuster UK Ltd, 2026

Copyright © Serena Kutchinsky, 2026

The right of Serena Kutchinsky to be identified as the author of this work has
been asserted in accordance with the Copyright, Designs and Patents Act, 1988.

1 3 5 7 9 10 8 6 4 2

Simon & Schuster UK Ltd, 1st Floor
222 Gray's Inn Road, London WC1X 8HB

For more than 100 years, Simon & Schuster has championed authors and the
stories they create. By respecting the copyright of an author's intellectual property, you enable
Simon & Schuster and the author to continue publishing exceptional books for years to come.
We thank you for supporting the author's copyright
by purchasing an authorised edition of this book.

No amount of this book may be reproduced or stored in any format, nor may it be uploaded
to any website, database, language-learning model, or other repository, retrieval, or artificial
intelligence system without express permission. All rights reserved. Enquiries may be directed
to Simon & Schuster, 222 Gray's Inn Road, London WC1X 8HB or RightsMailbox@
simonandschuster.co.uk

www.simonandschuster.co.uk
www.simonandschuster.com.au
www.simonandschuster.co.in

Simon & Schuster Australia, Sydney
Simon & Schuster India, New Delhi

The authorised representative in the EEA is Simon & Schuster Netherlands BV,
Herculesplein 96, 3584 AA Utrecht, Netherlands. info@simonandschuster.nl

The author and publishers have made all reasonable efforts to contact
copyright-holders for permission, and apologise for any omissions or errors in
the form of credits given. Corrections may be made to future printings.

Simon & Schuster strongly believes in freedom of expression and stands against censorship in all
its forms. For more information, visit BooksBelong.com.

A CIP catalogue record for this book is available from the British Library

Hardback ISBN: 978-1-3985-3284-7
Trade Paperback ISBN: 978-1-3985-3285-4
eBook ISBN: 978-1-3985-3286-1

Photograph on Pg.iii © Rio Tinto. Used by permission. Courtesy of Rio Tinto.

Typeset in Bembo by M Rules
Printed and Bound in the UK using 100% Renewable Electricity
at CPI Group (UK) Ltd

For Brenda,
who taught me that all that glitters is not gold.

Contents

Preface 1

1. The Promise 11
2. The Journey 27
3. The East End 44
4. The Secret 60
5. The Golden Age 86
6. The Escape 101
7. The Rise 123
8. Riding High 144
9. The Deal 171
10. The Creation 186
11. The Mission 211
12. The Grand Tour 226
13. The Sale 253
14. 'The Garden' 276
15. The Call 301
16. The Finding 319
17. City of Ghosts 341

Notes 355
Acknowledgements 357

Main Characters

Benjamin Hersh Kutchinsky (Kuczynski) and Leah Marmenstein
Parents of Moshe (Morris) and Frimit (Fanny).

Moshe Arron Kutchinsky and Hannah Wetzlar
Parents of Henry, Solomon (Solly), Gertrude and Joseph (Jo).

Joseph (Jo) Kutchinsky and Lily Diamond
Parents of Roger and Paul.

Solomon (Solly) Kutchinsky and Hella Thaler
Parents of Danny and Joshua.

Roger Nicholas Kutchinsky and Yvette Elder
Parents of Tanya and Natasha.

Paul Samuel Kutchinsky and Brenda Bruce Strachan
Parents of Serena, Katrina, and Hollie.

Philippa and Nick Cooper
Philippa: Brenda's best friend;
Nick: Paul's close friend.

Len Sanitt
Co-founder of the Sanitt & Stein workshop, which manufactured jewellery exclusively for Kutchinsky during its heyday.

Nat and Peter Stein
Nat: business partner of Len Sanitt; Peter: son of Nat, later ran Sanitt & Stein with Gerald Earle.

Anna Vainer (née Powell)
Former partner and business partner of Paul.

Vainer Family
Milos Vainer founded M Vainer Ltd, a Hatton Garden diamond dealership, and was father of Richard and Martin Vainer who linked Argyle with the House of Kutchinsky.

David O'Connor
David was the former Kutchinsky head of sales.

Leo de Vroomen
Dutch goldsmith whose manufacturing firm, De Vroomen Alexander, were commissioned to make the egg.

Nasser and Ferri Ghahramani
Nasser Ghahramani was a Kutchinsky salesman who accompanied the egg to Tokyo. Married to Ferri, a close friend of Brenda.

Alisa Moussaieff
Long-time owner and managing director of Moussaieff Jewellers. Bought the House of Kutchinsky in 1991.

Terry Walker
Friend of Paul's from his tennis holidays in Antigua.

Tadashi Kageyama (Tad)
Senior Managing Director, Forensic Investigations and Intelligence for Kroll (Singapore). He helped Serena locate the egg.

Preface

The man with the golden egg

BBC Television Centre, 2 May 1990

'Who would spend seven million pounds on an egg?'

The question echoes around the TV studio. The audience is silent, uncertain how to respond. At home, 6 million people are watching.

Terry Wogan, Britain's favourite chat show host, smiles knowingly down the lens of the camera. His brown eyes twinkle. 'Seven million pounds,' he repeats in his Irish brogue. 'And you can't even eat it.'

The audience laughs. A heckler shouts that he'd offer a fiver for it. The live band strikes up. At the back of the studio, two burly bodyguards stand silhouetted. The egg's diamond-studded shell sparkles under the bright lights.

'It was no silly goose that laid this, the world's biggest golden egg.'

Wogan is dressed in his chat show best of a mismatching tweed blazer and beige chinos with a bright burgundy tie. He gestures towards the giant jewelled object, his voice infused with pantomime-style levels of excitement.

'And let's welcome the man who made it,' Wogan says smoothly. 'Paul Kutchinsky.'

Polite applause escalates into cheers and even whoops as the tinkly show music reaches a crescendo. Two grey chairs are set up on either side of the egg. With the bodyguards hovering in the background, the studio suddenly feels more like a scene from a James Bond movie than a BBC chat show.

My father saunters out, beaming from ear to ear. His shiny new loafers glide across the studio floor and he stretches his arm out towards Terry to steady himself. Paul might not have the celebrity status of the other guests, but he is at ease in the spotlight. With his unruly mane, slender build and gold-rimmed glasses, he looks a bit like a mad professor.

The camera zooms in on the egg atop its golden pedestal. At 2-feet tall, it's the size of a small child. Its surface shimmers with thousands of pink diamonds, casting shadows across the studio floor. Its heavy gold shell is open to reveal the first of its surprises: a glittering miniature library topped by a tiny diamond clock.

Paul can feel the buzz of the whisky he downed backstage. Packed into the green room alongside the crooner Engelbert Humperdinck and the champion boxer Nigel Benn – the night's star turn – he'd felt suddenly invisible and snuck off to his dressing room for a hit from his hip flask. After taking a swig, he'd closed his eyes and rested the flask against his sticky forehead.

The past few days have been a whirlwind, and the enormity

PREFACE

of what's happening is only just sinking in. His lifelong ambition is being realised – but somehow, alongside the elation, he feels piercing darts of dread.

The egg is everywhere. On display in a museum. Splashed across the pages of national newspapers. Starring on breakfast TV. Suddenly, everyone wants to know who these London jewellers called Kutchinsky are. The press is comparing Paul to the legendary Carl Fabergé, whose ornate jewelled eggs won him the patronage of Russia's last tsars in the late nineteenth century. Just that morning, a letter had arrived from the Guinness World Records confirming the status of Kutchinsky's egg as the world's largest jewelled egg.

Still, it was a struggle to get a slot on *Wogan*. In 1990, there were only four channels on British television and this show was one of the BBC's most popular programmes. Paul had resorted to turning up at BBC Television Centre in West London with his multi-million-pound egg concealed in Harrods shopping bags. Once he'd persuaded the producers to let him on air, he'd called his wife in a panic, asking her to buy him a new suit and shoes.

Then he'd called his father to tell him to record tonight's programme. I imagine the response was characteristically curmudgeonly. Along the lines of, 'Your mother will want to watch it, I suppose,' before the line went dead.

The cameras are now rolling, and the chat show host is standing over the egg, fiddling with its controls. 'How do I turn this thing on?' The jeweller leaps out of his chair, flicks a switch and settles back down, smiling proudly, as the egg spins seductively. As the two men watch, its jewelled library is replaced by a portrait gallery filled with exquisite blue enamel frames, ringed with ribbons of diamonds, waiting to be filled with the future owner's family photographs.

'Look at that,' marvels the host – just the faintest hint of sarcasm in his voice – 'going round in all its sparkling glory.'

Peering intently at his guest, Wogan pauses, as if the question had just occurred to him.

'How long did it take you to make this, Paul?'

Paul smiles and gives the short answer: 'From the drawing board to completion, two years. First, you sketch it, then you make a model in brass. About forty of Britain's finest craftsmen were involved in the process at some stage,' he says, puffing out his chest.

He could go into more detail. He could explain how the idea of making 'the egg to end all eggs' had obsessed him for well over a decade. How he'd first sketched it on a hotel napkin after a drunken night out. How finding the craftsmen with the right skills to build it had been the biggest challenge of his career. But he holds back.

'And why did you decide to make it?' Wogan asks.

Paul fixes his eyes on his creation as it glistens under the studio lights. A joke, inspired by recent political events, pops into his head: 'To be truthful, Terry, the Egg Marketing Board was having a rough time after the salmonella crisis so we thought we'd give them a helping hand.'

His laugh is nervous and seal-like. The audience chuckles politely.

'Does Edwina Currie know about this egg?'

'I've written and told her all about it,' Paul bats back.

A couple of years earlier, in 1988, Edwina Currie, a government health minister, was forced to resign after sparking

PREFACE

fears of an egg-based food poisoning epidemic. It had been a serious matter; should he really be making jokes about it on national TV?

Paul fidgets, crossing and uncrossing his legs, aware his joke is wearing thin. 'We're very pleased with it,' he says, casting a loving glance at the egg.

'It's a stunning thing,' says Wogan, adopting an awestruck tone. 'Hang on, I'll start it again,' he adds, noticing that the egg has stopped turning. Bending down, the presenter fumbles with its hidden controls. Nothing happens. This is the moment Paul had feared most, that the egg's secret would be revealed in all its vulnerability on live television. He had gotten away with it so far, but was his luck about to run out?

'I think I pressed the wrong button,' Wogan murmurs, furrowing his brow. Leaping out of his chair, Paul forgets everything the producers have told him about where the cameras are. His back briefly fills the screen.

Just then, the egg jolts into life and starts to turn.

'It's going. It's going! Get your head out of the way,' Wogan scolds, making a shoo-ing motion.

'I'm sorry, I'm only trying to be helpful,' Paul responds, sounding briefly like a rebuked schoolboy.

'I know but we're trying to do a television show here,' the presenter drawls, as the audience politely chuckles. Paul fidgets nervously, clenching his fingers together.

In a bid to smooth over the momentary awkwardness, Wogan leans conspiratorially towards Paul as if they are two old mates sharing a pint. 'That's not just sparkly stuff, is it?' he says, waggling his fingers towards the egg's diamond-encrusted crown. 'That's not just the stuff that boxers like Nigel Benn put on their shorts. Those are rare pink diamonds. More than twenty thousand of them! You handpicked each diamond, didn't you?' he adds. It sounds almost like a challenge.

'I did. I worked very hard to produce it. Hope ya like it,' Paul says, almost coquettishly.

The truth was, he hadn't just worked hard. He'd risked everything to make this egg. He picks the scab on his thumb and shivers, cold suddenly despite the heat of the studio lights.

'Well, it's paid off,' Wogan replies. 'It's not just a lump of gold with diamonds on it – it's got everything. Talk us through it.'

Just then the egg, which was briefly frozen, jerks back into life. 'It started of its own accord. I pressed nothing,' says Wogan, looking bemused.

Squirming in his seat, Paul cracks a joke. 'I think you pressed the automatic rather than the manual, Terry,' he says, a hint of the Jewish East End audible in his voice. Keen to steer the conversation back to the egg's jewelled attributes, he dives forwards.

'These picture frames are removable and you can even put your name on it here,' Paul says, wrestling one out and cradling it in his palm. The back of the double frame is coated with blue enamel and it folds over to resemble a book.

Wogan reaches forward and jokingly puts it in his suit pocket. Paul takes the bait.

'I knew it was dangerous to bring it here,' he says, gesturing towards the bodyguards. 'But I didn't realise just how dangerous!'

For his next trick, Paul waits until the library spins back into sight and pulls out a tiny gold drawer from under the

PREFACE

bookshelves. 'You can hide your private diamond collection in there, Terry,' he teases. 'And you can take out the books,' he says, extracting a tiny gold volume which opens like a locket to reveal a secret portrait inside.

'It's a wonderful piece of work – worth every penny, I'm sure,' Wogan says dryly, arching an eyebrow. 'Have you had any bids for it yet?'

Paul gulps. It's still early days, but he had hoped for at least one advance bid. He's come close but there is nothing concrete. Yet.

'I was hoping this could be the big moment!'

'Don't look at me,' Wogan demurs.

'We all know you're very highly paid,' Paul prods, referring to the recent revelation in the media that Wogan is the BBC's highest-paid presenter. The news of his six-figure salary had attracted controversy from the taxpayers who were funding it.

'How can you talk about seven million pounds and my paltry salary in the same breath?' he says.

Paul looks fully relaxed now, his smile crinkling the corners of his eyes.

'Let's talk about your wonderful egg instead,' says Wogan. 'It really is a triumph – a tribute to British craftsmanship.'

Paul nods. 'Thanks, Terry. For too long in this country we've had no belief that we can make beautiful things.'

'Are you saying our jewellers aren't well regarded?'

'Well, name a few famous British jewellers,' Paul says, his voice becoming louder, more staccato. 'There aren't that many. They're mainly French or Italian.'

'So, the rest of Europe doesn't think too much of us?' Wogan is pulling a thread, goading his guest.

Paul nods. He wants people to know the egg is changing everything. That Kutchinsky is equal to the likes of Cartier. That the artistry of British jewellery is finally being recognised. Conscious he is running out of time, he squeezes in a reference to his new sports watch range, which Wogan declines to pick up on.

'But why did you decide to do this?' says the host, focusing on the beautiful absurdity of the egg. 'Was it to restore faith in British craftsmanship? How has Europe received it?'

Looking gleeful, Paul relates the story of how his creation was the star turn at the Basel Fair, the biggest event in the industry calendar. 'I couldn't even get on the stand myself to see it. We had more jewellers, retailers and wholesalers standing around it than any other exhibit!'

Paul laps up the audience's applause, leaving the first part of Wogan's question – the why – unanswered. Any worries about who might actually buy his egg momentarily forgotten, he excitedly details its forthcoming world tour when it will travel to Tokyo, New York and Australia, where it will appear at the Melbourne Cup, one of the world's most prestigious horse races.

The presenter watches him, waiting for the right moment to land his next blow.

'So, how much did it cost to make?'

Paul is caught off guard. 'Seven million pounds,' he blurts.

'That's what it *costs* but I'm asking how much it cost to make. A bit of an unfair question maybe,' Wogan concedes.

For a split second, the image of his desk piled high with envelopes containing final demands from suppliers pops into Paul's head. He pushes it aside, casting around for an answer that doesn't betray too much.

PREFACE

'How do you put a value on art? It really is art . . .' he says, with a flash of defensiveness that passes as quickly as it comes. 'We'll take an offer, Terry. How about six million, nine hundred and ninety-nine thousand?'

Their time is almost up. Paul feels exhausted and exhilarated – like he's gone twelve rounds with Nigel Benn and somehow survived. But Wogan has one final question:

'Is this a one-off?'

Paul looks out at the audience. His wife is seated at the front. He knows she thinks his obsession with the egg has gone too far already.

'The idea is to make an egg a year. We want to get people speculating about what the next egg might contain, finally revealing it at Easter,' he says, conscious that he is speaking fast, lisping slightly. Despite hours of elocution lessons, his 's' sounds still crumble when he's under pressure.

He catches his wife's eye. His business partners have warned him not to discuss any future plans until after the first egg has sold. He swallows, suddenly painfully aware of what he's just committed himself to on national television.

She quickly switches her face into a supportive smile but he could have sworn she was grimacing a second ago.

The host is winding up now, waxing lyrical about how lucky the studio audience is to have come so close to such a priceless piece of craftsmanship. 'Don't sell it in too much of a hurry,' he says, sounding sincere this time. 'It really is a beautiful piece of work.'

1

The Promise

Glastonbury Festival, June 2009

'My dad made the world's largest jewelled egg,' I said, flirting. My sexy new friend smiled back. *Be careful*, my brain whispered as I took a sip from his silver hip flask. The fiery liquid burned my throat. The world shimmered and tilted. It was too late.

It was early morning at Glastonbury. We were sitting on rickety deckchairs near the Stone Circle, watching the sunrise, swapping life stories. His dad was a rock 'n' roll drummer who had played Glastonbury once in the Seventies. I was impressed, but trying to hide it. We'd been trying to outdo each other all night, in that competitive way that's code for 'I want to rip your clothes off'.

'What is this? A dad-off?' He smirked, passing me a spliff. Our fingers brushed — and lingered. I found myself staring too long at his lips.

Around us lay the colourful detritus of the festival: discarded balloons, empty cider bottles, a glittery tutu, a single muddy welly. A bicycle-powered sound system pumped out tribal beats. Middle-class hippies fought for a turn on the rope swing. A semi-naked man dressed in a sarong and adorned with UV body paint pummelled a pair of bongos. The campfire's embers flickered and smoked.

'It's not a competition,' I joked. 'But I still win.'

'We'll see about that,' he said, in his Scottish accent. 'Tell me about this egg.'

I fell silent. My brain blurred. Fragments of memory danced in the distance. I stared at his face, fixating on the flecks of pink glitter in his beard.

I'd said it so flippantly, my tone almost celebratory. But that wasn't how anyone in my family normally spoke about the egg. It was a taboo subject, only to be discussed in solemn tones, imbued with an air of dark regret. It was a cursed object, a bad thing.

Follow the first rule of journalism, I thought: stick to the facts.

'Erm. It was big, and golden,' I stuttered. 'Lots of diamonds. Thousands. Like a giant Fabergé egg. But . . .'

I groped for the right words. My desire for this stranger made me want to preserve the connection between us. He extended the flask in my direction and I tilted my head back, letting it drip slowly into my mouth, feeling his eyes on me. Electricity surged. A string of words tumbled into semi-coherent sentences. I told him I came from a family of Jewish jewellers that once upon a time had celebrity clients like Elizabeth Taylor and Elton John. Dad made watches that tennis players wore at Wimbledon, and once sponsored a polo team that played against Prince Charles (as he was at the time).

He caught my eye and smiled. 'You didn't tell me you were rich.'

'I'm not,' I protested. 'Not anymore, at least.'

He reached out and held my hand. *Act cool.*

'Anyway, the point is we had this historic, hundred-year-old business and it was all going smoothly, until my dad decided to make this massive gold and diamond egg . . . and it . . . smashed everything to bits.'

I cast a glance in my suitor's direction, conscious that I might be boring him, but to my surprise, he looked spellbound.

I hadn't expected this.

I'd come to Glastonbury nursing a broken heart. My boyfriend of almost five years had moved to Berlin and, inevitably, met someone else. He broke the news that he had feelings for this other woman in an email to me, which I unfortunately read at work. Then we met up at a music festival in Barcelona for a miserable few days of reminiscence and recrimination, broken by moments of bittersweet sex. After which, I spent most of the flight home crying and drinking red wine. Thank God for sunglasses.

That had only been the previous weekend. Now I was at Glastonbury and, it's safe to say, I was not in the mood. I'd been making the musical pilgrimage to Worthy Farm since I was fifteen, but this year I was desperate for some time to process my break-up. And was worried that, for once, escaping reality by dancing in a field might not be the answer. But the friend who'd got me a free ticket wasn't taking no for an answer. *It will be cathartic, get it out of your system, make you stronger.* All the clichés.

So, here I was. Newly single, aged almost thirty, with

tingly limbs and lack of sleep clouding my senses, sharing my family secrets with this seductive stranger. He was dressed like an extra from a trippy version of *Top Gun*, his slim frame draped into a brown leather aviator jacket with a fur collar and colourful patches on the arms. A silver sequinned sailor's hat balanced jauntily on his head, dark curls bouncing underneath it. His swirling chestnut eyes were filled with mischief. I'd been jokingly calling him Maverick all night.

We'd met earlier, collided on the dancefloor. A moment of connection. He was dancing too close and offered to buy me a drink. An apology, or something more? I followed him to the bar, pushing and shoving through the flailing crowd. We downed sticky shots of sambuca and introduced ourselves, shouting into each other's ears. We filed back to our spot, holding hands to tether us, but his friends and mine had vanished. Instead of looking for them, we danced together, his hands snaking around my waist. Then we strolled around, waiting for sunrise, in search of adventure.

'What happened to the egg?' Maverick asked, pushing his neon orange sunglasses off his face and wriggling around in his deckchair to stare directly at me.

'It's lost,' I mumbled. 'It cost millions to make. Then it didn't sell. The business collapsed, so did my parents' marriage. It was a bit like Pandora's egg . . .' My voice trailed off. Discomfort seeped into my brain, and weariness invaded my limbs. The magic energy gifted to me by the silver flask was wearing off, as was my ability to detach this extraordinary object from the emotional carnage that followed it.

'How do you lose a multi-million-pound egg?' Maverick

asked, incredulous. 'It's not like losing your phone, or your keys – or even your mind, temporarily. It's a massive golden egg! Your dad must know who has it.'

He dropped my hand to fumble in his coat pocket and produced a packet of cigarettes. I shook my head, ignoring his crestfallen expression. There were nicotine stains on his fingers, I noticed, and recoiled slightly. We sat in silence as he took a drag.

'My dad's dead.' I delivered the death knell to our romantic overtures in a whisper, staring out at the distant tent city that was sparking back into life below us.

'I'm sorry.'

'It's okay.' I shrugged. 'The egg broke him.'

I felt him scan my face, searching for the right words, fearful he'd shattered the spell. We lapsed into silence.

The sun's warmth slid across my neck, melting away the mystery of the night. It revealed that his jacket was missing several buttons, and the dirt under his fingernails.

'Do you ever wonder where it is now?' he asked. A final attempt to draw me back. His questions, at first flirty and intriguing, grew increasingly irksome. Maybe we weren't soulmates after all.

I didn't have answers. I didn't need answers. I needed sleep. I needed my ex-boyfriend. I didn't need to be stripped naked by this man. Grief jangled at the back of my brain.

I pushed back the deckchair and tried to excuse myself. Instead, I tripped and fell straight into Maverick's lap. He laughed awkwardly. 'You should be proud of your dad,' he said softly, brushing my knotted hair out of my eyes. 'Keep telling his story.'

I kissed him farewell and set off down the hill, resolving to do just that.

*   *   *

Growing up, my mother used to refer to the egg as 'your father's ego', while to the rest of the world it was known as the Argyle Library Egg by Kutchinsky. I felt a mix of pride and bafflement towards my father's creation. I was thrilled to take its Guinness World Records certificate to school to show my friends, but I didn't understand why anyone would want an egg that big which wasn't made out of chocolate. And I was left frustrated when my repeated requests for a puppy were deflected with the refrain, 'After the egg.'

But 'after the egg' life was never the same. This breathtaking object caused such devastation that for a long time, my family decried its existence. Mum raged against it as if it were human. A Maleficent-like villain that stole her livelihood and her husband and robbed her children of a father. I was meant to hate it too. But I couldn't. Just like I couldn't hate Dad when he left.

After that sunrise moment at Glastonbury, it became a late-night story I reserved for after-parties, when dawn was breaking and disinhibition was at its peak. It was a way of keeping my father close, of introducing him to friends and lovers. I had my performance nailed: I would keep it light and rattle past the tragedy, focusing on the eccentricity and mystery. At the right moment, I'd pull out the photo of Dad caressing the egg that I kept in a box of keepsakes under my bed, eliciting cries of disbelief: 'WTF? It's massive!' or 'Mate, your dad was a proper legend.'

'You look so much like him.'

'Where is it now?' people would inevitably ask. I'd shrug. *Dunno. Don't care. Let's have another shot.* Like my father, I told myself, it was lost to me forever.

I confessed to a new fling that I'd give anything to see the egg again, to understand why it had so possessed its creator. Even saying those words aloud felt like a betrayal of my family and what the egg had cost us.

'Have you tried therapy? It might be easier than looking for a giant golden egg,' he suggested, only half teasing.

'This is my therapy.' I leaned over and swigged from the bottle of lukewarm Prosecco on the bedside table. It sounded hollow, but that was how I felt. He stroked my back, working his way down my body in slow, seductive strokes until my longing was focused elsewhere.

The fling turned into a boyfriend and life became more settled. I pictured our life for some time as a rom-com montage where the starry-eyed couple wanders around Ikea, strolls through parks at sunset and kisses in doorways. We moved in together and even got a kitten. Beneath the soft filter, it wasn't perfect – but it was enough, for a while.

He was captivated by the glamour of the egg story. He would ask questions about the family business, and I would stare blankly back. Holes in my history. For our first anniversary, he found a vintage Kutchinsky advert from a glossy magazine on eBay and hung it in our bedroom. Later, he bought me a tiny replica of a Fabergé egg. Both gifts made me cry, in a good way. It was the first time in decades that anyone had wanted to talk about, let alone celebrate, that part of my life. When I mentioned the anniversary gift to Mum, her reaction surprised me. It irked her, as if I were prising open a past that didn't belong to me. Dragging her back into an emotional abyss.

*   *   *

I started secretly collecting House of Kutchinsky memorabilia: adverts, photos, newspaper clippings. The jewellery was easy to find. It was all over the internet, with rare pieces from the Seventies fetching tens of thousands of pounds at auction. Occasionally, I recognised some of my grandparents' favourite pieces in catalogues or on social media. Was that Grandma's gold tiger brooch with its emerald eyes? Had that oversized diamond once graced her hand? Was that Grandpa's pocket watch? I became fascinated by the idea that jewels possess an immortality that eludes their maker. The world changes but jewels endure, holding up a mirror to society at the moment of their creation. Sometimes they decorate flesh, sometimes they gather dust for decades, sometimes they are lost. They travel through time and space. But they are rarely destroyed.

The thought that Dad's egg was out there somewhere gnawed at me. If I could see it again, then I might finally understand why he risked so much to make it. My work as a journalist suffered. I stopped researching other stories and devoted all my free time to delving into my family's past.

The boyfriend, understandably, got fed up with my obsession intruding into our weekends. I cancelled plans, spent mornings buried under a pile of books and joined a throng of American tourists on a walking tour of London's Jewish East End, the latter in an attempt to connect with the world my Polish immigrant ancestors inhabited when they first arrived in London fleeing persecution in the nineteenth century. But I still hadn't shared the story with anyone else while sober. Until, one day, I blurted it out in a packed room of newspaper colleagues. It was the day of our regular ideas meeting – an agonising, stilted affair where everyone, regardless of rank, was expected to present their best pitches. Our ash-blonde editor, whose icy stare terrified me, would note them down, asking questions when her interest was piqued. A blank look was bad news, especially if accompanied by an awkward half-smile.

'My dad made the world's largest jewelled egg,' I stuttered when it was my turn, 'like a Fabergé egg but bigger and with lots of pink diamonds.' I scanned my editor's face for a reaction. Stony silence. But after I told her about the egg's prime time TV debut and how it travelled the world by plane, occupying three first-class seats with my parents forming part of its entourage, she broke into a smile. 'It's perfect for our Father's Day edition,' she said. 'How fast can you write it?'

I was elated. All those years I'd spent scrabbling for ideas and I'd been sitting on the best story of all. I called Mum as soon as I got out of the meeting. Normally my biggest supporter, she baulked at the idea of canonising my father and his egg. 'It's not your story to tell,' she rebuked down the phone. 'You were only a child, what do you know?' Nobody would talk to me, she warned. There was a code of silence around the egg and the collapse of the business, that I would never be able to break.

Hoping she was wrong, I plucked up the courage to call the House of Kutchinsky's unofficial archivist, David O'Connor, who had been close to my parents. When the business was sold to a rival jeweller in 1991, he had stayed on as the head of sales.

My nerves evaporated as soon as David answered the phone. Greeting me warmly, he suggested I meet him for lunch at the Kutchinsky showroom that coming Saturday. My stomach clenched. I hadn't set foot in the shop since the egg wreaked such havoc on my family's life. I knew it was still there, a few doors down from Harrods. The showroom was the West End 'theatre' where my family had once worked their magic, persuading shoppers to adorn their bodies with precious jewels. Our name still hung above the door, but my family had long since departed, and without their driving force, the brand had lost its lustre. It used to make me so proud, driving past it as a child. But now it felt like a cruel taunt.

I dressed up in a navy blue polka dot dress, a blazer and heels that squeezed my feet painfully. I felt absurd hobbling through the streets of Hackney on the weekend at an hour when I was more accustomed to heading home from a party. Repetitive beats blasted through my headphones as I sat on the Tube, feeling the same nervous energy as I did before a big night out. When I reached the shop and its grand, gilded doors swung open, I halted, frozen to the spot. It felt as if someone had pressed pause on the day the business was sold. The sapphire blue and gold carpet with its pattern of interlocking K's, in which my grandfather had taken so much pride, was still there, as were the crystal chandeliers. Jewels sat marooned on soft leather pedestals in glass cabinets. Taking a breath, I imagined myself as a returning character in a TV drama, stepping onto the set, ready for a showdown with the usurper of my family seat.

Then David, smartly dressed in a navy suit and silk tie, appeared and enveloped me in a hug. A chameleonic salesman, he inhabited the persona of his clients, dressing, talking and acting like them – except at parties, when he would burst into either song or tears, or sometimes both. Sliding his slender frame behind one of the shop's gilt-edged mahogany desks, he motioned me to sit down. We swapped idle pleasantries, then I explained that this was a sleuthing mission to piece together the clues that led to my father's self-destruction.

It felt so strange being back here. The fleshy creases on David's face and the deafening emptiness of the shop, on what should have been a busy Saturday, were the only signs that time had moved on.

Twenty-five years ago, the shop's main attraction, in the eyes of my younger self, had been its proximity to Harrods' amazing toy shop. I would skulk in the back office eating biscuits until it was time to visit this treasure trove of unobtainable items like toy Ferraris, giant teddies and creepy porcelain dolls. The designer's office was another favourite retreat due to its enticing selection of colouring pencils in every shade imaginable, each pencil perfectly sharp. At least they were until I got near them. But my most cherished memory was the time we were allowed to stay up late for a cocktail party. These soirées were designed to woo clients, create a media buzz and reward staff. The first time I was allowed to attend, I must have been about eight years old.

I loved everything about that evening, except my outfit. Mum insisted on dressing my younger sister Katrina and me in ruffled white shirts with huge, lace collars, black velvet jackets and silk tartan skirts. I remember sitting atop this same mahogany desk, my long curly hair frizzing over my shoulders, sipping apple juice from a champagne flute. Mum hovered behind me, keeping a watchful eye. She looked the embodiment of Eighties glamour, with big, blow-dried hair, red nail varnish and a black velvet dress, adorned with a hedgehog-shaped jewelled brooch. Dad flitted around the room, moving between family and clients, stopping occasionally to ruffle my hair.

The canapés were the source of much excitement: mini burgers and fish 'n' chips wrapped in tiny paper cones and served on silver trays. But what stuck in my mind most of all was seeing my family all happy and smiling together in this room. My laughing parents, my glamorous, if sometimes ferocious, grandparents; even my aunt and uncle were smiling. All the various cousins and hangers-on were also there, downing champagne and celebrating our shared success. A mood of togetherness filled the air. Before the egg.

As David and I shared memories, my gaze kept flicking over his shoulder, as if I were expecting to see Dad bounding down the steps towards us. I blinked. Tears throbbed behind my eyelids, and my jaw tightened. Perhaps sensing the direction of my thoughts, David's voice pulled me back to the present. Did I want to try on some jewellery? he asked, with a mischievous grin. Before I could answer, a diamond necklace shimmered on a velvet tray in front of me. I gasped; shaped like a string of icicles held together by swirling snowflakes, it was wildly extravagant.

Twisting my hair up, I let David clasp it around my neck. My heart thudded in my chest. Its beauty was undeniable but, priced at £90,000, it cost more than twice my annual salary. I could imagine it gracing the neck of a leading actor on Oscar night, but I was a 33-year-old journalist who was more comfortable in a gold chain and hoops. I stared in the mirror, the weight of it constricting my throat, and ran my fingers over the platinum claws constraining the gems. Maybe in another life. Then it was gone. Sphinx-like, David had slunk up behind me and whisked it away. 'Didn't want you to run off with it, darling,' he tittered. The clasp had left a small imprint. I rubbed my neck, fleetingly sad to lose this glittering link to my past.

After rifling through old House of Kutchinsky catalogues, scrapbooks of glossy magazine adverts and dog-eared press cuttings, some pertaining to the egg, David announced that it was time for lunch. But there was still one place left to look for clues: Dad's old office. It too was eerily familiar, with its teetering stacks of papers. Framed photos of Nineties celebrities in Kutchinsky jewels lined the walls. There was Prince Charles with our polo team; Mum at a charity ball attended by Princess Diana. But there was no trace of the egg. In fact, nowhere in the shop was there any mention of the House of Kutchinsky's greatest and most catastrophic creation.

'Why?' I asked David as he guided me to a nearby Italian cafe, where he seemed to know everyone. He shrugged and avoided the question, bantering with the waiters to get us a good table. Over a bottle of wine, he reminisced about the adventures he had shared with Dad, travelling the world selling jewels and extravagant *objets d'art* for hundreds of thousands of pounds to the super-rich. 'It was a time of unbelievable excess,' he said sentimentally. 'We were all young. We partied. We had fun. We were naughty, darling,' he said, winking. 'The Eighties were amazing – everyone was making money.'

The waiter briefly interrupted us, setting down our plates. Then David went on spinning tales of exotic adventures in far-flung places like Dubai and Brunei, where he'd once found himself perched on the end of a Middle Eastern queen's bed, trying to persuade her to buy his jewelled wares. 'That was unheard of back then,' he exclaimed, flapping his arms for emphasis. 'For Western gentlemen to enter a queen's bedroom – outrageous!'

Between mouthfuls of club sandwich, he spoke warmly of my dad, framing the egg as the pinnacle of the jewellery firm's success. 'Your dad was a bit crazy but he had great creative flair. He didn't give a fuck what people thought of him,' David exclaimed, as mayonnaise seeped out the side of thin white bread and plopped onto the tablecloth. 'He took risks. Your grandfather just let him get on with it, especially after the first few big sales.'

I listened, entranced, as David explained that Kutchinsky's egg wasn't made in isolation. In the late 1980s, Dad successfully made and sold a string of jewelled objects to private clients for hundreds of thousands of pounds apiece. These buyers were often sultans and sheikhs in search of ostentatious ornaments to decorate their palaces and private jets. Huge sums were lavished on everything from emerald-encrusted golden pistols (which the House of Kutchinsky wasn't initially licensed to sell) to toy drums made from mother-of-pearl, hand-carved jade desk sets and even a pair of gold and ruby handcuffs, for one of the firm's kinkier clients. David roared with laughter at that particular anecdote, transported back to a more carefree time.

I must have flinched slightly, which he mistook for upset. He reached over and patted my arm. 'Your dad dreamt of making his family name world-famous. The egg would have been a huge success if the timing hadn't been so terrible.'

THE PROMISE

It was nice to think it was the mercurialness of fate that had brought down Dad, and turned his family against my mum and, by extension, me and my sisters. But I sensed there was something more sinister at play. An image of my Glastonbury liaison, Maverick, in his neon sunglasses, popped into my head. Emboldened by the wine, I asked the same question he had at the Stone Circle. 'What happened to it? Surely, it's hard to lose a multi-million-pound egg?'

David swirled the wine slowly around his glass. 'The thing is, darling, discretion is everything in our business. Trying to find it would be like searching for a giant golden needle in a haystack,' he warned. After the family business was so dramatically sold, Dad's Australian business partners assumed ownership of the egg. Then the trail went cold.

Amid the emotional and financial upheaval, Kutchinsky's egg had simply vanished.

But I wasn't giving up.

'I bet you I can find it,' I mused, twirling my hair around my fingers.

'How much?' David asked, playing along.

'Seven million quid?' I laughed, echoing the egg's original price tag.

'Call it £100 and you've got yourself a deal.' Suddenly serious, David extended an arm across the table, his hand wriggling out of the sleeve of his starched white shirt. Heavy gold cufflinks – Kutchinsky, of course – protruded from the cuffs.

I grasped his thin fingers. We shook. The hunt was on.

*   *   *

That was thirteen years ago. Since then, my egg hunt has led me across continents and time zones and into a web of conflicting rumours. Did it fall into the hands of organised crime? Did a greedy owner prise out the precious stones then melt the egg's golden shell for cash? Or was it still intact, locked away in a safe on the other side of the world?

In the hunt for the egg, I would spend money I didn't have on private detectives, consult countless experts and fire off emotional emails to jewellers and diamond firms around the world. I would go through periods of presuming it lost forever and grieving that my dad's story would never be told. But despite repeated dead ends and my family's grinding opposition, something inside me wouldn't give up.

'It's my life, not yours,' Mum would say as I picked at emotional sores. That was true, of course, but this isn't just her story. Neither is it just Paul Kutchinsky's story, although his life is woven throughout the egg's rich tapestry. It is the story of my quest to find this mysterious, destructive object, one of the most valuable artworks made in the British Isles in the twentieth century, and to understand what it was that drove my father to risk everything – his livelihood, his marriage and his family – to make it. It is a story of our family: of love, betrayal and obsession.

Unable to find answers in the present, I travelled back in time. The seed that eventually led to my father's golden egg was sown over a century ago, by those who laid the foundations for the rise of the House of Kutchinsky.

2

THE JOURNEY

> 'Into the heart of East London, there poured from Russia, from Poland, from Germany, from Holland, streams of Jewish exiles ... all rich in their cheerfulness, their industry, and their cleverness ... devout yet tolerant, and strong in their reliance on Faith, Hope, and more especially, Charity.'
>
> ISRAEL ZANGWILL, *Children of the Ghetto*

In these pages, I've attempted to breathe life into the long-buried story of my ancestors, shadowy figures from my family's past whose ingenuity, creativity and persistence carried them to this country, and helped them succeed. Those traits were fossilised down the generations, but by the time they reached my father – the first generation born into wealth – they mutated into a corrosive ambition that consumed him.

All I had at the outset were fragments of information, dug up during the egg's creation and printed in the glossy brochure that accompanied its launch. Was my family originally Russian or Polish? Was Kutchinsky even our real name, and why did my great-great grandfather's bid to make it to America, the so-called land of opportunity, end in failure?

To answer these questions, I spoke to family members and consulted researchers in Britain and Poland. I also buried myself in the National Archives, searching for the vestiges of my ancestors' lives, browsing documents dating back more than a century.

The only name I knew to look for was my great-grandfather, Moshe Arron, who the family firm was named after; MA Kutchinsky Limited being its official title. But despite my best efforts, I found no trace, until a panicked phone call to my mother reassured me that the stories I'd grown up with weren't just the product of Dad's febrile imagination.

'The focus for the Jews back then was on assimilation,' she explained. 'They wanted to become as English as possible, as quickly as possible. That was seen as the key to success. Moshe changed his name to Morris.'

I typed the anglicised version of his name into the search box of a genealogy website and waited, holding my breath. A list of results appeared, scrawled on ink-splattered paper and arranged in clinical columns. The skeleton of their lives.

This is how their story goes – a mixture of history and family lore, embellished no doubt by my own imagination. In the late nineteenth century, my great-great grandfather, Hersh, lived with his family in the small Polish town of Grabów in Kalisz province, which was under the rule of the Russian Empire. Situated east of the River Warta in central Poland, it was surrounded by endless fields and marshland.

THE JOURNEY

Grabów took its name from the forest of hornbeam trees that surrounded it. A hub for agriculture and craftsmanship, by 1890 the population had grown to just over a thousand, with a significant Jewish community. Among the hundreds of Jews who called it home were my great-great grandparents. Every autumn, they would watch as the forked seeds of the hornbeam trees fluttered like paper gliders across the town's muddy streets and thatched rooftops, landing on horse-drawn carts and at the feet of weary merchants. In winter, the hornbeams stood braced against the cold, their grey, muscular trunks exposed.

When the sun began filtering through the trees, illuminating the new leaves with their serrated edges, my great-great grandparents, Hersh and Leah, would celebrate surviving another long, cold winter. But in late 1892, with anti-Semitism spreading like a virus across the Russian Empire and the nation's economy locked in a deep freeze, Hersh's mood was different. He was sick and tired of just surviving. During winter, while their children slept, he and Leah sat by the fire lamenting their situation, discussing what a new life in the West might look like. He didn't want to leave. He loved Poland. It was their home. Their family was there. He had a good trade as a watch- and clockmaker, but the Russian regime's harsh anti-Jewish laws threatened to destroy it all, and he had his children's future to think about. The death in childhood of his eldest daughter, Sura – named after his mother who died in childbirth when he was young – haunted him. He couldn't risk losing another child.

* * *

The trouble for the Jews in Russia had begun more than a decade earlier, when the brutal assassination of Tsar Alexander II in 1881 was wrongly traced to a Jewish conspiracy. The false rumours were sparked when the Jewish seamstress, Hesia Helfman, was identified as a member of the revolutionary group responsible for the murder. This triggered outbreaks of anti-Semitic violence across Russia. And pogroms. A word imbued with fear for the Jewish people, which translated literally means 'wreak havoc'.

The Warsaw Pogrom was among the worst of these. On Christmas Day 1881, the city, which was the administrative and cultural centre of Russian-controlled Poland, exploded in violence after shouts of 'fire' triggered a stampede inside a church. A rumour circulated suggesting the crush was sparked by a Jewish pickpocket seeking to create a distraction. In response, an angry mob attacked Jewish residents and raided their shops. Blood was spilled. The mob was on the hunt, seeking out the devil in their midst. It was three days before the Russian authorities bothered to intervene. Two Jews were killed, twenty-four people were hospitalised and thousands of Jewish families were left in dire financial straits after looting destroyed the livelihoods of many, from market traders to tailors and kosher food sellers.

In the years that followed, blood-soaked tales of rape, murder and pillaging seeped out of the Pale of Settlement, the region of Russia where millions of Jewish families were forcibly relocated. Whispers of marauding Tsarist troops murdering fathers, terrorising mothers, molesting daughters and sending sons off to be cannon fodder in the Russian army, bred a climate of fear. At night, Jewish families huddled in their homes, listening for the ominous drumbeat of hooves on cobblestones.

Hersh held out longer than most, perhaps because he feared being labelled a traitor of the shtetl by his countrymen. Scores of friends and relatives, tired of oppression and hardship, had already travelled to America. In letters home, they painted a picture of a land of opportunity (the 'Goldene Medina') where Jews could make their fortune and live free from persecution. I'll never know exactly what was in Hersh's mind when he decided to leave, but what is certain is that if any of his direct descendants had been left in Grabów during the Second World War, they would have been forcibly taken by the Nazis to the nearby Chełmno death camp, to be murdered alongside at least 172,000 others. Today, there are no Jews left in Grabów.

Crossing the North Atlantic in winter was fraught with danger, so Hersh and his family waited till the spring or summer of 1893 to embark on their adventure. Dressed in their best travel clothes with their hair neatly combed, they crammed into a wagon, fidgeting with fear and excitement. Clutching their possessions, they set off for the nearest rail station, enduring a five-hour journey along bumpy roads. Their likely destination was Kutno, which was about 30 kilometres south-west of Grabów, where they could catch a train bound for a town on the German border. A symphony of sad farewells from a throng of handkerchief-waving neighbours, who whispered warnings about the dangers that lay ahead, followed them as the familiar outline of the hornbeam trees dwindled into the distance.

If, like the vast majority of Polish Jews, Hersh, Leah and their children – Moshe, fifteen, and Frimit, eight – were travelling without papers, they would have been a prime target for the people smugglers who prowled the train stations along the route to the main ports of Hamburg and Bremen. Enlisting the help of criminals to cross the border illegally was common practice among migrants in this period. Terrified of being captured by patrolling soldiers, my great-great grandparents may have paid smugglers for guidance and protection. Those who took this option would follow their professed guides until they reached a village on the German border. Once they neared their destination, however, the smugglers would melt into the night, and their accomplices would materialise from the shadows to threaten and extort more money from desperate migrants. Among the most notorious of these villains was a man named 'Fishl'[1] who posed as a rabbi, jumping into wagons, befriending travellers and extracting money with promises to aid the next stage of their crossing.

Crossing the border was the most high-stakes part of Hersh and Leah's journey, and many lost their lives at this critical juncture. Only once they had made it into Germany could they draw breath. Sinking wearily onto the hard, wooden seats of a train bound for a major German port, they had little to do but stare out of the window at the undulating landscape. Occasionally, Hersh might have lifted his head out of his religious texts to share stories of the wonders that awaited them in America. The kosher shops with shelves so stacked they groaned under the weight of food. The warm welcome in store from people of all faiths. The gifts he would shower them with once his business started to boom. Silk dresses for Leah and Frimit, an illustrated copy of the holy book for Moshe. After a long night in a cramped carriage, they would have awoken to find the blur of forest and marshland morphing into factories and warehouses as their train screeched towards their next stop, the seething metropolis of Berlin.

The memoir of Jewish American author Mary Antin, *The Promised Land* (1912), helps us conjure an idea of what happened next. Antin made the journey from Russia to America in 1894, around a year after my ancestors, and under similar conditions. Thinking their train would stop at one of the German capital's grand stations, Hersh and Leah readied themselves to disembark and push through the crowd of unwashed, filthy bodies. But instead, the train carried on, finally coming to rest several miles outside the city. Shepherded off the carriage, through the station house and into an adjoining yard, men and women were separated into different lines by sinister-looking, white overall-clad officials who squawked orders in German. Their precious possessions, all they had left in the world, were piled carelessly in a corner.

Antin records how the female passengers were taken to a small room where a giant kettle boiled on a small stove. Forced to undress, they were commanded to scrub their bodies. When near-boiling water rained down on their heads, the women gasped. Amid the steam and shame rising from their amassed bodies, there was a sense of helplessness – they were no longer in control of whatever fate lay in store for them. Ordered into a different room, they were handed woollen blankets to dry and cover their bodies. Bags of clothes were tipped onto the floor and women searched frantically for their skirts and stockings. After dressing, to their relief and surprise, they were returned to the relative safety of the train, their fears of rape and murder evaporating like the shower steam that had blinded and choked them.

The source of their humiliation was a lethal germ: cholera. Hamburg, then Europe's busiest port, had suffered a devastating outbreak of the disease in August 1892, which killed 8,600 inhabitants. My ancestors were among the roughly 2.5 million Eastern European Jews who emigrated to the West during the late nineteenth century, the majority of whom departed from German ports, particularly Hamburg and Bremen. The harsh disinfection measures described by Antin were designed to contain the spread of the disease.

If Hamburg were their destination, further humiliation would have awaited Hersh and Leah. They would have been lined up, questioned, disinfected and charged per head for enduring a further purifying process. Unfounded rumours linking Jews to the spread of the disease meant they were often treated more harshly than other travellers. Those showing signs of cholera, and those who got on the wrong side of a medical officer, were forced to endure prison-like quarantine conditions for weeks. If they sailed from Bremen, which had escaped the cholera epidemic, they would still have undergone a medical inspection before setting sail but conditions would have been more relaxed.

It's likely that Hersh's funds would have been running dangerously low by this stage. In the camp near the port, they waited anxiously for their day of departure, along with the other migrants. Friendships formed. Prayers were shared. Plans were made to meet again. Binding them together was a shared terror. For the Eastern Europeans, used to journeying across the sprawling Russian plains, the ocean was unfamiliar and unpredictable. They feared the sea, a natural phenomenon beyond their control. They had heard horror stories of ships

THE JOURNEY

wrecked on rocks, passengers tossed overboard by cruel waves, water flooding the lower-class cabins.

But it wasn't the sea that stole Hersh's dream of a new life in America. The story that has carried down the generations is that my ancestors were victims of a scam, that their hopes shattered when they realised that the tickets they were travelling with were forged and would only get them as far as London. Hearing this story as a child, my imagination would run wild, picturing Hersh, overwhelmed by the noise, stench and bustle of a big city, falling into the clutches of the thieves and thugs who worked the ports filled with steam ships bound for the North Atlantic, or being bewitched by one of the Yiddish-speaking con artists who prowled night and day looking for victims at their lowest ebb, enticing them with promises of special ticket deals, meal vouchers or private cabins.

However, there likely was no grand deceit. No moment of shock or crushing humiliation. During the cholera epidemic, migration to America ground almost entirely to a halt, and the best option available to Hersh and Leah would have been to buy a ticket to a staging post, such as London, and wait it out. It's also possible that Hersh lacked the funds to pay for him and his family to make the journey. The full adult fare was about 120–200 German marks (roughly US $30–50); even with half-price tickets for children under twelve (which they likely tried to pass Moshe off as), it still amounted to several months' wages for the average worker in Europe at that time. My great-great grandfather would have known that England was a free country, where he could work hard and, eventually, save enough for their onward passage to the new Promised Land. But for him, America would always remain a distant fairy tale. A promise of good fortune, frozen on the horizon.

A comparatively small ship would have carried them to England, dwarfed by the ocean liners that, before the cholera epidemic, had sailed regularly to the Land of the Free. I imagine Hersh, Leah and their children joining the throng of excited passengers on deck, clapping and cheering as the ship ploughed out of the harbour, until the first wave of seasickness hit and left them clinging to the railings, or staggering back below deck. The ship was dark and crowded. Squashed below deck in steerage with around fifty other passengers, they had to shout to be heard above the deafening roar of the steam engines. Sanitation was deplorable and sleeping conditions were basic; a noxious odour of stale vomit and rotting stew filled the nostrils of passengers as they tossed and turned, desperate for respite.

Fortunately, it was relatively short-lived. Less than two days after they set sail, as the sun hauled its shimmering bulk over the River Thames, the shrill blast of the ship's whistle pierced the air, warning of their imminent arrival. Disoriented and sleep-starved, the passengers congregated on deck as the vessel carved a path through the narrow entrance of St Katharine Docks to Iron Gate Stairs. As they disembarked, strange aromas wafted up from the quayside: manure mingling with pea soup, eel pies and fried fish. The symphonic clatter of a busy harbour grinding into life assailed their eardrums, punctuated by the wail of a street organ. A sketch from the time, entitled *Just Landed* by the artist William Rainey, which appeared in an essay collection entitled *Living London* (Cassell, 1901–03) detailing life in the capital at the turn of the century, shows a crowd of new arrivals ('greeners') shuffling through the narrow streets of the slum. Their heads are bowed and their faces forlorn. Women, scarves wrapped tightly around their heads, cradle squalling infants to their chest. Men, battered felt caps pulled down low, clutch bundles containing their worldly goods. Some are empty-handed, having been robbed along the way. Wide-eyed children hover by their parents' sides, as the light from the street lamp slices through the fog. There's an innocence about them, these strangers on the cusp of a new life.

Bewildered, my great-great grandparents picked a path through the port, watching as some of their fellow passengers were met by a friendly face and taken to lodgings. Although Britain operated an open-door policy for migrants in the late nineteenth century, the growing numbers of Eastern European arrivals had led to officials being stationed at the ports for health and safety purposes. Travellers were inspected for signs of disease and entry could be refused to those suspected of carrying smallpox or cholera. A handful of customs officials and police officers also milled about searching for smugglers and troublemakers.

Somewhere along the way, Hersh and Leah's original Polish surname was misspelled – forever anglicising it to the phonetically spelled 'Kut-chin-sky'. For more than a century, nobody in our family knew what the Polish version was, but from consulting the birth and marriage records in Dąbie, a town not far from Grabów where Hersh was born, I have discovered that it was in fact Kuczynski.

On the fringes, a gaggle of peddlers, beggars and missionaries stood alert, ready to pounce upon the new arrivals.

KUTCHINSKY'S EGG

A place to sleep? How about a hot cup of cocoa? Could you spare any change?

Questions fired into the blank faces of people who, when they began this journey, were individuals with homes and lives, people from different professions, different social classes. Now they were all labelled the same. *Aliens.*

Except Leah was hiding a secret. Buried in the hem of her thick wool skirt that was crumpled and stained with vomit, herring juice and filth, were a few pieces of jewellery – family heirlooms handed down the generations. Described by my grandmother as the 'brains behind the business', I've often wondered if Leah acted alone. Did she sew the jewels into her skirts in the dead of the night, while Hersh snored beside her? Did she suspect her husband, who by all accounts had a weaker character, might be lured into a scammer's trap, or that if they encountered robbers the only way to keep her hoard safe was to ensure it remained a secret – even from her own family?

Leah's priority upon arriving at the docks would have been to find a safe place to liberate her jewels. They couldn't take any risks. Her treasure was their last bulwark against destitution. They needed money to feed their children, pay for lodgings and buy Hersh tools so he could get to work mending watches and silverware.

As they stood on the quayside, London waking up around them, a Yiddish-speaking guardian angel sidled up and asked if they needed help. At first they were unsure, fearing he might be another Fishl, preying on their vulnerability. But their options were limited, and in the end they had no choice but to trust him. Fortunately, it turned out that Hersh and Leah's angel was genuine, and he guided them to safety through the bustling side streets. He worked for the Poor Jews Temporary Shelter, a charity that helped new arrivals. In 1885, a Polish immigrant known as Simon Cohen turned his East End bakery into a shelter for Jewish migrants. At night, the new arrivals curled up on flour sacks spread across the hard floor and imagined themselves back home in the shtetl. Cohen, who paid for it all out of his own pocket, became a local hero, so there was uproar when the shelter was labelled unsanitary and shut down that same year. Three wealthy Jews stepped in to save the shelter, reopening it in a nearby townhouse. It was still in the slum but at least there were beds and regular kosher meals to help those with no family awaiting them, free of charge. Between 1885 and 1914, the shelter helped tens of thousands of Jews to settle in London[2].

Hersh and his family spent their first night there, gulping down soup and slices of bread slathered with pickled herring at the shelter's long dining table, before settling down to sleep in different dormitories – Hersh and Moshe in one room, Leah and Frimit in another. The children passed out as soon as their bodies touched the thin mattresses on the dormitory beds, while their parents tossed fitfully, kept awake by the heavy breathing of the other residents, their minds racing. Leah would have been painfully aware that there was nowhere suitable at the shelter to unstitch the jewellery from her skirts.

A few further sleepless nights followed, until they managed to secure basic lodgings near the docks. Her heart racing, Leah's hands ran back and forth across her hem, praying that her precious cargo hadn't somehow vanished during their journey, pinging out unnoticed into the corner of a train carriage or robbed from her while she slept. As she teased out each piece, I picture her smiling sadly at the memories they evoked, her stoicism suddenly crumbling. Pressing her forehead into the coarse grooves of the wooden table, she closed her eyes. Then the tears came. A hot, salty trickle that spilled down her face, pooling beneath the crumpled collar of her blouse. She'd done everything in her power to protect her family. Now it was up to Hersh to haggle hard to get a good price for the precious jewellery.

The next morning, at first light, he pulled on his overcoat, scooped the jewellery up into his inside coat pocket and stepped out into the city's polluted passageways. The East End, an immigrant hub for the past 800 years, was stirring. At the turn of the twentieth century, estimates suggest there were 150,000 Jews in London, with the vast majority living here in the capital's biggest slum. Amid the clatter of carts and babble of foreign tongues, the familiar musical echo of Hebrew verses floated up from the hundreds of tiny synagogues lining its back alleys.

Everywhere Hersh looked there were Jewish grocers and Jewish bakers. Jewish butchers and Jewish tailors. Jewish theatres and Jewish food stalls. But as he picked his way through the narrow passageways, he would have been struck by the hostile stares, spitting and swearing that followed him. I picture him shading his face with his felt hat and dropping back into the shadows until he found himself in a crowded market street filled with Jewish traders selling everything from clothes to live chickens. They might have shared a faith, but the market folk could tell when a new arrival was fresh off the boat. Nobody would make him a decent offer for Leah's jewellery.

THE JOURNEY

Finally, an older woman with grease-stained skirts and a toothless smile took pity on Hersh and pointed him in the direction of an antiques dealer who ran a small, cupboard-like shop on a nearby street. Dark and airless, it smelled of dust and chemicals and was crowded with old clocks, battered pocket watches and silverware. For the first time since he'd stepped off the steamboat, Hersh felt a twinge of familiarity. This was his world. Striking up conversation, he launched into his carefully prepared spiel about the origins and quality of each piece, holding them up to the light so the shop owner could appreciate their full radiance. A bout of good-natured bartering followed, at the end of which an acceptable price was struck. Hersh even persuaded the dealer to let him have a go at mending the creaking grandfather clock that loomed over the shop floor. Whistling happily, he wove a path through Whitechapel's putrid back alleys, eager to get home and share his good news.

Slowly, Hersh and Leah set about rebuilding their family's life. They'd risked everything to get to London, suffering trauma and sickness along the way. It would take time for them and their children to adjust.

The first snapshot of their new life comes in the 1901 census. Home, by this point, was Montefiore House, a tenement block in the heart of the slum. Their first names, like their surname, were now anglicised. Hersh is Harris, Moshe is Morris and their daughter, Frimit, is Fanny. Leah refused to change hers. The census lists Hersh as a 46-year-old, self-employed watchmaker who works from home, helped by his 23-year-old son. Frimit is sixteen and has left school to work as a tailor.

Montefiore House served as a portal to the Pale of Settlement. Overcrowding was rife, with about eight people crammed into each two- or three-room dwelling. The stink of shared toilets, thick and sour, curled up the staircase, mingling with the aroma of fried fish and the damp reek of mould. Yiddish filtered through the walls with many of the older residents, like Hersh, not yet learning English. By day, the kitchen table was transformed into Hersh's workbench, piled high with his new tools: screwdrivers, files, chisels and a small hammer. After securing that first job, work began to trickle in from neighbours whose watches and silverware had been damaged during the long journey from Eastern Europe. Slowly but surely his reputation spread. Hersh schooled his son in his trade, while Leah busied herself shopping, cooking and cheering up their shabby surroundings. Each evening, she would scrub away the scratches and stains on the table, before serving food that reminded them of home: chicken soup with matzo balls; potato latkes and chopped liver. Later, she would do Hersh's accounts, while Moshe read the holy texts aloud and Frimit sewed. In bed at night, curled against Leah for warmth, Hersh stopped dreaming of buying another passage to America and started making plans to open a shop there in London's East End.

Then in 1906, just as his dream was within his grasp, Hersh fell ill with stomach cancer. Getting a diagnosis would have been difficult due to the language barrier, and he declined rapidly. He died at home, surrounded by his family, aged fifty. Leah was devastated, but Moshe's grief was double-edged. Now in his late twenties, he had fallen under the spell of the Austro-Hungarian activist Theodor Herzl, the father of modern Zionism. Herzl, an imposing figure with a dark, protruding beard, travelled to London in 1898 and held a series of public meetings in the East End. Moshe adored his father, but Hersh's death also meant abandoning his plan to travel to Palestine to help found a Jewish state. He would now be needed, here, to look after his family. He was torn. As Hersh took his last shallow breath, his lungs rattling, his mind lost to morphine, Moshe had to make a choice between pursuing his dreams and taking over his father's business. Grasping his father's thin fingers, he leaned over his bed and whispered a promise in his ear. He would stay in London.

3

THE EAST END

Four months after Hersh's death, the Kutchinsky family bid farewell to Montefiore House, their home for the last seven years. This time, instead of an arduous trek across land and sea, they travelled a few hundred metres down the road. Hersh's death had left Moshe with a small inheritance, and that, combined with his own savings, gave him the means to open the first Kutchinsky shop at 171 Cannon Street Road. It was a small watch- and clockmakers, and the family lived above it. It wasn't long after the move that Moshe's thoughts turned to marriage. A striking German girl had caught his eye, Hannchen Wetzlar, whose family owned a prestigious jewellery and silverware shop in southern Germany and were a supplier to the Bavarian royal family. Moshe resolved to tell Leah to send for the matchmaker (*shadchanim*) once their mourning period was over. It was time.

At the start of the twentieth century, Hannchen, who was in her early twenties, had come to London to follow in the footsteps of her older sister, Bertha, to find a husband there. Her late father, Solomon Wetzlar, had inherited his father-in-law's jewellery business, and after his death in 1895,

THE EAST END

Hannchen's formidable mother, Pauline, took the helm. At the time, her oldest sister, Helene, was unmarried and, although there were no laws against it, socially it was perceived as disrespectful for younger siblings to wed first, and so Bertha and Hannchen had to, tactfully, look further afield. An introverted character, Hannchen likely loathed the idea of leaving her home and relocating to a big city like London, but it was the only way to widen her pool of potential suitors.

The 1901 census shows her living with her cousins, Menki and Clara Zimmer (the sister of Bertha's husband Michael Lebrecht), and their five children in a townhouse on the edge of the slum, close to the green oasis of Finsbury Square, one of the first public spaces in London to be permanently gas-lit. An importer of gold leaf, born in London to immigrant parents, Menki and his family were part of the burgeoning middle class. At the time, German Jews were typically better educated and more literate and culturally assimilated than their Russian counterparts, and Hannchen would have enjoyed a more comfortable lifestyle than the majority of Jews living just streets away in the heart of the slum.

It's hard to know exactly when Moshe first laid eyes on Hannchen, or Hannah, as she became known. Perhaps her cousin, Menki, was a business associate and introduced them sometime in 1907, hopeful of a match. By then, Hannah had been in London for more than six years and was approaching thirty. Perhaps she suffered from a lack of well-off suitors, or at least those with prospects other than working in the textile workshops that filled the East End. Back in Bavaria, her oldest sister, Helene, had by now been married off to her widowed half-uncle, Moses Tobias Wetzlar, a pious eccentric who founded a famous silverware shop in Munich. In the East End, the average marrying age among Jewish immigrants was late teens or early twenties. While Hannah was happy living close to her sister, and was fond of Clara's children, she would have started to wonder if she was destined to remain a spinster.

Until now, Moshe had been more interested in religion than romance, but there was something different about Hannah, with her wavy brown hair, high cheekbones and slender frame. There was an elegance to her that he rarely saw among women in the East End. Her family's elevated status also presented an opportunity to sprinkle some gold dust on the Kutchinsky name. Hannah and Moshe would have had little control over their courtship, meeting maybe a handful of times over several months to see if they were suited. Since Hannah's mother tongue was German, and Moshe spoke mainly Yiddish with a spattering of English, communication would have taken some effort. It's possible they exchanged only a few words before their wedding day.

They were married on 31 May 1908 in Sandys Row synagogue. Tucked away down a winding lane, its blue and white wooden doors a colourful beacon for worshippers, it was the largest of the East End's prayer houses and a popular spot for weddings. It still stands today, an anomaly amid the skyscrapers and sandwich shops of London's financial district and is the last remaining place of Jewish worship in Spitalfields. The only downside to his marriage, as far as Moshe was concerned, was his new wife's cooking. Hannah's admission that she was a vegetarian caught him by surprise, coming as it did after their wedding night. Prone to bouts of ill health, Hannah sought solace in aspects of the German natural health movement,

Lebensreform (life reform), which preached abstinence from meat and alcohol, alongside bouts of barefoot walking and nature worship. Being vegetarian also made it easier for her to keep a kosher kitchen, eliminating the risk of ever mixing meat with dairy.

Over the years, Hannah's cooking became the butt of family jokes but she resolutely ignored the noses that wrinkled in disgust as she brought out pickled beetroot instead of the customary lamb on Passover. Although Moshe would later follow her example, the rest of the family remained resolutely carnivorous, sneaking off for salt beef and chopped liver sandwiches at Blooms, the popular East End kosher eatery.

Their marriage got off to a happy start with the birth of their first child, Henry, eighteen months later. The following five years were taken up with growing their family and the business. Each new arrival brought joy but put pressure on their already cramped living quarters. Leah's adult nephews, Joseph and Mendel Wolkovitch, also lodged with them. When the 1911 census was completed, the Wolkovitches were aged twenty-two and nineteen respectively. While Mendel was listed as a tailor, Joseph worked for Moshe, who made him a company director when the business took off; a decision that would later stir tensions among his sons. When Hannah broke the news that she was pregnant for the fourth time, Moshe decided to take action. In January 1914, they moved to a more spacious shop with four rooms above it, where there was almost enough space, although the Wolkovitch brothers still slept in the living room.

It was here that my grandfather, Joseph, was born. As the youngest of four children, with two older brothers, he had to fight to be heard from the minute he drew his first breath. The way he told it, for the first years of his life, he was referred to only as 'Baby Kutchinsky' but his birth certificate confirms he was given a name, even if it wasn't used. This sense that he was somehow overlooked lingered into adulthood, instilling in him a dogged determination to outshine his older siblings.

Just days after Joseph (Jo) was born on 27 September 1914, a letter arrived for Moshe from the Home Office. Seven months after submitting his application, he was finally a British citizen. His bid was supported by a mix of friends and neighbours, including a local cinema owner, a grocer and a warehouse worker. The file containing his Naturalisation Certificate is held in the National Archives. Stretched across twenty tightly bound pages, it paints a picture of a 'respectable man', who was committed to building a life in his adopted country. As I peered at the yellowing paper, the Home Office stamp asserting its authority and Moshe's signature scrawled across it – so like Dad's – I felt a sudden swell of emotion. I wished I could have known him and acknowledge the debt of gratitude I owe him, one that has allowed me to enjoy a life of middle-class privilege in twenty-first-century Britain.

* * *

The new Kutchinsky shop was billed as a jewellery manufacturer and diamond merchant, a step up from their previous incarnation as watch- and clockmakers. It occupied a prime position on Commercial Road, a smog-filled artery that pulsed through the heart of the East End. Making his thrice-daily trip to the synagogue to pray, Moshe skirted around colourful wooden trams and traders unloading carts piled high with barrels and baskets of beer, pickled herrings, fruit and flowers, while in the distance the domed clock tower of Gardiner's department store loomed, marking the gateway to the slum.

Across the road was Frumkin's, a family-run wine shop, founded by the great-grandfather of the future Chief Rabbi Jonathan Sacks, which was always packed in the run-up to Jewish festivals. The Frumkin family, like Moshe, were respected figures in the community and the two families happily sent trade back and forth. A few doors down, the Yiddish-run pub, the Mackworth Arms, served what were rumoured to be the best potato latkes in the slum. Another nearby hotspot was Oscar Baumgart's photographic studio, The Empire, at 118 Commercial Road, where families marked special occasions with stiff, formal portraits.

Moshe and Hannah were photographed in a similar style, alongside their family, soon after their wedding. The grainy, sepia image was sent to me by Judy Wolkovitch, Mendel's daughter-in-law. While it's unclear if it was taken by Baumgart it bears the hallmarks of his work. Set against a sweeping terrace scene with marble pillars and a dreamy forest backdrop, my great-grandparents look like time travellers. Moshe is a familiar stranger, in whom I see aspects of my grandfather and other family members, reflected back: the formal black suit, the bulbous eyes, the protruding ears, the wisp of hair captured beneath his fez-like hat. Hannah is seated in front of him, elegant in a silk dress with a spray of fresh flowers pinned to her chest. A half-smile plays on her lips. Alongside them are Moshe's sister, Fanny, and her dashing new husband, Nathan Williams, who would become a wealthy banker. Sandwiched between the two couples is Leah, trussed up in a silk dress with a frilly ruffle obscuring her neck. Her cheeks are round, her stomach is doughy and she has a double chin, a sign that prosperity was finally on the horizon.

But any hope of a more settled life was dashed when the First World War broke out in July 1914, and the Kutchinskys' world spun once more on its axis. Suspicion of strangers surged across London. East End Jewish shops with German-sounding names were targeted. Speakers of Yiddish, with its Teutonic inflections, suffered abuse in the street. Whether your family history was Russian, Polish, it didn't matter. Exempted from military service, because he wasn't yet a British citizen when war broke out, Moshe could have volunteered but he chose to stay in the cocoon of the East End. He wasn't alone. In 1914, many of his fellow Jews declined to fight, a stance which led the right-wing *Daily Mail* newspaper to label them unpatriotic parasites who were living a good life (in the Stepney slums, no less) while others sacrificed themselves at the front. The reality was that many of those who had fled the pogroms in Russia weren't willing to fight alongside the nation that had persecuted them. Enlisting also meant sacrificing aspects of religious life – there wasn't much time for translating the Torah in the trenches – and for Zionists like Moshe, who were largely based in Europe, it went against their initial position of neutrality. Moshe also felt a need to be present to protect his family, especially his German wife. In the eyes of her fellow Londoners, Hannah was now the enemy.

In May 1915, disaster struck. Hannah's brother-in-law, Michael Lebrecht, a wispy man with dark hair, a neat moustache and protruding ears, who made a successful living as a luxury goods broker, was arrested on suspicion of being a German spy. Her devastated sister Bertha was left to look after their five children on her own. In those dark early days of war, Hannah ventured out only to visit her grief-stricken sister who lived nearby in Stoke Newington, then a leafy East London suburb. After five months of uncertainty, Michael was released and life resumed a semblance of normality – until bombing raids brought terror to the East End in 1917.

The Kutchinskys would have joined the terrified crowds seeking shelter below ground in the Tube stations as German bombs laid waste to the streets above them. This was the first time Londoners had faced this deadly threat. By 1918, the bombs had killed an estimated 670 people in the capital. Shocked by the changed view of the German people, who went from being hailed as one of Europe's most educated races to one of its most reviled, Hannah felt increasingly isolated. She hadn't been back to her hometown of Bamberg for almost fifteen years, and now she might never see the rest of her family again. It was around this time she started talking about going home. After the war, Moshe promised, kissing her cheek. After the war.

But it wouldn't be until the mid-1920s that Hannah got her wish, when news of her mother's ailing health spurred the family into action. Pauline had outlived her husband by three decades but now she was frail. Plans were made for the whole family to travel together, leaving Joseph Wolkovitch in charge of the shop under Leah's watchful eye. They would only be gone a few months, Moshe reassured his mother. Setting off with his family by boat to Hamburg must have evoked memories of the journey he had made as a young man, in the opposite direction. The conditions aboard were somewhat improved: steerage had been replaced by tourist class and there were better facilities and cabins for families. However, there was still no kosher food available, so they had to take their own salt beef sandwiches and bagels. Not that it mattered to Moshe, who spent much of the journey bent over the rail, groaning, flakes of vomit clinging to his beard – his seasickness as bad as ever.

From Hamburg, they travelled south to Bavaria by train. For my grandfather Joseph, aged twelve, the journey was a great adventure. It was the first time he'd set foot outside of London's East End. Taught German at home by Hannah, Jo and his siblings felt a connection to their mother's homeland. But for Moshe, there would have been apprehension. A nagging concern that despite his status as a business owner and scholar, his wealthier in-laws would think of him as a poor man from the shtetl.

Moshe's fears were soon allayed. The Wetzlars welcomed them with great excitement and after Pauline's death, aged eighty-five, in February 1927, the family decided to stay on. A few months turned into a few years. Life in Bamberg, where the population totalled 45,000 in 1925, felt relaxed after the relentless pace of London. It was a charming town with a towering cathedral, colourful frescoes and romantic timber-framed houses, the most striking of which was the cream- and gold-coloured town hall that sits on an island in the middle of the River Regnitz. To Jo, Bamberg looked like something out of a fairy tale. This was a golden period for him, with sunny days spent cruising around the cobbled streets with his cousins or swimming in the river. The world felt safe and free.

THE EAST END

By the early 1900s, Jews across the German Empire had been granted full legal equality and played an increasingly visible part in public life, progress that would later spark a devastating backlash. But for now, in Bavaria, Jewish freedoms were at their peak. The Jewish population in Bamberg was small but thriving: in 1910, the national census recorded about 1,181 Jewish residents, just under 3 per cent of the town's total population. When war broke out in 1914, Jews from Bamberg, including Hannah's older brother Max, fought in the German army, demonstrating their loyalty to their homeland.

The Wetzlar jewellery shop was located on Lange Strasse – a bustling thoroughfare in Bamberg's historic town centre – inside the upmarket Hotel Drei Kronen, which attracted a monied clientele. The hotel's grand arched entrance was marked with elegant pot plants and a uniformed doorman, who stood to attention outside. Bicycles leaned casually against the sandstone exterior. The name 'S Wetzlar' was proudly emblazoned above the shop's glass front, a testimony to Hannah's father, Solomon, or Solly, who had established the business, which was now run by her brother Max. The windows were filled with a dazzling array of gold- and silverware from candlesticks to coffee sets and platters. A narrow entrance, separate from the hotel, led to the workshop at the back of the shop. Adverts from the late nineteenth century in local Bamberg newspapers spoke of S Wetzlar's reputation for exceptional craftsmanship and jewellery made with 'diamonds of the highest quality', and in 1907 they were named a supplier to Prince Rupprecht of Bavaria. Electric lights illuminated the sparkling goods locked away inside dark wood cabinets carved with ornate floral and geometric designs in the regional style. Behind the counter, Max held court, chatting up wealthy locals and tourists as they passed by.

Here my grandfather began learning his craft, alongside his siblings. I picture Jo helping out in the workshop, sweeping gold filings off the floor and peering over the shoulders of craftsmen as they soldered metal into shape. Meanwhile, Max schooled Moshe in the art of cultivating a higher class of clientele: how to identify their exact desires before they articulated them, whether it was a necklace for a wife or mistress, gold cutlery for a christening or a silver coffee set for a wedding. Seeing this level of sophistication up close would have been eye-opening for Moshe and his children. For the first time, they were part of a family that catered directly to the elites. This sense of entitlement took root deeply in Jo, fostering a belief that he was born to success.

While life for Bavaria's Jews was still carefree and prosperous on the surface, a political storm was brewing. Radical anti-Semitism was spreading across Germany, stirred up by Adolf Hitler's Nazi Party. In violent speeches and hate-filled propaganda, Hitler and his cohorts characterised Jews as a money-grabbing, corrupt race that had conspired to bring about Germany's defeat in the First World War. Hitler's attempt in 1923 to overthrow the Bavarian state government, known as the Beer Hall Putsch, ended in failure and bloodshed. Arrested, along with nine of his fellow conspirators, the Nazi Party leader changed tactics to focus on seizing power through the parliamentary system and published his autobiography-cum-manifesto *Mein Kampf*, placing the extermination of the Jews at the core of his political beliefs.

THE EAST END

I imagine Hitler's name being raised during Friday night dinners in Bavaria. Heavy silver cutlery scraping against dinner plates, as silence descended on the extended family gathered around the long wooden table, followed by a mix of scorn and speculation about his political chances. It was in Bamberg in February 1926 that the Nazi Party gathered behind closed doors to resolve ideological tensions within the party and assert Hitler's leadership and focus on anti-Semitism and nationalism. Moshe and his family may well have passed uniformed Nazi Party officials scuttling through the streets, gathering in beer halls to drink Bamberg's famous dark, smoky *Rauchbier* and tuck into a tasty *Blauer Zipfel* (blue sausage), which turns a curious pale colour after being poached in vinegar.

Jo's older brother Solomon (named after Hannah's late father) claimed that while he was in Germany, he saw Hitler speak at a rally, and that he was 'magnetic'. Terrifying, sinister, but also strangely impressive. Nuremberg, the old imperial city where the Nazi Party rallies were held in August 1927 and again in August 1929, was about an hour's drive from Bamberg. Solly was probably not the only Jew who, curious and fearful, crept into the city park where Hitler, his arm outstretched, spewed hate to an enraptured crowd of uniformed supporters. Better to know your enemy, Solly thought.

But it wasn't until the Great Depression of 1929 that Hitler's path to power opened up. Alarmed by the political situation and financial downturn, which hit Germany hard due to their dependence on foreign loans and trade, the Kutchinskys said emotional farewells to their Bavarian relatives and returned to London. According to family myth, Moshe and

Hannah brought with them a framed copy of the royal warrant letter granted to Max Wetzlar in 1907, which hung in the Commercial Road shop – although if this is the case, it was long gone by the time the shop moved to the premises I knew. Moshe put what he'd learned from his German in-laws into action, focusing on high-quality goods and cultivating an air of grandeur which set him apart from his Black Lion Yard rivals. He also extended his business repertoire, starting a side-hustle as a private landlord buying up properties in the East End and renting them to fellow Jews.

Just a few years later, back in Bavaria, the Wetzlars' lives changed forever. After the Nazis introduced laws aimed at restricting Jewish-run firms, Max struggled to keep his business afloat. First, he moved to a smaller premises in 1935. Then, in the wake of the Kristallnacht attacks in November 1938, when Jewish synagogues, shops and homes were destroyed in a wave of state-sanctioned violence, the family's situation spiralled. The attacks claimed the lives of at least ninety-one Jews, with an estimated several hundred more later taking their own lives, and 30,000 Jewish men, including Uncle Max, being sent to concentration camps like Dachau and Buchenwald. Upon his release, a month later, Max was forced to sell the jewellery store under the new 'Aryanisation' laws that banned Jews from owning or managing businesses, effectively bankrupting them. Max fled to London to join his sisters, bringing his siblings Gustav and Regina with him. Their eldest sister, Helene – widowed nearly twenty years earlier – had died at her home in Munich in 1937. Their other sisters, Henriette Rabinowitsch, Brendine Hainemann and Elise Jürgens, stayed with their respective families in France and Germany.

I always believed that our family, who were mainly based in Britain, survived the Holocaust relatively unscathed. There was a story, whispered by my grandmother, Lily, that one of Jo's aunts, most likely Elise, narrowly escaped deportation because she was married to a German, who became a Nazi officer. After checking the database of Holocaust victims, it's clear she didn't perish in the death camps but I have no way of knowing what fate befell her. The story goes that she was cut off from the family for betraying her own people, and disappeared without a trace.

Henriette, however, had no such escape. She died, aged sixty-six or sixty-seven, in Auschwitz in 1942. I never knew Henriette or heard her name growing up, but seeing her listed among those who died in that place of unthinkable horror moved me. Her name is etched on the Wall of Names memorial in Paris. I have stared at those slabs of dark grey Jerusalem stone, feeling overwhelmed by the scale of the loss, not knowing that Henriette was among the estimated 76,000 who were taken from France. Intriguingly, there appears to be no record of her husband's fate. Did Abraham, who was likely older than his wife, die on the journey to Auschwitz? Or, did he too collaborate with the Nazis to save himself? It's possible that if he survived, he adopted a more gentile-sounding surname and disappeared.

Before I started searching for my father's lost egg, and delving into our family history, I had never even heard the Wetzlar name, let alone felt an emotional connection to them. Our family had taken ownership of their story. Their royal warrant became the House of Kutchinsky's royal warrant. Their historic tradition serving the Bavarian court became part of our heritage. It was as if the Wetzlar name itself had been erased, overwritten by Kutchinsky.

Later, Jo would turn his family's royal credentials into marketing gold – weaving them into promotional materials and casually name-dropping them in interviews. My grandfather had just the right blend of charisma, creativity and street smarts to pull it off. His father, Moshe, was too serious, too principled and too burdened by Hannah's family tragedy to exploit it – and Jo's older brothers had inherited that same earnestness. But he had no such qualms. After their return from Germany, he trained as a diamond setter. 'Leaving school at fourteen never did me any harm. What do ya need an education for?' he'd croak, pulling out a handkerchief with two pound coins tightly wrapped in it and dropping them into mine and my sisters' small, sticky palms. His message was clear: money talks.

But it wasn't just a hunger for wealth that motivated him. Grandpa Jo had an eye for beauty. He would sit at his bench for hours, his eyeglass scrunched into his eye, staring at a single diamond, searching its transparent depths for the tiniest flaw. Once he'd mastered his craft, he started thinking about how to grow the business. With the increasingly fierce competition from Black Lion Yard, he thought their firm needed a gimmick, but one that felt genuine. Moshe had always believed in founding a business on trust and this was a value he'd instilled in his sons. What if, thought Jo, that trust became their calling card?

Occasionally, Moshe would allow an excited bride-to-be to take home a ring to show her fiancé, before she'd paid a penny. No rush to return it, he'd say, smiling warmly. But while Moshe was motivated by his faith in their tight-knit community, Jo publicised it as a service which no other jeweller offered. Suddenly everyone in the East End wanted to buy their engagement ring from Kutchinsky's.

With business booming, Moshe, now in his sixties, turned his thoughts to retirement and his lifelong goal of translating one of the Torah's holy books. The question of succession was looming. Moshe's oldest son, Henry, turned his back on the jewellery business entirely. The rumour is that there was a family row and he stormed out of the shop, although Henry's son denies this. The middle son, Solomon, was dispatched to Antwerp to buy diamonds and set up an office there. And there was no suggestion that their only daughter, Gertrude, would do anything other than make a 'good' marriage. Which left Jo, who I suspect greased the wheels of his own ascent, planting the seed in Moshe's mind that Solly would do best overseas and causing friction with Henry. However it occurred, by the late 1930s, the nameless baby of the family was now the boss. Jo had triumphed.

Until one morning in 1940, not long after he was married, the Metropolitan Police burst into the shop with a warrant for his arrest.

4

THE SECRET

Although they grew up just streets apart in the East End, Jo and Lily Diamond first met miles away, in Torquay (an upmarket seaside resort on what is known as the English Riviera) in the summer of 1939. There, on the south-west coast with its elegant hotels, sandy beaches and palm trees, their eyes locked. For Jo, who was on holiday with friends, it was love at first sight. Everyone else paled in comparison next to the woman he would later call his beloved 'Choochie'. I picture Lily perched on a blanket on the yellow sand, sandwiched between her elder sisters, her movie star looks marking her out. Stretching her tanned legs out, adjusting her sunglasses and staring at the waves, trying to ignore the rumours of impending war swirling around the town.

Jo's gaze, trained as it was to spot beauty, fell on her as he larked about on the shore. Mustering his best salesman's charm, he approached and offered to buy them all an ice cream. Lily smiled and accepted the offer of this dark, moustached stranger, defying the disapproving glare of her sisters. When he returned, holding her vanilla cone aloft like a beacon, they fell into easy, flirty conversation. When he discovered her surname, he laughed and said it was proof they were a perfect match. Writing down the name of her hotel, he promised to call on her that evening and strolled off to rejoin his group, glancing back over his shoulder to cheekily blow her a kiss. He spent the remainder of the afternoon counting down the hours until he could see her again, the tall, slender brunette with the beauty spot and mischievous laugh.

The rest of the holiday was a romantic blur. Walking arm in arm along the picturesque promenade, seagulls screeching above their heads, they shared their hopes and dreams. Like Jo, Lily was ambitious – determined that being Jewish and from the East End wouldn't hold her back. Her dream was to become an actor but a badly timed bout of jaundice had robbed her of the chance to take up a scholarship at a prestigious London drama school. But she wasn't giving up, she told him tearfully. Jo squeezed her hand and silently swore to give Lily the glamorous life she dreamed of.

When Jo returned home, his skin aglow and an irrepressible smile on his face, his parents were horrified to discover the source of his good mood. Despite Lily's name having the shimmer of wealth, as the daughter of a tailor she lacked both money and status. The 'rag trade', or *schmutter* in Yiddish, was a key source of employment for East London's Jews. Lily's family was fairly successful but she still wasn't good enough for the Kutchinskys, for whom marriage was a source of social and professional elevation. Love came later. If at all. Hannah, who could be haughty and snobbish, refused to acknowledge Lily's existence, absenting herself whenever she came to the house. Lily wasn't easily intimidated, but Hannah's disapproval stung. Jo soothed her fears; he didn't care what his parents thought – he was determined to marry her. But their courtship faced another obstacle when the Second World War broke out in early September 1939, and the government rushed through a law conscripting all men aged eighteen to forty-one into the military. Suddenly, the bright future they'd conjured during that carefree summer looked uncertain.

* * *

The winter of 1939 was bitterly cold. A thick fog, colloquially known as a 'pea souper', hung over London, shrouding the streets in a swirling, damp haze. People struggled to catch their breath as it choked their lungs and muffled their footsteps, adding to the mood of oppressive unease as the nation's war effort ramped up. By nightfall, the capital was in darkness – all lights dimmed or covered under blackout regulations – creating the perfect setting for nefarious activities. Desperate not to be parted from Lily and fearful about what might become of the family business in his absence, Jo looked for a way to evade the draft. With Solly still abroad and Henry out of the picture, there was only Gertrude left to help the ageing Moshe. The rollout of conscription was slow and staggered, and it took almost six months for call-up notices to be served to men, like Jo, in their mid- to late twenties. During that time, he stood behind the counter of the Commercial Road shop and listened for whispers.

It wasn't long before he heard that, for the right price, a man known as 'Uncle Edward' could get you certified as unfit to fight. Elias 'Edward' Myer Lipschitz was an imposing figure who owned Stylish Gowns Limited, a thriving textile business with eighty employees based in Whitechapel, close to the Kutchinsky shop. Lipschitz was in his mid-forties, married, with two grown-up daughters. He was clean-shaven, taller than many of his peers and well built, verging on stout. A fan of boxing, he was often seen at the big fights around the East End. He had come over from Poland as a baby but, unlike Moshe, never became a British citizen. A customer of Kutchinsky's over the years, perhaps he saw Jo as the son he never had. They certainly shared an entrepreneurial spirit and together forged a conspiracy that made them both rich.

I only uncovered the truth about what my grandfather did in the war when his government file was released under a Freedom of Information request. After being given a hint by the former manager of the Kutchinsky workshop that Jo spent time in prison, I found a record of his internment in the National Archives. It took months for the Home Office file, entitled 'Lipschitz – Kutchinsky Conspiracy', to be released but it was worth the wait. Inside were reams of dog-eared paper of different shapes and sizes, some were typed, some were covered in scrawled ink, but together they painted a compelling picture of the crimes that led to them being branded traitors of the realm.

The bulk of the police evidence against them was held in Lipschitz's file, which was spread across three bulging folders, their brown covers frayed and torn. Inside were reams of handwritten and typed notes containing detailed testimonies from twelve men, which showed how the scam unfolded over an almost seven-month period. Leading the charge against them was Chief Inspector Salisbury of Scotland Yard, supported by a cast of fellow officers, senior government ministers and top barristers. Salisbury's moral outrage at this 'dangerous and widespread conspiracy' run by 'these ruffians' bristles below the surface of his extensive reports. Closing my eyes, I could almost hear his chubby fingers furiously pounding his typewriter. And his disgust wasn't just reserved for the conspirators; Salisbury described the young men lured into their web as 'crafty and unscrupulous Jews', who were 'completely lacking' in 'courage'.

Raised with a market trader's mentality, my grandfather was always alert to the opportunity of making a fast buck. Not only did he inherit Moshe's aversion to war, but he was painfully aware that his absence would harm the family firm, just as he was starting to build it up. I imagine, as he reluctantly handed over hundreds of pounds to buy his way out of the army, an idea sparked. Did Jo approach Lipschitz and suggest he use his shop as a cover for his illicit activities? Earnest young men were often sighted in the shop, hovering nervously over trays of engagement rings, so nobody would notice a few extra faces coming and going. Plus, if everyone paid in cash, he could easily fiddle the books to hide their ill-gotten gains from the taxman.

By early 1940, conscription was well under way. The British armed forces swelled to more than a million personnel, with hundreds of thousands of new recruits aged between eighteen and twenty-one. But those in the older age groups were left in limbo, waking up every day fearing the arrival of the letter that could lead to their doom. The uncertainty fostered anxiety and desperation. Crooked doctors hinted to their patients of a way out, rumours spread during dances in the West End, knowing glances were exchanged in coffee rooms and numbers scribbled surreptitiously on cigarette packets. The premise of the scam was simple: anyone suffering from epilepsy was ruled unfit to serve. For about £300 (about £20,500 today), Lipschitz and Kutchinsky could get healthy men a set of false certificates stating they were suffering from the 'grand mal'. Several medics were involved, some of whom were in their pay, while others were duped into providing misdiagnoses.

Elias Lipschitz casts an imposing shadow over the case files, emerging as the ringleader with Jo cast as the junior partner. It was Lipschitz who arranged for the young men to fake seizures, issuing a stream of instructions about how to dupe unwitting local doctors, and later accompanying them to see a specialist in the West End. At times, he even persuaded his wife to pose as their concerned mother. Most of the cases listed in the file follow the same pattern, but occasionally Jo and Lipschitz had to get creative. In the case of Bernard Oberman, a 23-year-old ambitious solicitor who had just started his own practice, there wasn't enough time before his medical examination to acquire the correct certificates. Instead 'our friend influenza' came to the rescue, writes Inspector Salisbury, the sarcasm dripping from his pen.

After faking a bout of the flu, Oberman was granted a delay. Next, he staged a fit under Lipschitz's supervision. The scene was enacted at Oberman's office, out of work hours, where another man assisting Lipschitz gave Oberman a 'sock on the jaw' to make his tongue bleed and water was poured over his trousers, to imply that he'd wet himself. A handkerchief was then stuffed in Oberman's mouth and a doctor was summoned. A series of meetings with different specialists followed, where Lipschitz would play the part of the concerned uncle, driving the younger man to appointments and coaching him on what to say when quizzed on his symptoms.

When the day of Oberman's army medical dawned, I pictured the earnest young solicitor, whose fears for his future had brought him to this point, wracked with guilt. Timing was still tight and Lipschitz had promised to meet him outside the Memorial Hall in Tottenham, North London, with the certificates. As he waited, his mind racing, he fretted over the realisation that getting caught posed potentially as great a risk to his career as the war. Lipschitz arrived at the last minute, sweating profusely and silently thrust a sheaf of documents in Oberman's direction. Sitting in the waiting room, wiping his clammy palms against his trousers, he considered handing himself in at Scotland Yard. All too soon, his name was called and he found himself sized up by four doctors, staring at him over their spectacles, looking both solemn and sceptical.

Handing over the papers, he kept his gaze fixed on the ground. Someone cleared their throat. A chair scraped against the floor. Then, as if by magic, Oberman was dismissed with barely a raised eyebrow. Astonished, he watched as his army registration certificate was torn up in front of him. When he emerged from the hall and shared his success with Lipschitz, the older man laughed: 'I think you ought to send me a box of cigars,' he quipped drolly.

As the harsh winter frost started to thaw, this illegal trade boomed and its masterminds grew bolder. For Jo, the money was a lifeline for the House of Kutchinsky, keeping the business afloat in wartime when jewellery was a remote luxury for most. Although I don't doubt he syphoned off just enough to buy bottles of his beloved whisky and gifts such as silk stockings for Lily, making her the envy of all the other East End girls.

THE SECRET

By the late spring of 1940, London was sweltering in the grip of a heatwave. As Nazi Germany drove the Allies out of mainland Europe, the threat of an attack on Britain loomed larger than ever, and yet the fighting still felt far away. Fears of a poison gas apocalypse, drummed up by the media, had faded. Deckchairs lined the banks of the Thames, inviting gas mask-carrying workers to take a break, while daytrippers crammed onto beaches licking ice creams, swigging beers and sunbathing. Those who had volunteered as air raid wardens found themselves with little to do but drink tea and castigate neighbours for letting in chinks of light through their blackout curtains.

When Jo wasn't at work or setting up dodgy deals, he spent every spare second with Lily. There was a hedonistic intensity to relationships in those early days of war; sex and romance serving as an anaesthetic against the tedium of rationing and the uncertainties of wartime. Lily always spoke dreamily about the night they saw the classic film *Gone With the Wind* in a grand West End theatre. Decades later, as she lay dying, ensconced on her brown leather sofa, still glamorous in a blue silk kaftan and gold slippers, her hairdresser having just visited her at home, she recalled the romance of that evening – how there was a live orchestra, drinks in the interval and a warning about what to do in the event of an air raid.

Soon after that magical night, they got engaged. It was becoming more common for Jewish men to choose who they married, without the interference of family or a matchmaker. Jo designed the ring himself, promising her a bigger diamond once the war was over. She said yes, crying happy tears and kissing him. As his family's brightest hope, he was prepared to gamble that, over time, his parents' disapproval would fade. She was already winning his father over with her winsome smile and sharp mind. As for Hannah, she didn't like many people (him and his siblings excepted), so he was used to navigating her haughty silences. For him, Lily was the rarest of all diamonds and he was determined to make her his wife.

Just five days after Hitler's troops entered Paris on 14 June 1940, they were married in an Islington registry office, followed by an Orthodox service. Jo was twenty-five years old and Lily was just twenty-three. They returned to Torquay for their honeymoon, where they tried to ignore the doom-laden news from across the Channel. Lying side by side on the seaside resort's golden sands, they dreamed of the life they'd have after the war. But neither of them imagined that within months, Jo would be bedding down in a draughty elephant house in a prisoner-of-war camp hastily erected on the site of a famous circus.

His arrest, just weeks after their wedding, came as a huge shock. The sun was already blazing across the capital on the morning of 12 July, when truncheon-waving police officers, gas masks hanging from their belts, stormed into the Kutchinsky shop looking for Joseph Kutchinsky. A few miles away, a similar operation was taking place at Lipschitz's home – the arrests co-ordinated to avoid alerting either suspect that the game was up. Jo was bundled, kicking and cursing, into a dark blue police van with barred windows and driven across the city to Rochester Row Prison, in Westminster, to await his fate. Back at their home in Stoke Newington, his bride lay in a blissful slumber, unaware that the fairy tale she'd been inhabiting since their wedding had just come to a crushing end.

THE SECRET

After spending a few days locked in the cramped cells at Rochester Row, the order came to transfer them across the river to Brixton Prison. They were being detained under a controversial new regulation, 18B, the arresting officer explained, which allowed the government to imprison, without a trial, anyone it deemed a danger to national security. Amid the paranoia and fear that followed the outbreak of war, there was a wave of these arrests. But unlike some of his fellow 18B inmates, my grandfather wasn't a spy or a Nazi-sympathiser. My feeling is that he was, at worst, a war profiteer or, more sympathetically, a pacifist with a capitalist spirit.

Reading through the documents, I pictured the police van containing Jo and Lipschitz pulling up in front of Brixton Prison's high, stone walls crowned with curled barbed wire. As the doors creaked ominously open, the conspirators' eyes met and they exchanged furtive, worried glances. Ushered out into the courtyard by two burly constables, Jo fell silent. All he could think about was how he'd let down Lily and his father, and brought shame on the Kutchinsky name. Behind him, he could hear Lipschitz being dragged away, shouting in vain for someone to fetch his lawyer. They had never believed they'd end up here, so great was their sphere of influence in the East End. But while violent threats and blackmail had silenced most of their 'customers', one man betrayed them to Scotland Yard.

Sidney Minsky, a 24-year-old trimming merchant, lived with his two older brothers on Brick Lane. After dodging the draft himself with Jo and Lipschitz's help, he'd suggested his brothers follow suit. All was well, until his eldest brother, Emmanuel, found a cheaper route out of the army and asked for the money he'd paid in advance to be refunded. Lipschitz refused. They had quarrelled and threats were made. On 4 July, Minsky went to Scotland Yard and told Chief Inspector Salisbury, who was already investigating the case, that he feared for his safety, and that of his brothers, if the two men were left at large. Shaking with fear, Minsky described Lipschitz as 'a powerful man with a reputation for violence'. Worried that the two men would terrorise other potential witnesses, Salisbury immediately ordered their arrests.

*   *   *

The conditions in Brixton, London's oldest prison, were grim. Although it had done away with the 'treadmill', a cruel device designed to rehabilitate prisoners through torture, the prison had barely modernised since the nineteenth century. The 18Bs, who were unconvicted and so technically innocent in the eyes of the law, were treated with marginally more respect than other prisoners, but overcrowding was still rife. Up to three prisoners were often crammed into a cell and the stench of their chamber pots and unwashed bodies filled the corridors with a noxious odour. At night, the wails of sedated prisoners awaking from their stupors in the mental health unit echoed across the courtyard, while bed bugs feasted on prisoners' blood. Jo struggled to sleep, his mind racing, desperate for a way out.

Among the inmates already settled into prison life, there was a familiar face: Oswald Mosley, the leader of the British Union of Fascists (BUF), who had been on friendly terms with Mussolini and counted Hitler among the guests at his second wedding in 1936 in Berlin. Born into an aristocratic family, Mosley was a tall, fashionable figure who walked with a limp, he was charismatic, well connected and a notorious womaniser. After serving in the trenches during the First World War, he entered politics, initially as a Conservative, and was elected to parliament aged just twenty-one. Married to an earl's daughter, he revelled in the power and influence of his new career. In the mid-1920s, he broke with the Tories and, after a spell as an independent, joined the Labour Party in 1924. He became a rising star on the left and a well-known political figure in the East End, where among the immigrant working class there was an appetite for socialist ideas.

His eventual split with Labour came not because he was too right wing – quite the opposite. His economic ideas were radically interventionist, aligning with those of the great economist John Maynard Keynes, who believed in investing in public works to create jobs and stimulate the economy. When Labour came to power in 1929, with Mosley as a government minister, unemployment skyrocketed as the Great Depression took hold. The party leadership, under Ramsay MacDonald, were far more economically conservative than Mosley. In February 1930, Mosley put together a detailed proposal for tackling unemployment which proposed a complete overhaul of the British economy and included suggestions such as borrowing £200 million to spend on creating jobs and bringing Keynes himself into government. When the Labour leadership rejected the memo, he was enraged and stormed out of the party.

In February 1931, he founded the short-lived, radical centrist New Party, which was built on his economic blueprint, and also advocated for sweeping powers to be granted to the government, with limited control by parliament – a foreshadowing of the fascist-style thinking that would follow. The

New Party attracted the financial support of a small number of wealthy Jewish businessmen and had several branches in the East End. According to his biographer Stephen Dorril in his book *Blackshirt*, Mosley would dine with Jewish associates such as Israel Sieff, the newly appointed vice chairman of Marks and Spencer, and even considered them friends. But when in 1932 the party rebranded as the British Union of Fascists, pivoting to a more far-right agenda and adopting an anti-Semitic stance, these individuals quickly withdrew their support. Mosley made it clear to those who had supported him that he wouldn't sanction any attacks on those he saw as 'good Jews', as he put it, by which he seemed to mean wealthy entrepreneurs who paid into the British economy.

It wasn't until several years later, when Mosley was running out of money, that he first crossed paths with my grandfather. It wasn't politics that brought them together; Jo wasn't interested in stepping into that arena. 'Bad for business,' he'd say with a shrug. 'We should all be Hungarians.' This was a classic Grandpa-ism which meant we should all act like Hungarian Jews whom he admired for their ability to integrate while holding onto their own identity. Instead, what brought Jo into the fascist leader's orbit was a desperate need to free family members from the threat of Nazi persecution.

In the late Thirties, his older brother, Solomon, was living in the Belgian port city of Antwerp, Europe's diamond capital, buying precious stones for the family firm. Solly and Jo were polar opposites. While Jo was a charismatic bon-vivant who loved money more than religion, Solly wore threadbare suits and lived a more pious life. Antwerp was then home to Belgium's biggest Jewish community and it was there that

THE SECRET

Solly met his Dutch wife, Hella, a shy, sweet-natured brunette, seven years his junior, whose father, Samuel Thaler, was a diamond merchant. Hella was as opposite to Lily in character and appearance as Solly was to Jo. But she had an inner steel. They were married in 1938, just before the Kristallnacht attacks sparked terror and outrage across Europe. It wasn't long after that Hella raised the prospect of bringing her parents and two younger siblings to safety in Britain.

In the wake of Kristallnacht, the British government eased its policy for refugees, albeit with some reluctance and strict limits on numbers. The flagship measure was the Kindertransport, which allowed approximately 10,000 Jewish children from countries including Germany, Austria and Poland to enter the UK between December 1938 and September 1939, but while many lives were saved, it did mean thousands of children were separated from their families. Elsewhere, bureaucratic hurdles made it difficult to obtain visas, and the right-wing press railed against the idea of letting in Jewish refugees at a time of high unemployment.

It was against this backdrop that Solly placed a call to Jo, asking his brother to help bring his in-laws to London. Through his networks, Jo had access to almost every wealthy businessman in the East End. He made enquiries and was told that for the right price, Mosley, who was desperate for funds to keep his fascist party going, could act as an intermediary between the British and European governments to negotiate the coveted visas. Records show that in late September 1939, Solly and Hella were in London to sign the National Register (a scaled-down census to aid the issuing of ration books and identity cards). When Solly returned to Antwerp for work,

Hella stayed behind. She was a Kutchinsky now, Jo told her, and they would look after her.

Jo had worked his magic, and Hella's parents, Samuel and Clara, and her siblings, Paul and Sarah, also appear on the 1939 register, living in the seaside town of Littlehampton, 60 miles south of London. Their address was Irvine Road, a desirable street with tall, semi-detached Edwardian houses, just minutes from the sandy beach. But the family weren't alone. Living with them were Moshe and Hannah, who had rented the house to provide their family with a retreat from the stresses of wartime life in the capital and the risk of air raids. I picture them all gathered in the blackout gloom for Friday night dinner: candles unlit, electric lights covered, heads bowed, blessings uttered with extra emphasis.

Meanwhile, Solly was still in Antwerp, wilfully blind to the growing threat of a Nazi invasion. The story goes that in early May 1940, with rumours swirling that Hitler might break Germany's pact of neutrality with Belgium, Hella risked her own life to return there and beg Solly to leave. She pounded on the British Embassy door until her knuckles were raw, desperate to secure passage on a boat to England for the two of them. It was too late, the official told her. Barely any ships were sailing and there were no tickets left. Hella thrust her marriage certificate and their newly issued British identity cards in the official's face, but he stood firm. There was nothing he could do. Turning on her heel, Hella vowed to return in a few hours and stalked off.

Was it then that Solly succumbed and, for the second time, called his brother for help? Did Jo reach out to Mosley again, just before the fascist leader's arrest? It's possible that

THE SECRET

Solly used diamonds to bribe the official of his own volition, but knowing his strait-laced character, this seems unlikely. Whatever went on behind the scenes, when Hella returned to the embassy a few hours later, their travel papers, including boat tickets, were waiting for them. But they weren't safe yet. Thousands of Jews scrambled to leave the country as news of the Nazi advance, which began on 10 May, spread like wildfire through Belgium, Holland, Luxembourg and France. The roads to the ports were packed with people fleeing in cars, handcarts and on rusty bicycles. Solly and Hella drove in a panic to Dunkirk, which was still under British control. The Germans weren't far behind. Throngs of refugees milled around the sea port, their eyes fixed on the sky, searching for the shadow of an enemy plane. As the number of ships sailing for Britain dwindled, Solly and Hella squeezed on board one of the last boats out. Others weren't so lucky. A fellow Jew, travelling without papers, tried to bribe his way onto the ship with diamonds. He got as far as the gangway but was turned away, weeping. Even once on board, they still weren't safe. The threat of deadly sea mines slowed their pace to a crawl, while a fellow passenger, suspected of being a German spy, was shot and thrown overboard. Eventually, after almost twenty-four hours at sea, their ship docked on England's south coast.

After their nerve-wracking adventure, Solly and Hella recovered in the relative luxury of Moshe's large family home at 88 Aberdeen Park, a private road in a verdant part of North London that would later be memorialised in verse by the British poet John Betjeman. The spacious, four-storey Italianate villa was a world away from the slums the Kutchinskys had first inhabited in this country, but the Jewish tradition of families living together endured: under the same roof were his elder brother Henry, their sister Gertrude, her husband – the rabbi Wolf Morein – and their two young children. A photo from around this time shows Moshe and Hannah sitting in the garden in striped deckchairs, the grass beneath them scorched by the summer sun. Moshe's suit jacket is unbuttoned and his trousers are rolled up to his calves. His stomach has spread with age, while his wife is still razor-thin and poised, her stocking-clad legs neatly crossed and her hands clasped in her lap. I picture the whole family, spilling out into the sprawling garden with its long, bushy hedge, to hear the story of Solly's great escape. Hella, however, harboured a simmering rage towards the Kutchinskys. She never knew of Jo's dealings with Mosley, and in her mind, the family, although kind to her parents, had abandoned her husband to his fate. What is certain is that without Hella's bravery, Solly would likely have been just another statistic. Before the war, there were 55,000 Jews living in Antwerp. When Belgium was liberated in 1944, there were only 800 left in the city.

* * *

In later years, my grandfather spoke openly about receiving Mosley's help to bring family members over, describing him as 'more rational' than the other fascist leaders who plagued Europe at that time. While there are no surviving documents to support this seemingly incongruous tale of a fascist striking deals with a Jew, there is a reputed precedent. In 1937, Mosley used his wife's contacts with Heinrich Himmler to negotiate the release from the Gestapo of an Austrian member of the wealthy Anglo-Jewish Rothschild family. The incident was relayed to Guy Liddell, MI5's wartime head of counterespionage by W.E.D. Allen – a former MP turned historian who drifted through Mosley's far-right milieu – and Liddell recorded it in his diary: 'He alleges that Mosley got some £40,000 for the part he played in arranging for the release of the Rothschild family on the continent in 1937,'[1] Liddell wrote. The episode is also referenced in Dorril's book, and word would likely have spread among Britain's tight-knit Jewish community that for those with means, Mosley's help could be bought. In Jo's case, I assume diamonds bought with the proceeds of his war profiteering were sold to raise funds; precious stones once again acting as the source of our family's salvation.

In prison, Mosley maintained a semblance of his usual aristocratic lifestyle. According to reports in the press, he and his cohorts quaffed bottles of wine, had meals delivered, hogged the radio and agitated for champagne. Jo was younger than the fascist firebrand by almost two decades but shared his love of the high life. It's possible he sought Mosley out, away from the gaze of his BUF disciples among whom anti-Semitism was rife, not just because he wanted diversion but because as a former minister and Labour MP, Mosley had a grip on how to play the legal system, particularly when it came to putting pressure on the government.

This is all speculation, but stranger things have happened in wartime and Jo's file does show that he repeatedly demanded for his case to be heard in a court of law and tasked his father with writing a direct appeal to the Home Office. Despite his ambivalence to war, Moshe was too religious to have condoned criminality, but he did write a heartfelt letter in October 1940, which is preserved in the archives, pleading for his son's release. When I read it, it was the first time I'd clearly heard my great-grandfather's voice. 'At the time of his detention he was a newly married man,' Moshe wrote of his youngest son. 'I am convinced that if he did as he is alleged to have done, it was from this reason alone and not from any disloyalty.' He went on to reference his own affection for his adopted homeland. 'I have been established here since 1893 – 48 years. I am well known and think I have an honourable reputation,' he added, imploring the Home Secretary to give his appeal 'your kindest and immediate consideration'.

As summer faded, Jo and Lipschitz were moved to Liverpool Prison. Conditions were even harsher up north in the 'Hornby Hotel', a nickname derived from the street where the hulking Victorian jail was situated. First built in 1855, it was the wartime home of a motley collection of serious criminals and men convicted of military offences, and one of the few prisons where executions were still carried out. The claustrophobia-inducing cells, sealed by heavy wooden doors, were no larger than a standard lift carriage and contained only a chamber pot and a wooden bench for sleeping. Cockroach infestations were rife, the manual labour was back-breaking and the stench of unwashed bodies eclipsed even Brixton. At night, the weeping and wailing of those condemned to the gallows echoed through the walls.

Back in London, the Blitz began on the evening of 7 September. German bombs set London's streets ablaze while hundreds of miles away, Jo languished in prison. Buildings vanished overnight, leaving smoking skeletons of twisted metal. People crouched in corrugated iron shelters buried in their back gardens. Commercial Road was badly hit, and vast craters filled the space outside the Kutchinsky shop where once traders, carts and trams all competed for space. Friends and customers were killed, buried beneath the rubble, as the East End bore the brunt of the bombing.

Listening fearfully for news, Jo may have felt a sliver of relief that at least his banishment had removed him from danger. But any sense of security was shattered on the night of 18 September, when the Luftwaffe's deadly load fell on Liverpool prison, obliterating an entire wing and killing twenty-two inmates. The body of one unlucky prisoner wasn't found until eleven years later when the last of the rubble was finally cleared. What must have flashed through my grandfather's mind, confined to his cell, as he heard the ghostly wail of the air raid siren followed by the blood-chilling screech of explosives hurtling towards him. Did he lie there in the dark, eyes squeezed shut, conjuring Lily's smiling face on their wedding day? Did he ever wonder if it had been worth risking his freedom to get rich?

After the prison was bombed, Jo and Lipschitz, shaken but unscathed, were moved again under military escort. This time, their destination was a prisoner-of-war camp on the edge of Ascot, a town in south-east England famed for its glamorous horse races – a symbol of the lavish lifestyle Jo had longed for. As the bombed-out cityscape gave way to fields of mulch and semi-naked trees, their leaves twisting in the wind, Jo peered through the mesh covering the train's windows. A few months ago, he'd felt invincible, now he was reduced to a mere number, shunted around the country like cattle. The lack of control over his life was galling, but even more tormenting was the thought he might never see his 'Choochie' again.

* * *

Fringed by pine trees, Ascot Internment Camp, also known as Winter Quarters, was one of several hundred hastily assembled camps around Britain to house more than 400,000 prisoners. Previously the winter home of the popular Bertram Mills Circus, inmates bedded down in huts that had been inhabited by lions, zebras and elephants. A barbed wire fence ran around the perimeter, gleaming forebodingly in the late autumn sun. Life was humdrum but orderly with prisoners summoned at dawn for roll-call, their breath shimmering in the dewy morning air. Stomachs were lined with meagre rations of porridge, kippers and bread – enough to sustain them for the day of manual labour that lay ahead. Amid the bleakness and isolation, close bonds formed between inmates from different nationalities, faiths and backgrounds. In the evenings, they staved off boredom by playing football matches, doing crafts and putting on plays.

As the war progressed, the initial wave of panic in which the glut of 18B orders were issued subsided. A government reshuffle saw Herbert Morrison, who had opposed the introduction of the 18B regulation, become Home Secretary. Advisory committees were set up to review cases in which the application of the new laws might have been overzealous. Working in Jo and Lipschitz's favour was the difficulty of obtaining witnesses willing to testify against them in court. By the start of 1941, it was clear a prosecution would be impossible as the men who had bought the fraudulent certificates had by now been sent to war, as had most of the doctors who had signed them.

THE SECRET

In early February 1941, Lipschitz and Jo were granted committee hearings (the transcripts of which are preserved in the archives), a privilege not afforded to all 18B prisoners. This gave them the chance to contest their internment. Under a hail of questions from Norman Birkett KC, the lawyer acting for the Home Office, Jo affected the outrage of innocence. 'I cannot understand why I am singled out,' he said incredulously. 'I am put away for six months and where is the justice of it? It is not only me; my wife is broken-hearted about the whole thing. You can understand,' he implored Birkett, who made it clear that he wasn't taken in by this performance.

'The reason is because they [the witnesses] say you are the man who did it,' the lawyer retorted. 'That is why you are singled out. They say this is what happened ... but if this is utterly false, made up by all these people, it is the most widespread conspiracy to defeat military service,' Birkett responded, adding, with a touch of sarcasm, that if there was no truth in all the testimonies against Jo, then his imprisonment would be the 'wickedest thing in the world'.

An anti-Semitic conspiracy was clearly at play, Jo retaliated, comparing himself, somewhat grandly, to Alfred Dreyfus (1859–1935), a Jewish artillery captain in the French army, who was falsely convicted of passing military secrets to the Germans. 'It is shoved on to me, it is to cover somebody else,' he told his accusers. 'They need a Dreyfus – here I am.'

Lipschitz, whose solicitor was already building a case that his client's health was too fragile for him to be imprisoned in such harsh conditions, was equally impassioned in pleading his innocence. He swore that he had only met Jo on a few occasions in the Kutchinsky shop, prior to being arrested, when he used 'to give him a necklace to mend or buy a trinket'. In his eyes, this was a conspiracy dreamed up by business rivals who were livid that his firm had won a lucrative government contract to manufacture uniforms for the military. 'There is a tremendous amount of jealousy,' Lipschitz said, affecting a humble air. When accused of making thousands of pounds from the scheme, he feigned shock saying, 'Oh my God,' while swearing his innocence on the holy book, the Torah.

I never met Lipschitz but knowing Grandpa's character, and having read all the evidence against them, I am convinced of their guilt. Still, I can't help smiling at the audaciousness of Jo's defence. I'm sure his desire to get back to Lily helped him steel himself against the relentless questioning. 'My freedom has been taken from me ... Everything is at stake. If only I could get to the bottom of things,' he told Birkett, who wrote to the Home Office: 'Frankly, I do not believe the statements of [Lipschitz and Jo],' adding that it seems impossible that such a 'volume of testimony' could exist and 'be quite without foundation'. But guilty or not, Jo was soon a free man.

Seven months after their ordeal had begun, they were released on 14 March 1941. Jo headed straight for Lily's parents' house in Reading, where she'd taken refuge after his arrest and had stayed while the German bombers laid waste to London. Eager to get their marriage off to a fresh start, Jo whisked her away for a second honeymoon in Bournemouth, a seaside resort on the south coast popular with the Jewish community. As soon as their holiday was over, he was back behind the counter of 171 Commercial Road. But his ambitions were stalled once more when he received a fresh call-up notice in October 1941, this time, somewhat ironically, from

THE SECRET

the Royal Army Medical Corps (RAMC). It was not a front-line posting, and he was stationed in Church Crookham, a sleepy Hampshire village about 38 miles outside London. His uncle Nathan, Fanny's husband, was a wealthy banker with connections at the War Office. It's rumoured that Nathan pulled strings to keep Jo out of the fighting, although the story he always told was that he was excluded due to his German heritage.

Black and white photos taken at the RAMC barracks in Church Crookham show young men in ill-fitting uniforms and floppy side caps on parade or smiling outside their quarters, their arms draped around each other, grins pasted across fresh faces and cigarettes hanging casually from their mouths. Their body language suggests that while the uncertainties of war lay ahead, for now this was all a big adventure. Some RAMC recruits were ashamed to be carrying a stretcher rather than a gun but Corporal Joseph Kutchinsky didn't share their patriotic zeal. For him, wartime service was a necessary evil to be endured before he could return to build his life with Lily. He was finally discharged in August 1944, after being deemed medically unfit for service. Was this one final deceit? For the moment this remains a mystery. The truth is locked away in the National Archives, in a sealed file that was released to me only after prolonged wrangling, with the 'confidential medical information' that led to his discharge from service redacted. I had to smile; Jo Kutchinsky was always one step ahead.

*   *   *

My grandfather never spoke about what happened to him during the war; never let slip, even after a few whiskys, that he had once been branded a traitor and imprisoned alongside Britain's best-known fascist, Oswald Mosley. After his release, and the end of the war, he buried his darkest secret beneath the trappings of wealth and warned Lily never to mention it to anyone. My father was fairly loose-lipped when it came to family secrets, so I am certain he was unaware that Jo had been in prison. Mum had never mentioned it either, so I assumed she too was in the dark until during one of our long drives through the Scottish countryside she revealed that Lily had confided in her. Prison had hardened Jo, Lily explained; her husband was sharper and colder when he emerged, a better businessman but a more distant friend and lover. 'It was spoken about on pain of death,' Mum told me, a note of fear still palpable in her voice. 'Lily always said Jo was different after, more detached. Nobody could get close to him. Paul spent his whole life seeking his father's approval.'

*   *   *

After the war, the Jewish East End was a ghost town; 'the worst place on earth,' according to the locals. Shops and businesses clung on but the community was decimated. Many of those who had been evacuated found they had nowhere to return to. Those who had remained were trapped by poverty, living in bombed-out buildings.

Among them was a talented goldsmith named Len Sanitt, who had covered himself in glory during the war, serving as an engineer and seeing combat on the deadly battlefields of El-Alamein in north-western Egypt. Len's mum ran a sweet shop in the heart of the slum and had known Jo and his brothers since they were small, feeding them kosher treats. Newly married and short of money, Len was working, fixing and making jewellery, out of his mum's kitchen, covering the counter with his tools and metal dust. Keen to help Len, and get her kitchen back, his mum paid Jo a visit and suggested he meet her son. Kutchinsky's was the best jewellers in the East End and her son was the best goldsmith – it was the perfect match, she reasoned. Jo agreed to a meeting and instantly connected with Len, but he made it clear that any agreement with Kutchinsky would have to be exclusive. He didn't want the likes of Fishberg's, their Black Lion Yard rival, getting wind of their designs. The deal was sealed on a handshake. That's how it was back then. Len brought his childhood friend, Nat Stein, in to help him on the manufacturing side, and so began a partnership that would change the face of British jewellery.

The final piece of Jo's puzzle was his brother, Solly. Lily, who saw Solly as a glorified dogsbody and loathed his lack of style, refused to be in the same room as her brother-in-law and sulked melodramatically whenever his name was mentioned. But Jo, for once, ignored her. Solly was family; he'd been lucky to get out of Belgium alive, and Jo would do everything in his power to help him. It was then, with emotions running high, that my grandfather made a decision that would come back to haunt him.

The House of Kutchinsky was a family business – that was his father's vision and the image Jo wanted to present to the world – so he made Solly an equal partner, much to Lily's annoyance. But Jo was adamant that there would be no rivalry between them. If only he had instilled that same principle in his own sons, the House of Kutchinsky's history might have turned out very differently.

5

THE GOLDEN AGE

From the moment he was born, Paul Samuel Kutchinsky was treated like the prodigal son. Cradling her squalling infant to her breast, Lily felt a rush of fierce, protective love – unlike any emotion she'd experienced before. It wasn't that she didn't love her firstborn, my uncle Roger, but the nature and timing of his birth worked against him. The world was a darker place when he arrived, on 11 July 1945, after a long and difficult labour that left Lily scarred, physically and emotionally. Once she had healed, she and Jo began to carve out their niche in post-war London, and as Lily told it, Roger was dumped in the arms of a ferocious nanny, while the couple strolled around town attending fashionable parties and functions. Until Paul was born, she and Jo only had eyes for each other.

After Roger's birth, Lily put off trying for a second child. But as the economy recovered and Jo worked ever longer hours, she found herself increasingly alone and restless. Every day, she would wave Jo off to work as his brown Rolls-Royce glided back towards the urban sprawl. Cooped up in their modern four-bedroom house in Ilford, an East London suburb popular with Jewish families, having abandoned her own dream of becoming an actress, and with a strict weekly allowance to spend, she sometimes felt like just another beautiful possession for Jo Kutchinsky to flaunt. Paul's arrival on 3 March 1950, almost five years after his older brother, gave her life a new purpose. A clingy baby, Paul latched onto his mother and refused to let go. If the nanny dared pick him up, he screamed inconsolably. Lily was equally besotted. While Roger looked more like the Kutchinskys, Paul, with his dark curls, olive skin and sweet pout, was the spitting image of his mother.

As the boys grew up, Lily's favouritism became common knowledge among friends and relatives. Paul was the handsome one. The funny one. The tall one. The slim one. Even being the naughty one only added to his charm. While his older brother played by the rules and was ignored, Paul broke the rules and was adored. Lily was determined that Paul would go to the best schools. Wear the best clothes. Mix with English high society. Take elocution lessons to cure him of his spittly lisp. And one day, marry the scion of a wealthy Jewish family. He would be anglicised but not assimilated. As she pointed out to Jo, when he accused her of spoiling the boy, the youngest son was always special in the Kutchinsky family. Jo had started life as the nameless, overlooked youngest child and risen to make his family's fortune, while Lily herself was the adored baby of her family, feted for her good looks and charms, who had made the best marriage. So, while it was the inverse of English tradition to prioritise the youngest child, it made sense within their family. In Lily's mind, Paul's future at the helm of the House of Kutchinsky was already mapped out.

My dad left a cache of old black and white family photos

in a black crocodile-skin box that once housed backgammon pieces, a game he taught me to play as a child. Among them are a plethora of pictures of him and his parents. His brother is a fleeting presence. It's the same when I speak to Dad's friends. They either never knew Roger or don't have anything nice to say about him. 'Paul had a terrible relationship with his brother,' an ex-girlfriend from his teenage years recalled. Despite going out with Paul for several years, and living near the Kutchinsky family, she never knew Roger.

While five years is a significant age gap, the gulf between them seems to have widened to a chasm as they got older. Dad rarely spoke about Uncle Roger to me and when he did it was usually with disdain, deploying an array of unflattering nicknames including 'Mr Pig'. The only childhood story he ever told was about Roger reportedly tripping him down a flight of stairs. Paul was rushing after his mother to stop her leaving the house when Roger stuck his foot out. Dad always saw what may have been a genuine accident as an act of malice, a precursor to the lifelong animosity that played out between them.

*   *   *

When I started my search, I knew that at some point I would need to contact my uncle. While our families weren't close growing up, I do have fond memories of playing with my cousins as a child and bouncing exuberantly on the Seventies-style water bed in Uncle Roger and Aunty Yvette's bedroom. 'We tolerated them,' is as warm as Mum gets when discussing her former brother-in-law and his wife, of whom my abiding memory is her long, glossy brown hair that stretched all the way down her back.

When I emailed Uncle Roger, he refused to engage with me; he just replied that he didn't see the point of 'raking over the ashes of distressing incidents' which had scarred the lives of all who were involved.

In a final attempt to build bridges, I reached out to one of my most elderly relatives, Ruth, who is the daughter of Henry, Jo's oldest brother, making her Dad's cousin. 'You don't look very Jewish,' she said, scrutinising my highlighted hair and bright clothes, as I sat nursing a slice of cake in her North London living room. I laughed awkwardly. But she was generous with her time and her memories of my grandparents. She was also full of kind words about Roger. Apparently, he was a regular visitor and a great comfort to her. Buoyed up upon hearing this, and hoping my uncle had mellowed, I replied to his email saying I understood if he wanted to avoid discussing those later events surrounding the egg and the fall of the House of Kutchinsky, but might he consider sharing childhood memories of my father? After all, he was his brother and knew him all his life. He had no comment to make, he wrote, sounding both icy and irritated, the malignancy of their relationship bubbling beneath his words.

What turned their sibling relationship into such a void of ill-feeling? Aside from the inevitable emotional fallout from Lily's favouritism, the brothers seem to have subconsciously defined themselves as the antithesis of each other from an early age. While Dad was the rebel, sneaking out at night and getting into scrapes, Roger spent his free time on charity committees, raising money for the Jewish blind and playing Scrabble in the evenings. His idea of adventure was a road trip with friends to visit Winston Churchill's grave in Oxfordshire, the day after the political giant's state funeral on 30 January 1965, when Roger was nineteen. Less sociable than Dad by nature, perhaps he felt that being the 'good son' would eventually win over his mother, whom he adored.

If Roger shared anything with his brother, it was an all-consuming desire to outstrip their father. Some friends of Dad's that I spoke to during my research recalled his older brother muttering, 'If I don't do better than my father, then I fail in life and business.' Aware, perhaps, that his younger brother was being groomed as the House of Kutchinsky's future frontman, Roger wanted to find something other than jewellery to define himself by. According to his friends, he had no desire to enter the jewellery trade and no passion for it. After the egg, this ambivalence towards the family profession seems to have been his salvation; he could retreat into a different life, immersing himself in local politics and becoming a Liberal Democrat councillor.

*   *   *

The post-war era was a frustrating time for Jo, its ethos of 'make do and mend' at odds with his burning ambition to transform the fortunes of his family firm. The Commercial Road shop had survived the Blitz but it wasn't unscathed. The front was badly damaged and its windows shattered during air raids, carpeting the streets in shards of sparkling glass. The nation was still bruised and battered, rationing was causing continued misery and there was an acute housing shortage. Banks were reluctant to lend money and there was little spare cash to splash on luxuries like jewellery, with even the wealthiest people only buying second-hand pieces or redesigning old heirlooms.

It wasn't until the end of the decade, just before Dad was born, that the economy finally began to recover and the government paid out the £357. 13 shillings (about £15,460) to fund the repairs. By 1950, the shop had been restored with a freshly painted cream exterior, and the Kutchinsky name picked out above the door in black paint. A retired education worker, Judy Keiner, who lived nearby when she was a schoolgirl, remembers being struck by the contrast between the grimy devastation of Commercial Road and the 'size and the beauty of the diamonds' in the Kutchinsky shop's windows. 'I saw them when I got off the bus home from school. The display was always clean and simple with modest stands and rings with diamonds as big as the Ritz on them.'

The business received a further boost when the Conservative government cut the tax on the sale of luxury goods in 1953, which at times had stood at 100 per cent during the war. Fun and fashion returned to people's lives. The next five years were a time of rapid change. Wages soared; it was a golden age for jobs; unemployment reached a record low of 1 per cent (215,800 people) in July 1955, shortly after Anthony Eden took over from Winston Churchill as prime minister. Council estates, tower blocks and shopping centres transformed city centres. The advent of supermarkets altered shopping habits. Britain's first motorway opened in 1958. The subversive spirit of rock 'n' roll gave birth to the cultural conceit of the rebellious teenager. And Britain went on a spending spree. By 1957, the Conservative prime minister, Harold Macmillan, was presiding over an unprecedented economic boom, declaring in a speech that most Britons 'have never had it so good'.

Aware of the opportunity this golden age presented, Jo and

Len worked on designs for a new style of modern jewellery that would get them noticed. They visited foreign workshops for inspiration, travelling to Stockholm to learn the art of enamelling from the House of Bolin who, like Fabergé, had made jewels for Russia's last tsars. But it was their trips to Paris, the world's fashion capital, that proved the most fruitful. There they visited the workshops of leading jewellers, studying their forward-thinking designs and manufacturing techniques, which were far ahead of anything being produced in London. While the men spent their days locked in meetings, their wives wandered around Paris's clothes shops and cafes. Lily looked down on Len's wife, Sonia, with the sort of snobbery that is often seen in those who have hurtled up the social ladder and don't like to be reminded from whence they came. These trips were the first time Sonia, a slender blonde with a tense smile who grew up on Brick Lane, had ever flown on a plane. She was terrified, squeezing Len's hand so tight his knuckles turned white. Every night, the two couples would dine together in fancy restaurants. Lily, decked out in the latest fashions and dripping in diamonds, was always perfectly polite but Sonia never felt welcome. There was no warmth in the other woman's smile, which occasionally veered into a sneer. Once they found themselves seated near the Duke and Duchess of Windsor, aka Edward and Mrs Simpson, and Sonia remembers Lily bursting into life, brazenly craning her neck to get a glimpse of the notorious pair.

As their fortunes rose, Jo and Lily cemented their status as London's Jewish royalty. Holidays at the British seaside were swapped for the fashionable French Riviera. In the late 1950s, they started visiting Cannes, home of the famous film festival.

Their hotel of choice was the luxurious Carlton, which was the location for the 1955 Hitchcock thriller *To Catch a Thief* starring Grace Kelly and Cary Grant, and where Kelly later met her future husband, Prince Rainier of Monaco. Jo's fondness for the luxuries of the Côte d'Azur was well known in the Kutchinsky workshop. If a worker was spotted going home with dusty clothes, he would fly into a rage. 'There's money in dust,' Jo would growl, insisting they wipe their overalls and shake out their trouser turn-ups. (Gold dust, a mix of filings and powder, is worth just as much as any other form of gold and can be easily melted back down.) 'That's going in my Cannes kitty,' he would say, a note of glee in his voice as the dust swilled around in murky water, regaining its sheen.

A reel on super 8mm film survives from one of their French holidays. A Mediterranean seaside scene flickers into view with a shot of the Carlton Hotel's grand white exterior, fringed by palm trees, silhouetted in the background. The sea shimmers an iridescent blue, as a speedboat cuts across the horizon. Dad, aged about ten or twelve, is stretched out on a sun lounger. His scrawny body is clad in eye-catching zebra-print trunks. His gaze is fixed on his mother, who looks typically stylish in a frilly blue swimsuit and cat's eye sunglasses, a book resting on her lap. The film jerks forward to nighttime, where it's difficult to discern much except the curved shape of cars and fashionable silhouettes stepping out of them. The next day at the beach, Jo appears looking like a Fifties Hollywood heart-throb with his dark hair, deep tan, a pipe dangling from his mouth and his shirt sleeves rolled up to reveal a chunky wristwatch. Lily laughs as Paul clambers on top of her, while she combs her brown tresses into a bouffant. She lovingly pats his chest, before shifting back to smile at her husband behind the camera. Agitating for her attention, Paul wraps himself around his mother, showering her with kisses and holding her neck in a chokehold. In the final frames, Dad stands alone at the water's edge. He hugs himself and looks forlorn, before noticing the camera is on him. Smiling, he scarpers off into the sea and swims away, fading into the distance.

There is no trace of Roger in that particular film. Perhaps he didn't go on the holiday, or is simply out of shot. What is striking is how at home Jo and Lily look amid the splendour of the South of France, as if this were the world they were born to. If they felt imposter syndrome, they certainly didn't show it.

The House of Kutchinsky was emerging as a creative force in British jewellery. Paris had expanded Jo's artistic horizons. He and Len deviated from tradition with their avant-garde, modernist designs which chimed with the futuristic aesthetic of the decade. Under Moshe, the firm had mainly sold engagement rings and silverware: candlesticks, cutlery sets and elegant teapots. Beautiful but with a practical bent. But Jo saw each piece of jewellery as a work of art. Forged from gold, which bucked the presiding trend for the more durable platinum with its ethereal hue, his creations were a riot of colour and fun. He paired traditional gemstones with semi-precious stones such as jet-black onyx, rich blue lapis and golden-brown, and natural materials like coral which were rarely used in jewellery at the time. Meanwhile Len and Nat worked out how to reproduce the quality of the French designs in the most cost-effective way. Jo was adamant that the key to success wasn't making one-off pieces but honing a signature style that would be accessible to Britain's burgeoning middle class and set them apart from their European rivals. That was how the House of Kutchinsky made its name.

*   *   *

By 1958, the firm had outgrown the East End. Jo was ready to take the risk and 'go up West' but not everyone agreed. While Lily saw it as the logical next step in her family's social elevation, Moshe, who was eighty-five and fully retired, just shook his head and fretted in Yiddish about opening on the Sabbath. Solly, who now worked full time in the shop alongside Jo, saw the move as a betrayal of their roots and feared it might alienate their loyal East End customers, like the grandmother who first bought her engagement ring from them and had just purchased silver candlesticks as a wedding present for her great-grandchild. But Jo insisted that it was a leap they were ready to make. Opening their first West End salon would make them a fully-fledged jewellery house, he added, soothing Solly's nerves, while subtly asserting his status as the big boss. The Jewish East End was already fading from view, the ripple of London life moving onwards, outwards. 'People said to the move: what courage! I said, to stay I would have to have courage,' Jo recalled, reflecting on his big gamble two decades later in a newspaper interview.

But while Jo acted as if he didn't give the East End a backwards glance, that wasn't quite the case. He was grateful for all it had given him. His wife. His family. His wealth. As a businessman too, he was steeped in its traditions. He continued to get his suits made with a secret pocket to hold a loaded pistol in case of a robbery. Lily, terrified he would blow off his testicles or accidentally shoot someone, pleaded with him not to carry it – after all, the new shops had electric shutters and alarm systems going straight to the police station – but he refused. The rumour was he'd got the gun from the gangster brothers the Kray twins, who had been customers when the shop was still in Commercial Road. Years later, acting on orders from Lily, my dad would secretly remove the gun's firing pin, rendering it useless.

Jo's timing for the move was perfect. It was the cusp of the 1960s, the economy was booming and London was starting to swing. The House of Kutchinsky opened its new showroom in October 1958 at 69 Brompton Road in the fashionable Knightsbridge neighbourhood. Harrods, one of the world's most exclusive department stores, was just a short walk away. The shop sat proudly among a litany of designer boutiques, antique dealers, art galleries and passageways leading to smart cobbled mews where Victorian coachmen once lived. The pavements were wide and clean, and there was none of the clatter and chatter of the East End. The clientele parading up and down outside were wealthy and well groomed in fur coats, high heels and smart suits.

The firm's artistic credibility skyrocketed after it was included in an exhibition of the world's best modern jewellery in London in 1961. Held at the prestigious Goldsmiths' Hall (the headquarters of the jewellery trade) and curated by the Victoria and Albert Museum, the display featured hundreds of treasures including jaw-dropping tiaras, gold masks and flamboyant pendants submitted by exhibitors from thirty-three countries. 'The point of the exhibition is to prove that all good jewellers are artists . . .' the catalogue noted, going on to describe the show

THE GOLDEN AGE

as 'a memorial to the creative thought of the 20th century'. To this end, the exhibition mixed artistic pieces by the likes of Picasso, Jean Arp and Salvador Dalí alongside works by leading jewellery houses such as Cartier, Bulgari and Harry Winston, and bright young things like Andrew Grima, renowned for making abstract jewellery for high-profile clients like Princess Margaret. Jo provided Kutchinsky jewellery worth £25,000 (more than half a million pounds today), including a twisted gold bracelet set with diamonds and turquoise, a Jaeger pocket watch hidden inside an exquisite golden shell and a selection of his signature chunky gold cocktail rings. The exhibition was a big success with 26,000 people visiting during its five-week run and was hailed as a pivotal moment in the development of jewellery as an art form in Britain and beyond.

The House of Kutchinsky's signature gold pieces were soon adorning the bodies of a new breed of celebrity – artists, musicians and socialites – who were rising up to challenge the old class order. They lavished money on luxuries that were once the preserve of the elites and wanted accessories that were as alternative as the fashion, music and art of that era. Jo's bold, playful designs were the perfect fit. Ahead of his time, he made waves designing a boundary pushing range of jewellery for men, including hand-carved gold signet rings, set with magnificent white diamonds, and matching cufflinks. The Knightsbridge showroom became a magnet for celebrities including The Beatles and their mini-skirted girlfriends, Hollywood royalty Elizabeth Taylor, British stars Diana Dors and Joan Collins, and politicians like John Profumo, who became entangled in one of the twentieth century's most notorious sex scandals.

KUTCHINSKY'S EGG

In 1965, the Pathé News cameras, which had previously reported on Kutchinsky's success in pioneering a new style of affordable, high-fashion gold jewellery, visited the firm in its new surroundings. This film, which is titled 'Super Sparklers', is more promotional than the previous news reel, and is festive, frivolous and teeth-grindingly sexist. It features a blonde model called Eve playing the part of a human Christmas tree, wearing a wispy, triangular-shaped chiffon dress and standing atop a desk under a grand chandelier, a diamond necklace dangling from her toes. Laid out beneath her is half a million pounds' worth of jewellery. 'Any of these little pieces would gladden a woman's heart for years,' the voiceover intones. As big band music plays in the background, Jo appears, grinning awkwardly, and reaches up to fasten a necklace. Eve beams back, apparently enjoying being turned into a life-sized bauble. A sea of suited arms fills the frame as every inch of her is draped in diamonds. A bracelet is clasped around her ankle, a ring slips over her toe, her arms are adorned and each neatly manicured finger shows off a sparkler. The camera travels seductively down Eve's bejewelled body, lingering on her feet, which look almost as if they've been bound together with an extravagant necklace. She is then carried off by a uniformed doorman and placed in the safe where, we are told, she will stay till Christmas.

Anything that happened at Kutchinsky was now news. A robbery the following May at their newly opened Bond Street showroom, during which thieves escaped with £15,000 worth of jewellery (more than £300,000 today) made the newspapers. 'Bond Street gems battle' was the headline in the *Evening Standard*, which dedicated almost a full page to its report. It transpired that Lady Shepherd, a widow of a knight of the realm, armed only with a brolly, and an elderly gentleman wielding a stick, had joined forces to fight off the 'axe-swinging diamond grabbers' who laid siege to the shop in broad daylight. Recovering from a bruised arm at her home in London's Belgravia, Lady Shepherd, who lost her umbrella in the fracas, said she had a 'jolly good go' at the thieves and had helped break the windscreen of their getaway car – a grey Jaguar. Meanwhile, inside the shop, Lily's nephew Lionel Dessar was one of six sales assistants on duty. 'I was standing face-to-face with one of the bandits,' he told the newspaper. 'Only the glass on our door separated us. I wasn't going to let him in and he wasn't going to let me out. The men were threatening to break through the door as well. They could have done too – they made mincemeat out of the window,' he recalled, badly shaken. Among the stolen items grabbed through the window was a diamond necklace, a ladies' wristwatch, seven rings and a pair of diamond earclips.

This wasn't the only theft that occurred in this period. As demand for Kutchinsky jewellery grew, Jo was flooded with requests from actresses and models to borrow pieces for film premieres and society parties. Usually, these pieces were returned intact but in October 1967, the *Daily Mirror* reported that £770 (almost £18,000) of Kutchinsky jewellery had vanished after a wild 'Chelsea champagne party' attended by the likes of supermodel Twiggy and the artist David Hockney. A glittering cast of socialites, actresses and models were all interviewed by police after the party, which was organised by the society bible *Harper's Bazaar*, but to no avail. The fate of those two missing gold and diamond rings is still unknown, lost in time.

But despite these small setbacks, Jo's gamble in moving the business upmarket had paid off. The House of Kutchinsky was now one of Britain's top jewellers. Delighted by her husband's success, Lily agreed to move the family to the West End, so Jo could be near work. This meant selling her dream house in north-west London and giving up her garden, but she was excited to be moving into one of the capital's most fashionable neighbourhoods near all her favourite shopping haunts and lunch spots. After surviving the devastation of war, Lily and Jo were finally living the life they'd dreamed of when they first met.

6

THE ESCAPE

Dad loved driving. It made him feel free. In that liminal space between departure and destination, he was unleashed from responsibility. He liked nothing better than spending a day speeding from somewhere to nowhere. His favourite drive was the coastal route from London to the remote tip of north-east Scotland. It takes about ten hours, covers over 500 miles and takes in some dramatic, craggy coastal scenes. He started driving it when he was a student at Aberdeen University and found that the further he got from London, the freer he felt. This came as something of a surprise, as it had never been his plan to study so far away from home, especially after enduring five miserable years at boarding school, an experience he could never speak about without shuddering.

St Lawrence College is based on the south-east coast in Ramsgate, Kent. It has a turreted facade and ivy-covered, red-brick buildings that, to the 13-year-old Paul, were reminiscent of a horror movie set. It was not a happy place for him. He hated being separated from his mother and spent long, lonely nights crying into his pillow, wishing he was back home with her and his beloved Scottie dog, Angus. His only respite came on the precious weekends, once or twice a term, when his parents were allowed to visit. Lily and Jo would appear and take him for lunch at a beachside cafe. His mother would buy him ice cream, brush his hair and generally make a fuss of him, ignoring Jo's disapproving glower.

Despite his parents registering him under the name Paul Kaye, he endured endless taunts about his olive skin colour and refusal to eat ham sandwiches. His only friend was an Iranian boy who was also an outsider. Being skinny and not terribly athletic didn't help, and he also struggled to keep up with the academic work. His school reports hinted at his isolation, describing him as 'temperamentally independent' or 'rather an individualist'. Every holiday, he begged Lily not to send him back to that 'hellhole' with its cold dormitories, church services and army cadet camping trips, not to mention the perpetual threat of a lashing[1] with the headmaster's 'stick'. At first, Jo stood firm. The Kutchinskys might be Jewish but they were also British; Paul needed to toughen up – after all, his father had survived not just the war but prison. 'It'll get better,' Lily told her son, as he wept down the phone. But it didn't.

Scribblings inside Dad's schoolbooks hint at his distress. I found a pile of these in Mum's loft, stashed inside an old chest that was buried under a pile of designer clothes. It was a strange experience, seeing his teenage self laid out in front of me. 'I hate this place, I hate these people because I'm a right case of loneliness and upset,' he wrote inside a 1965 term calendar, angrily scratching the word 'FUCK' in blue ink across the grey cardboard cover. A horned skull with demon eyes and forked teeth decorated the inside cover, opposite a hippie with sideburns smoking a joint. Amid these angsty expressions were some more puerile acts of rebellion like crossing out the school's Latin motto *In Bono Vince* (Good Will Conquer) and replacing it with 'In Good Wanking'. There were lists of girls' names too. Long-forgotten crushes. Margaret. Alix. Liz. Janice. Jane. A few had blue ticks beside them.

Eventually, in 1965 an attempt was made to send Dad to St Paul's, a private day school in London. Addressing Paul's unhappiness in his letter of recommendation, the headmaster attributed 'young Kaye's' desire to leave the school to the fact that his parents 'are Jews and there is the usual strong family relationship'. In the end, they never went through with the move, likely because Dad's grades weren't up to the standard required for St Paul's, one of the top schools in the country. Resigned to his fate, he finally settled at St Lawrence's, started playing rugby, where his slender frame gave him an advantage as a winger, and made the chess team. He learned to play the joker, mocking himself mercilessly before others could. He was never happy, but learned to survive.

*   *   *

Paul suspected his schooling was all part of Jo's grand plans for the business. He watched as his father seized every chance to court the high-society parents who packed the grounds for prizegivings and sports days, festooning Lily with jewels and handing out his card to anyone who complimented her. Paul would squirm watching Jo, dressed up in top hat and tails, playing the English gent, the Yiddish lilt of his accent betraying him. In those moments, Paul hated his father. His anger was enhanced by the unspoken rivalry between them for Lily's love. Paul could see it burning on Jo's face whenever he was the focus of his mother's affections – sending him away to boarding school got rid of the competition. His father never admitted it, but Paul was convinced. Jo had sold the idea to Lily on the basis that it was a chance to erase the last vestiges of the East End from their family and win new clients in the upper echelons of English society. While Roger was being schooled in a local, Jewish-majority comprehensive, Paul would be a beacon of anglicisation. It was the best for everyone, Jo assured a distraught Lily.

But despite his parents shipping him off to this illustrious school and hiring a tutor to boost his grades, Paul still flunked his A levels. 'His potential is impaired by a lack of self-discipline,' his teacher wrote in a report. Dad's take on it was more straightforward: he'd smoked too much weed and skived off. After all, what did exams matter when your future was already set? 'You get your brains from your mother,' he'd joke to me whenever the subject came up.

After he scraped a D in maths and an E (the lowest possible pass) in physics, none of his chosen universities would take him. Going straight into the jewellery business would have pleased his parents, but he didn't feel ready for the pressure. Jo Kutchinsky was so well known in the trade, how would he ever measure up? Paul liked the idea of taking time out to experiment with a new life, a new identity. Grabbing the phone book, he started flicking through it alphabetically and called the first university he found, which was Aberdeen. He was shocked when they offered him a place to study science, a broad-base degree which would allow him to specialise in his final year. He had little interest in Scotland and even less

THE ESCAPE

desire to continue studying, but once he realised it was about as far from his family as he could go without leaving Britain, he accepted. It was a chance to escape the pressure of his father's expectations and his mother's stultifying love.

For the first time, Paul felt in charge of his own life. Finally, he had an existence that was nothing to do with jewellery and very little to do with being Jewish. Feeling confident in his resolve, he set off for Scotland in his souped-up, brown Ford Cortina, accelerating towards a new life of friends and freedom.

But there were some aspects of his London life that he found harder to leave behind. I was rifling through my mum's attic, rails of her old designer clothes crammed into the eaves, the Scottish wind howling and the waves lashing the cliffs below, when I unearthed more of Dad's old photographs stuffed into a battered King Edward's cigar box. Among them were pictures of him, aged about nineteen, with his arms wrapped around a beautiful blonde girl accompanied by a trove of love letters. This was Adele, his girlfriend before Mum, whom he affectionately called his 'darling Dellykins'. The letters date from autumn 1969, the start of his second year at Aberdeen University. I knew Adele. Her daughter had been in my year at secondary school, and somehow we worked out we had this slightly awkward connection. Occasionally, our families would collide on skiing holidays or at elaborate Jewish weddings. When, in the course of writing this book, I reached out to ask her to share her memories of Dad, I was touched by how warmly she spoke of him. I visited her in her elegant West London home, and she produced copies of the same photos Dad had saved of them together, as well as a few I hadn't seen before of a heartachingly young Paul, all skinny limbs, velvet flares and roll-neck jumpers.

They had first met in July 1969. Paul was home for the summer holidays, after finishing his first year at university, and Adele was dating his friend Gary. Paul picked her up one evening, at Gary's request, to drive her to a party the night after Neil Armstrong became the first man to walk on the moon. Adele's family were watching the Apollo 11 mission in their living room on their black and white TV when Paul sauntered in. 'Hello Moon,' he quipped.

'I thought he was fantastic,' Adele told me, recalling that moment. 'It was just chemistry. Suddenly I didn't want to be with Gary.' But it wasn't until fate put Paul and Adele on the same plane headed for the same resort in Italy a few weeks later that any lingering loyalty to Gary was put aside – by both of them. She was holidaying with her family at a grand hotel while Dad, who was travelling on a budget with his best friend Leon, was down the road in what Adele described as 'a dump'. On their first night, she invited them over for drinks in the hotel bar. A storm blew up which left the boys stranded, so they slept over in her room. After that Paul and Adele were an item.

On paper, Adele was perfect. Her family lived nearby in the West End, they shared friends and were members of the same synagogue – not that Dad went often. But nobody was good enough for Lily's 'prince'. Despite the frosty reception she received, Adele, who harboured dreams of a career in fashion, was impressed by Lily's matriarchal glamour. She recalls my grandmother doing domestic tasks like cooking and washing dishes while wearing a lilac and green Pucci mini dress, silver kitten heel slippers and large diamond earrings. 'She was very chic,' Adele gushed admiringly. 'My mother always wore an apron when she cooked.'

Paul and Adele were serious about each other, in the way first love feels like it will last forever; Adele remembers owning a Kutchinsky ring which she thinks Dad made for her – a delicate gold band topped with an acorn-like tiger's eye bead. But Paul couldn't shake the feeling something was missing. For him, Scotland was a retreat. Not from her, but from what he saw as the narrowness of London Jewish society, where even his generation, though more anglicised than his parents', still lived, worked and dated in an almost impenetrable social bubble. Going away to university had opened his eyes to the possibility of a different life. He felt torn.

A few nights before he left to begin his second year, a bitter row erupted over the dinner table after Lily made some rude remarks about Adele, making it clear she wasn't wealthy enough to be a suitable partner for a Kutchinsky. This snobbishness was Lily's worst trait. Jo, not wanting to be on the receiving end of his wife's acid tongue, stayed out of it. Once she had finished eviscerating Adele, Lily switched to lamenting Paul's decision to study in the wilds of Scotland and his failure to keep his promise to call home on Friday nights. Paul, wearily familiar with this line of attack, simply rolled his eyes. It's all my fault for sending you away to boarding school, she sobbed, pushing back her chair and clattering out of the room in tears, while Jo puffed silently on his pipe.

On the morning of his departure, Paul crept out of his parents' flat at dawn. He'd packed the night before, while they were out at a charity ball. The back seat was crammed with his belongings: records, books, paints, a chess set and a few bottles of spirits pinched from his father's collection. On the passenger seat sat a framed photograph of him and his mother on holiday. He'd grabbed it as he was leaving in a sentimental moment. Lily looked elegant in a pale blue patterned swimsuit and sunglasses, her hair piled on her head. Paul sat next to her, a pensive teenager, his shirt unbuttoned and feet bare. Sliding around on top was a rectangular black leather box that he had found left outside his bedroom door, which he suspected contained a peace offering from his parents. Too late.

Streaks of sunlight criss-crossed the sky as he approached the Midlands. Hunger stabbed at his gut, reminding him he hadn't eaten since sunrise. He stopped at a roadside cafe where he found a quiet corner in which to guiltily devour a bacon sandwich. Ketchup squirted from between the slices of soft white bread and dripped onto his black velvet flares. Shit. He rubbed it with a napkin but the stain only spread across the soft fabric. Karma for indulging in his favourite non-kosher treat.

Back in the car, he tuned the dial until Jimi Hendrix came crackling through the radio. At home, his mother always nagged him to turn his music down. Anything with guitars made her wince. She liked swing and jazz and watching musicals in West End theatres. It was a toss-up as to what she hated more – rock music or his new girlfriend.

Careering northwards up the motorway, Paul found himself marooned behind a large white lorry. He accelerated to overtake but a gust of wind buffeted its awning, blocking his view of the road ahead which was slick and slippery from rain. As he swerved back in front, he worried for a moment that he'd misjudged the gap. The car in front was perilously close. He

THE ESCAPE

slammed on the brakes and stopped just in time. Tired and shaken, he gripped the wheel and breathed out slowly.

Darkness had fallen by the time he reached the ancient stone bridge over the River Dee that marked the gateway to the Silver City, as Aberdeen is known due to its wealth of grey granite buildings that sparkle in the all too rare sunshine. Scotland's third-largest city was at a crossroads. The discovery of North Sea oil, or 'black gold', off the coast in December 1969, at the start of Paul's second year, transformed the city from an ancient port, reliant on traditional industries like fishing and shipbuilding, to the oil capital of Europe. Aberdonians looked on bewildered as Stetson-sporting American oil barons poured into the city, snapping up houses, boosting the economy, bringing with them hamburger joints and sugary treats like Lucky Charms cereal. Paul would witness the rapid pace of change over the coming decades but at first all he noticed was the biting cold, the cheap price of a pint of beer (once he learned to mimic the local accent well enough to get served) and the stench of fish wafting from the harbour through the city's narrow streets.

In his first year, he'd rented a room in a shared house. Nine Belvidere Crescent was a two-storey granite villa in Rosemount, a fashionable part of town popular with more well-off students. The location was good and he liked his housemates, so he'd decided to stay on in his second year. He parked up in the street outside and started hauling his possessions up the front garden path. It was late, around 11 p.m., according to the clock on the dashboard. A sea mist had settled over the city and there was an eerie chill that made him feel even more detached from reality.

KUTCHINSKY'S EGG

Back in his room with its single bed, small desk and patterned carpet, he flicked the gas heater on and crouched over it. He ran his thumb over the leather box that his mother had left outside his room and pressed the hidden catch. Nestled on the luxurious white silk lining which bore the House of Kutchinsky logo in grey was a men's wristwatch with a gold dial and black alligator-skin strap. It was exactly the sort of watch he wished his father made more of. Jo's watches were extravagantly designed, with clusters of gemstones obscuring the dial, making it hard to read the time. If a customer dared to point this out, Jo would just stare at them wide-eyed. '*The time,*' he'd say, feigning shock, his eyes twinkling. '*If you can afford this watch, you don't need* the *time!*' It was a classic Jo routine.

Fastening it around his wrist, Paul stretched his arm out and admired it, feeling a wave of guilt for being so sulky with Lily before he left. But was it a generous gift or a golden handcuff?

*   *   *

Mum used to tell me an edited version of how she and Dad met, but when I was ten years old, I snuck into my parents' book-lined study and found hints of an unabridged love story in an old diary. After he left, I knew better than to open that wound and it wasn't until one Christmas, two decades later, that the full story came pouring out.

Mum's university friend, Maria, had arrived to spend the festive period with us. A retired fashion executive who had enjoyed a jet-set career, I used to joke that her and Mum together were like the lead characters from *Absolutely Fabulous*, Patsy and Edina, minus the vodka swigging and cocaine snorting.

THE ESCAPE

On Christmas Eve, we were seated in the kitchen of Mum's seaside home, with its dramatic cliff-top vistas, preparing the meal for the big day around the long wooden table. Mum and Maria fell into the intimate conversation of friends who have known each other for almost half a century.

'Your dad looked like a Jewish Cat Stevens,' Maria said, when I asked what he was like at university, where they all first met. The comparison took me by surprise but after googling the Seventies folk star, I could see the likeness. 'He used to come to lectures wearing a long cashmere coat,' Maria continued. 'Your mum fancied him but wouldn't do anything about it. She drove me mad!' Mum rolled her eyes in Maria's direction, wrestling the giant turkey into a roasting tray ready to be shoved in the oven at daybreak. Vegetables were chopped and dropped into bubbling pans on the stove.

I filled the silence by searching for Cat Stevens on the ancient iPod dock that served as a stereo in the kitchen, and pressed play on the first track that appeared. 'The First Cut Is the Deepest'. Ethereal guitar chords and a soft, beguiling baritone filled the kitchen. Mum stiffened in recognition. As the song played, she refilled her glass and started to talk, transporting me back to Aberdeen University in the early Seventies.

Brenda Bruce Strachan wasn't Paul's type. He liked blondes with perky breasts who laughed at his jokes. Brenda was twenty, a year older than him, striking-looking and cool in a bookish kind of way. Her light brown hair flopped across her face, cloaking deep-set turquoise eyes and high cheekbones. She dressed in hippyish clothes – long velvet skirts, embroidered blouses and Afghan coats. She'd grown up in Peterhead, a bleak fishing port on the north-east coast. Her parents had moved to Aberdeen and she was living at home with them while she studied, to save money. Her plan was to graduate, move to Edinburgh and become a writer.

With his wild, dark hair and slim frame, Paul stood out in Aberdeen. He was clean-shaven and his face was framed with round spectacles with thin, gold rims. He went about with a small set of wealthy English friends and, like Brenda, he dressed in the fashion of the time, except that his flares were designer, his long coat was cashmere and his platform boots were made of Italian leather.

Brenda noticed him first. At the start of his second year, Paul switched to an arts degree which, in his case, meant swapping long days in the lab for supposed study sessions in coffee bars punctuated by the odd lecture. Their paths crossed when they found themselves in the same psychology lectures. Brenda was single and had several men buzzing around, but for her it had to be a big love or it wasn't worth the emotional risk. Instead of making a move on Paul, she pumped Maria, whose outgoing personality complemented Brenda's more introverted nature, for information as Maria had briefly dated a friend of his, Adrian. Over coffee in their favourite haunt, The Dungeon, Maria gave her the lowdown. All she knew was that his name was Paul K, that he was rich, from London and while fancied by girls, he wasn't a 'lothario'. Then Maria turned the conversation back to the gig they were organising at the student union in a few weeks' time with Hawkwind, a space rock band who were big on the underground scene. Brenda sighed. The last gig she'd helped Maria organise at the union had ended with her drinking too many snakebites (a potent mix of lager and cider with a dash of blackcurrant cordial) while Maria stood at the front making eyes at the singer.

At first, Paul kept his promise to write to Adele several times a week and received exuberant letters back covered in spidery kisses and filled with updates on her job hunts, social outings and latest fashion purchases. He made regular trips back to London and they spent holidays together, with their families, in Bournemouth and the South of France. But distance eventually caused the spark to fizzle.

Meanwhile, Brenda still fancied Paul from afar but there had been no opportunity to find out if the feeling might be reciprocated. The closest they'd come was a brief, flirty chat during a night out at a bar with mutual friends. She had walked home that night feeling confused. At first, he'd seemed interested but had then pulled away. Perhaps the rumour that he had a girlfriend back home was true. Busy with studies and student parties, she pushed all thoughts of the 'Jewish Cat Stevens', as Maria insisted on calling him, to the back of her mind until one snowy afternoon in January 1971, when Paul walked into The Dungeon and sat down with a friend.

Brenda and Maria were seated nearby, gossiping about the previous weekend's parties and the guys they were sort-of seeing. Trying to pretend she hadn't noticed him, Brenda kept talking until Maria grabbed her arm and pointed in the direction of the seat Paul had just vacated. Lying forgotten on the table were a pair of black leather gloves. It was a gift from the gods, Maria said, urging Brenda to go and retrieve them. When she refused, Maria got up, grabbed the gloves and stuffed them in her friend's bag with a satisfied grin. 'I've given fate a helping hand, now it's your turn,' she said teasingly.

Brenda grimaced. 'Thanks,' she hissed sarcastically. But secretly, she was pleased. Finally, she had an excuse to speak to Paul, to find out if there was actually a spark there. When she got home, Brenda unfolded the gloves from her bag and smoothed them out, her fingers surprised by the softness of the leather. Folding them away in a drawer, she pondered the best course of action. She didn't want Paul to think she was so desperate that she'd stolen his possessions to secure a date. She could explain that Maria picked them up, she consoled herself, cringing at the thought. Slamming the drawer shut, her cheeks flushed; she resolved to do nothing.

A few days later she ran into Paul at a gig. Surprised by how pleased she was to see him, she left her friends downstairs and spent most of the night chatting to him but failed to mention the gloves. The moment never felt right and he was giving her mixed signals. Maybe, she thought, she could drop them back in The Dungeon or send them anonymously in the post; anything that would avoid looking like she might have a crush on him. Almost a fortnight passed before fate brought them together again. She was back in The Dungeon with Maria, when he walked in, this time alone. Maria watched as Brenda's gaze honed in on him. 'You still haven't told him, have you?' she demanded.

'I don't even know his full name,' Brenda said defensively. 'And I think he's got a girlfriend in London.'

'If you don't let him know you've got those bloody gloves, I will!' Maria said, tossing her long brown hair over her shoulder emphatically.

'Remind me why we're friends?' Brenda groaned, wriggling out of her seat. 'Alright, I'm going!'

THE ESCAPE

The gloves were still at Brenda's house, which was slightly out of town, so she and Paul arranged to meet the next day at 6 p.m. outside the Psychology Library. Brenda spent a long time getting ready, doing her make-up, curling her hair and choosing her outfit. She ran the short distance from the bus stop to the library in her high-heeled platform boots, just to make sure she wasn't late. But when Paul showed up, he just grabbed the gloves and scurried off, promising to buy her a coffee sometime. Freezing in her short skirt, Brenda stared in disbelief at his retreating figure.

Paul was holding back. Adele was coming to visit him in Aberdeen for the first time, flying to Edinburgh and then driving almost a hundred miles.

The relationship had cooled but their lives were intertwined in a way that his non-Jewish university friends didn't quite understand. He felt he owed it to her to at least try to make it work. But suddenly, he found he kept bumping into Brenda on campus, going for coffees after lectures and giving her lifts home. Brenda, who'd been hanging out with another guy she liked called Eric, started writing in her diary about Paul K again but was still convinced nothing would happen between them. Although he wasn't flashy, he was clearly from a wealthy family – why would he be interested in Brenda Bruce Strachan? It's true that her dad, Johnny, was a local celebrity in Peterhead. In 1959, he had scored the winning goal for their local team, Fraserburgh FC, in a historic football match against Dundee United, who were a top-tier club. Their defeat in the first round of the Scottish Cup by the much lower-ranked Fraserburgh, who were only a semi-professional team, is still cited as one of the greatest upsets in Scottish football. But that fleeting moment of glory didn't compare to a lifetime of riches. It was a lost cause, she told herself glumly.

Adele's visit crystallised the fact it was over between her and Paul. Her new fur coat, which she'd been so excited to show him, looked horribly out of place in the student union. He felt on edge the whole time and found himself mocking her for liking Stevie Wonder and other 'soppy' music. He hated himself for being mean to her but it was clear to them both she didn't fit into his life there. The worst part was when, arm-in-arm with Adele, he bumped into Brenda on the steps of the union. Terrified that Adele would see how much he liked this Scottish girl, he avoided eye contact and rushed past her. Confused and hurt, Brenda assumed he was too busy with his glamorous girlfriend to notice her existence.

It was the last week of term before their paths crossed again. Paul spotted her in the union bar and, feeling bad for blanking Brenda, bought her a drink. They spent the rest of the night locked in conversation. Then Brenda invited him and Maria's ex, Adrian, to a house party. After a few hours, she and Paul left there and walked back to Belvidere Crescent where they sat huddled in his room by the heater, smoking and talking until the early hours. Paul confessed he had been intimidated by her because she was part of the hip music crowd. He walked her home and after that they were inseparable.

Their first proper date was on the last day of the spring term at the St Machar pub in Old Aberdeen. Mum still remembers every detail. It was lunchtime and Paul was due to get the train back to London that evening. The narrow bar was buzzing with people drinking and playing darts, while the rain poured down outside. Squeezed into a corner table by the steamed-up window, Paul sat on a red leather banquette nursing a pint and a plate of stovies (a hearty potato stew), glancing up every time the door swung open. He felt strangely nervous. What was it about this Scottish girl that had gotten under his skin? She was different to anyone he'd ever dated. She had no idea who the Kutchinsky family were, had no interest in designer clothes and loved talking for hours about politics and books. She was smart too – although not punctual. Glancing at his watch, he realised she was now an hour late. Was she coming?

Just as he was about to leave, Brenda crashed through the door, soaked to the skin. Her long brown hair was plastered to her face, her thrift shop blouse was soaked through and mascara ran in leaky dark pools down her face. 'I was like a drowned rat,' she recalls. As she scanned the throng of people lining the bar, disappointment crept across her face. She was too late. He'd given up and gone.

Smiling, Paul stood up and called her name, waving to catch her eye.

'Sorry,' she panted, blushing. 'Buses were late. So much rain!'

Despite the shaky start, the date was a great success. The first thing he would do when he got back to Aberdeen after the holidays, he promised, was take her out for dinner on a proper date. He still felt guilty about hurting Adele but he was resolved – it had to be done.

Sleet-soaked streets and a brisk wind, with tantalising chinks of sunlight, greeted him when he returned to Scotland at the end of April. Aberdeen's granite buildings seemed to blend into the ominous skies, but not even the Scottish weather could dampen his spirits. The first thing he did after unpacking was call Brenda. Do you like Indian food? he asked, after her initial excitement at learning he was back in Scotland had subsided. He'd missed her birthday a few weeks earlier and wanted to take her somewhere special. People didn't really eat Indian food in north-east Scotland, Brenda said, laughing. Intrigued, she agreed to try it.

They started going out officially after that night. My parents fell in love hard, fast and completely, forming a partnership that would last almost twenty years. But it would take a long time for Paul to pluck up the courage to tell his parents about his new, non-Jewish girlfriend. When they first visited Aberdeen for his graduation that summer, Paul sheepishly introduced Brenda as his friend. He'd explained to her about his religion, how it only mattered to his parents, but she couldn't help worrying about what this meant for their future. In the photos from that day, one of which I keep framed on my wall, Paul's thick, frizzy hair hangs past his shoulder; with his long hair and big lips he looks as much like Lily as I look like him. Seated in a studded leather chair, his black gown draped over a neat suit, he is smiling nervously at the camera, his mortar board on his lap.

It wasn't until Brenda moved to London in late 1972 that Paul told Lily and Jo the truth about their relationship. Paul begged his parents to meet his new girlfriend, convinced they would warm to her charms. A meeting was arranged at their new house in an affluent part of north-west London. At the time, Brenda and Maria were working in a West End restaurant while figuring out what to do with their lives. Their uniform consisted of a top hat and long skirt with a split up the side, and they made a lot from the tips. Brenda used her wages to buy a new dress for the occasion but it wouldn't have mattered what she wore. The meeting was less afternoon tea and more a ruthless interrogation, designed to send her scurrying back to Scotland. Lily was vicious, almost as if she felt compelled to prove her own position within the family by casting aspersions on those who might wish to join. Any hope Paul had harboured that his mother's own experience of being disapproved of might spark empathy was soon extinguished. In Lily's eyes, Brenda being both Christian and working class were far greater crimes than coming from a family of insufficient wealth. 'I was persona non grata,' says Mum, half smiling at the memory. 'Lily was terrible to me but I wasn't intimidated. They were just people underneath it all. Paul was her favourite. They had planned he would marry somebody well established in the Jewish community, but your dad wanted to escape all that.'

When they got engaged in 1974, Lily was incandescent with rage. Determined to put an end to it, she sent her nephews, Stanley Dessau and David Morein, who both worked in the Knightsbridge shop, to Aberdeen with instructions to force Brenda's parents to break it off. It's rumoured that Lily told her nephews, if all else failed, to buy them off. The Strachans had to understand that Brenda, a working-class Scottish 'shiksa' (non-Jew), was not a suitable match for her Paulie. If the marriage went ahead, their children wouldn't be Jewish, since the religion passes through the mother. It was an unthinkable situation for the Kutchinskys to be in. The fact that Brenda was converting to Judaism, a two-year process that included studying Jewish history, learning some Hebrew and keeping a kosher kitchen, wasn't enough in Lily's eyes.

I spoke to Stanley over the phone in 2024, when he was cocooned in his Marylebone flat, isolated from the world and still understandably fearful of Covid-19. At ninety-four, he was one of the last survivors of their generation. 'Lily always said Brenda was born a Christian, and she would die a Christian,' he told me, his voice slow and scratchy. 'I didn't want to carry out her dirty work. I had no choice. I was told to get on a plane to Scotland, find the Strachans and get rid of Brenda.

'Lily was furious because your mother wasn't Jewish,' he said. 'The Kutchinskys were a famous family in Jewish circles. This was a humiliation. I understood where they were coming from, but I still felt horrible, turning up at a stranger's house like that.'

Dressed in expensive navy suits and clutching leather briefcases, Stanley and David stood out at Aberdeen Airport. Stanley had never been this far north. The thick Aberdonian accent sounded like a foreign language to him, and the bracing North Sea wind lashed his skin.

'We didn't know where the Strachans lived or what their phone number was, but we knew we couldn't go back and say we'd failed at the first hurdle. So we called every Strachan in the phonebook and asked them if they knew Paul Kutchinsky. Most of them slammed the phone down on us. I couldn't really understand what they were saying, but I assume they thought we were practical jokers.'

Finally, Brenda's parents, Maud and Johnny, answered the phone. Not fully comprehending the situation, they invited these strangers round for tea. After hiring a car and struggling to decipher the directions Johnny had given them, they eventually found Raeden Crescent, a sprawling housing estate built into a grassy slope, where blocks of flats mingled with neat rows of terraced houses. Each had the same pebbledash exterior and tiny front garden with its own iron gate. Johnny's bedding plants lit up the grey landscape with splashes of purple, pink and red.

'They received us very kindly, warming us up with tea and a tasty cake,' Stanley told me. 'But they refused to get involved. We tried to explain about the religion, but Johnny just puffed on a cigar and said, "That's a strong kirk (church)." He was a character. I could tell he was fond of Paul. They just wanted their daughter to be happy, but I don't think they fully understood the world she was entering into.'

When she heard that the plan had failed, Lily went ballistic. She threatened to cut Paul off financially. The business would go to his brother, Roger, she said. Brenda would never be accepted. When that didn't work, she tried a softer approach, promising that if Paul cancelled the wedding, they would make an effort with his girlfriend. Paul, who hated confrontation, bowed to the pressure. The first Brenda knew of it was when he came home that night to the flat they shared in West London with a box of 'wedding cancelled' cards. Upset by Paul's cowardice, Brenda gave him a deadline of six months. Either he stood up to his parents or she would leave London for good.

Caught between the two women he loved, he made a final decision. Paul defied his mother and married mine on 30 November 1975, at a Central London synagogue in a low-key ceremony followed by a party in a grand country house hotel, a short drive away. Brenda had taken her white wedding gown, which she'd saved for months to buy, back to the shop after the original date was cancelled. Instead, she wore an elegant blue smock dress with a cream silk blouse underneath. Her auburn hair was cut into a long bob that danced around her cheekbones. Paul wore a black velvet suit, with a wide-brimmed hat and big spectacles. Their faces glowed with matching, jaw-aching grins. Lily and Jo refused to attend. It was a snub that my father learned to live with but never forgave.

After the wedding, Brenda set about winning over her frosty in-laws. She observed all the Jewish holidays, attended synagogue and dutifully took her mother-in-law's advice on furnishings and fashion. Slowly, Lily began to thaw. Jo worked long hours, and she was lonely. She had a chauffeur-driven Rolls-Royce at her disposal and would turn up and take Brenda shopping, to see an art exhibition, or for a trip to the seaside. United by their love of Paul, the women slowly forged an unlikely alliance to mastermind his ascent.

7

THE RISE

After university, Dad had heated debates with Jo over his future. Secretly, he dreamed of returning to Scotland and striking out on his own, an ambition fuelled by his family's stubborn refusal to accept Brenda. He talked about opening a gallery in Aberdeen selling antiques and glass objects. Jo, of course, had other ideas; he had raised his son as heir to the House of Kutchinsky. Jo won – with caveats. If Paul was going to be forced into his father's trade, he was adamant that he didn't want to wear a suit every day and stand around like a performing monkey. He wanted to do something creative. In early 1972, a deal was struck. Paul had enjoyed helping out in the workshop during university holidays, learning the jeweller's craft, and it was agreed he would spend a year there as an apprentice. Unlike the other salesmen, he would learn how to make a Kutchinsky collection in its entirety, from start to finish.

Dad looked back on that time as the happiest of his career. The forty-strong workshop, which was tucked behind a winking neon Coca-Cola sign in the heart of London's theatreland, was a place where he could be one of the boys rather than the boss's son. He liked the banter, the smell of sweat mixed with smouldering gold, dust and chemicals, and the physical nature of the work. His seat on the bench – a long wooden table that ran through the middle of the room – was next to a large window and he would spend his spare time gazing out at the winding streets of Soho, London's red-light district. After work, the men would head across the street to the Piccadilly Theatre bar. They never went to a show, most of them couldn't afford it, but would amuse themselves by spotting famous actors coming and going.

The founders of the workshop, Len and Nat Stein, treated Paul like family. They nurtured his talent and taught him their secrets. Then, two decades later, he betrayed them.

*   *   *

From the minute I was born, on a warm summer night in 1979, I was undeniably Daddy's girl. As the eldest I benefited from the full force of his attention, and while my younger sister, Katrina, clung tightly to my mother, I was different. Later, Mum would describe the bond between my father and me as a 'poisoned chalice' that divided me from her and my sisters.

My arrival was big news. Mum's hospital room filled with cards and flowers. Jo and Lily came to coo over me, remarking how much I looked like Paul with my feathery dark hair and brown eyes. Dressed in a stylish white nightdress, Mum cradled me and smiled sheepishly as Dad snapped endless photographs. Her style had evolved from her student hippy days to a more timeless look. The hair framing her face was dyed a soft buttery blonde, and she wore a gold necklace with a butterfly pendant around her neck. After almost a decade with Paul, she'd settled into life with the Kutchinsky family but still kept her own identity, working as a psychiatric social worker right up until my birth.

Lily signalled her new closeness to Brenda by insisting the chauffeur drive us home from hospital in their Rolls-Royce. The majestic vehicle pulled up outside Seven Garthside, a newly built detached house in a tree-lined cul-de-sac on the edge of Richmond Park in south-west London, which my parents had bought with Jo and Lily's help. For Mum, who'd grown up in the countryside, it was a perfect compromise. Dad loved the leafy exclusiveness of the area and quickly made friends with the neighbours, including the charismatic Italian fashion executive and his dancer wife who lived next door.

Dad, like a lot of men back then, didn't really get involved with the late nights or nappy changing. Instead, he painted a fairy-tale castle mural on my bedroom wall and, as I grew older, enjoyed buying me clothes including a mini fox fur coat, which I wore with a Parisian-style beret. I was horrified to find pictures of my toddler self swaddled in animal skin, but furs were a status symbol back then and a staple part of the Kutchinsky women's wardrobe. Every weekday morning, Dad would kiss Mum and me goodbye, jump into his navy blue BMW and drive the 11 miles to the House of Kutchinsky's Bond Street salon, where he was now manager.

*   *   *

Home movies of my early childhood – 'the innocent days' as Mum calls them – were languishing on VHS tapes in her shed in Scotland until I excavated them. It's a miracle they survived the decades of harsh winters and salty sea air. Watching the footage now, I am struck by my father's almost journalistic attention to detail as he documents happy moments in our lives like holidays, carol concerts and birthday parties. A fan of gadgets and technological wizardry, he bought one of the first home video cameras and carted it around everywhere, his eye glued to its lens. The result is hours of footage in which he is present but invisible – an absence in our midst.

I have vivid memories of him skiing backwards down the Alps with the camera around his neck, filming me. He and Mum had learned to ski as students on the slopes of Britain's tallest mountain, Ben Nevis, and they had me on skis almost before I could walk. What he lacked in finesse, he made up for in enthusiasm. Like him, I would bomb down the training slopes, often landing in a snowy heap. I especially loved going on chair lifts with Dad, our legs dangling in the air as we ascended the mountain, pine trees and people shrinking below us. I would nestle next to him in his white woolly hat and orange goggles and pretend I wasn't scared. Back at our apartment, with its Seventies-style animal-skin rugs and low-slung leather chairs, he would film the sunset over the mountains as Katrina and I danced around the balcony, brandishing Barbie dolls.

These videos are full of ghosts. In one, recorded in late June 1983, we are on holiday in a villa in the South of France with Mum's family. Mum is tanned, topless and slender, a pearl and diamond necklace sparkling at her throat. She is floating in a blow-up boat with two-year-old Katrina, while I splash around in the pool with my cousins. There is the tinkle of lazy laughter. At one point I walk right up to the lens and ask for an ice cream, smiling. Watching it now, I'm struck by the flirty intimacy between my parents, a closeness I barely remember.

Dad's fondness for the South of France shines through in his David Attenborough-esque commentary, as he films a sunset over the bay. The camera sweeps across the horizon and back onto the cobbled streets, ending with a close-up of our blue Volvo station wagon. He is still filming as he arrives at the restaurant and I trot towards him, the lilt of a saxophone echoing around the square. Katrina is enthroned on Mum's knee. Mum looks stylish with her long dark-blonde hair, big glasses and yellow-striped sundress with a split at the back. Our symbiotic father–daughter dance continues into the night, as I twirl around a palm tree and jump off it with a flourish, all the while checking he is filming me. Watching it now, I envy the way my childhood self is so blissfully secure in his presence.

'Was that good, Daddy?' I ask, sounding almost tipsy in the way children do when they are high on tiredness.

'Marvellous, Cece, it was marvellous.'

Watching these clips is like rewatching old episodes of a soap opera when you know the tragic fates that befall your favourite characters. Of the ten people in the video, four are now dead, and Mum has since severed all ties with her sister. I'm there as part of the cast, Cece or Sub (short for Yellow Submarine, which is what happens when ex-hippy parents dress you in a yellow sleepsuit), but these aren't my memories. I barely recognise the smiling, self-assured man playing the role of my father. I press pause and scrunch my fists into my eyes, scared that if I start crying, I won't stop.

KUTCHINSKY'S EGG

*   *   *

Slowly, Dad's resistance to his father's dynastic dream had evaporated. He had even started to see similarities between the art of salesmanship and his psychology studies. Four years before I was born, he had given an enthusiastic interview to the *Jewish Chronicle* newspaper on this subject. 'What happens in this shop is directly related to psychology,' he explained. 'You have to find out not just the needs of your customers but why they want something. You can't eat expensive jewellery. It won't keep you warm. So why do people buy it? For some it means status and position. Among sheikhs today, for example, if a woman is not drowned in all the latest jewels, people look down their noses. Then there are other people who love jewellery for its own sake. They always want more.'

The jewellery market was booming at the start of the 1980s. The surge in the post-war oil industry had brought spectacular wealth to the Middle East. Now, the princes of these newly independent nations travelled to the West in search of jewels for their wives and exquisite *objets d'art* for their palaces and private jets. When they arrived in London, they found a natural home in the House of Kutchinsky. Grandpa Jo fervently believed that the Jews and the Arabs, despite their differences, shared an understanding of the importance of haggling. This was what gave him the edge over his more traditional competitors: the ability to spend days locked in leisurely negotiations with Middle Eastern royalty. Unlike other jewellers, who saw it as insulting, Jo, with his East End roots, was happy to engage and he instilled this ethos in his sons.

Meanwhile, Dad matured into his role as the frontman of

the Bond Street shop. He had the same instinctive appreciation of beauty as Jo, coupled with the unshakeable confidence of youth. It wasn't long before he started leading sales trips to the Middle East. While he was serious about closing deals, he also relished the adventure and opulence of those trips. Once in Oman, he stayed up drinking the night away in the bar of the country's newest five-star hotel – one of the few places you could buy alcohol. The next day, there was no sign of him at breakfast. Just as the salesman was about to give up and head to the royal palace alone, his boss staggered into the lobby, his skin several shades of green and his shirt untucked. He'd just 'christened' the toilet bowl of his new bathroom, he said proudly, wiping the back of his hand across his mouth and snorting at his own joke. Despite the inglorious start, they ended the day on a high – securing several high-value sales.

In a tender postcard home, addressed to 'Teddy' (his nickname for Mum) from one of these trips, dated March 1982, Dad wrote: 'Working hard here, my feet are killing me from all the time I have spent on [them] ... We have made all the right contacts and I hope they will pay off.' He also asked after me, joking that I was too busy to come to the telephone to speak to him. I savour these fragments of him. The messy scrawl. The sentimental jokes. The flash of neediness. There's a picture of Dad, in a faceless hotel room, doing a military salute in front of a poster of one of the Sultan of Brunei's wives. It's one of the few pictures where he's not wearing glasses. He looks exposed, like a fish whose shimmering scales have been scraped off.

Back in London, he made plans to create a new style of jewellery that would capture the imagination of the English upper classes. Elegant, dainty, feminine, it would break with Jo's orthodoxy that bigger was better. Kutchinsky could easily be as famous as Cartier, Paul would tell Brenda, drumming his fingers in frustration on the low black coffee table they'd bought on their travels around India. Dad was fixated on the idea that the firm's Jewish heritage held them back. He cringed whenever his father instinctively referred to their less expensive jewellery as 'shlock' (Yiddish for low-quality goods) in front of clients. They were never given a British royal warrant, Paul complained, because they were seen as glorified market traders. After a few drinks, his usual cheery warmth would give way to sullenness, a sense that no matter how far he ran from his Jewishness – marrying Mum, avoiding synagogue except on high holy days, shunning the North London suburbs – it would always hold him back.

Dad's other frustration was Jo's refusal to get rid of Uncle Solly. Despite being fond of him, Paul would bemoan his scruffy suits and shaggy hair. Why were the old man's flies always undone? he lamented. It would be funny if it wasn't such a terrible look for the business, especially when he clambered onto the desks in the showroom to dust the chandeliers, almost giving clients a full frontal. Solly didn't fit with the modern, international look he wanted the House of Kutchinsky to project. While Jo retained a lingering loyalty to his brother, Lily shared Dad's view. In her mind, the business belonged to Jo and there was no way that Solly's sons, Joshua and Danny, would ever inherit it. 'Over my dead body,' she would pronounce, eyes flashing, stamping her dainty foot with her arms folded defiantly across her chest.

As time passed, the mutual dislike between Lily and Solly

had hardened into a visceral loathing which neither tried to hide. 'The day he married that woman, madness came into this family,' Solly would hiss whenever Lily was in the shop. Once, she overheard him and snapped, attacking him with her Chanel handbag in full view of the shop floor and insulting his 'fat cow' of a wife. Luckily, Jo managed to drag her off him before she did any lasting damage to either Solly or her expensive accessory.

In a luxury magazine article from 1981, there is a photo of the House of Kutchinsky's key players. I found copies of this black and white portrait, plus outtakes, in a folder of press cuttings in Mum's study. Five suited men are arranged around a desk. Dad sits casually in front, a soft smirk playing on his face. His suit jacket is unbuttoned, and his hair curls almost to his shoulders. Behind him, his older, more formally attired relatives stand at attention. They look awkward and ill at ease. Solly's sideburns sprout wildly from the sides of his head; Stanley Dessau is grim-faced; and although David Morein is smiling, his shoulders are tense. Enthroned between them, a cigar clasped in his hand, Jo signals that he is still in control — for now. Perched on the end of the desk, slightly apart from the other men, Roger clasps his hands tightly, though he too is smiling.

Solly's sons, Danny and Joshua, aren't mentioned in the article. I sensed from Danny, a portly man now in his eighties with a shock of silver hair and a blustery air, that they were aware of being looked down on by their more sophisticated cousins. Unlike his younger brother Joshua, who rejected both jewellery and Judaism, Danny aspired to a career in the family trade but instead of a place in the family business, he ended up working for a diamond merchant in Hatton Garden. 'I was lonely,' Danny recalled. 'Dad asked a few people to keep an eye on me but it wasn't my scene – every day after lunch, all the traders in the diamond bourse would pack up and start playing cards.' Being excluded clearly rankled – he had the Kutchinsky name but none of the wealth or status.

Danny was closer in age to Roger but since the families barely socialised, there was little love lost between the cousins. Once, when they were both teenagers, Danny got wind that Roger was throwing a party in his parents' palatial West End flat and decided to surprise his cousin. 'I had a friend called Colin who liked gatecrashing,' Danny said, chuckling at the memory. When they turned up and knocked on the door, Roger was unimpressed. 'What do you want?' he asked abruptly, opening it barely a crack. 'You are not invited.'

'Do your parents know you are having a party?' said Colin, sensing an opportunity. Realising that Danny could pass this incriminating information back to his uncle, Roger reluctantly let them in.

Danny might have won that small battle but in the mid-Eighties, Lily won the war for her branch of the family. Solly was now in his early seventies and with Jo also over retirement age, a plan for the succession was urgently needed. Adding to the uncertainty was the question of who truly held the power. Solly and Jo had assumed they were equal partners, until it emerged that Moshe had once gifted a share of the business to Joseph Wolkovitch. His family were unlikely to claim it, but on paper it left one of the brothers as a minority. When Solly pressed again for Danny to be brought in, it proved the final straw. Jo's response was blunt: either the company would be broken up or they would strike a deal to buy Solly and his sons out – the ultimate aim being for Paul and Roger to take full control.

'There was a big *oy gevalt* (kerfuffle),' Danny said. 'My father stayed longer than he should have done. It was his life, he loved it.'

I've come to think it was Moshe, with his focus on family, who was the driving force in ensuring Solly was looked after. Did Jo make his father a deathbed promise in early December 1959 to always provide for his siblings, just as Moshe had to Hersh all those years ago? In the end it was agreed that Solly would receive a lump sum of more than £800,000 (equivalent to more than £3 million today). This would be paid in five annual payments tied to inflation. It didn't seem a huge amount, given the opulence of the Kutchinsky brand, but when Solly and his sons scrutinised the company accounts, they got a shock.

'The figures were really bad,' Danny said. 'The overdraft was very high and the sales were very low ... We thought it was a scam to put the price down. As it happened, they probably were the figures.'

After Solly's departure, Lily's next target was Jo's loyal nephew, David Morein, the oldest child of Jo's sister, Gertrude. His father, Rabbi Wolf Morein, died in 1941, aged just thirty-three, when a simple operation for appendicitis proved fatal. Wolf's death had affected the family deeply. Moshe was devastated to lose a son-in-law whose piety far exceeded that of his own offspring. Gerty never remarried, and David grew up worshipping his uncle Jo, who became a surrogate father to him. After he left school, Jo took him into the business and taught him how to smoke cigars, drink whisky and close a deal.

While David wasn't a jewellery man in the way that Jo was, and my father would become, he had a sharp business brain and helped orchestrate the move to the West End. Later, he devised a successful marketing strategy, setting up glossy magazine shoots in glamorous locations with the likes of legendary fashion photographer Norman Parkinson. When Jo and Lily left their West End flat for a new home in north-west London, it was in part to be close to David and his family. Every morning, he would call for his uncle Jo and drive him to work in his brown Rolls-Royce, making sure he had his ear.

Paul bore a deep grudge against David for his role in trying to pressure Brenda's parents into ending their daughter's relationship with him. And as the struggle for the succession ramped up, he revelled in his cousin's discomfort. In mid-1981, after some cajoling from Lily, Jo agreed to move Paul to the flagship store in Knightsbridge, on the proviso that he started on the shop floor and proved his worth like any other employee. Additionally, he was given the coveted responsibility of selecting which gems would grace their designs. Seated in an alcove at the back of the showroom, Paul would pore over packets of precious stones, searching for flaws and sorting them into glittering piles, his mind whirring with ideas and ambitions for the future.

A few months after Paul's promotion, armed robbers raided the Bond Street store, making off with more than half-a-million pounds' worth of jewels. The theft, which occurred on the morning of Tuesday, 22 September, hit the headlines as the burglars' getaway vehicle was a £40,000 Rolls-Royce owned by comedian Mike Yarwood, who hosted a primetime

BBC show. The number plate had been changed to read LSD 777 (LSD was old-fashioned slang for cash and 777 was the winning line on many slot machines).

It was about 11 a.m. when two smartly dressed, briefcase-carrying men, estimated to be in their mid-thirties, slid out of the Rolls and headed towards the shop's double glass doors. After a quick once-over from the uniformed doorman, they were allowed to enter. The staff's anticipation turned to horror as one man put a gun to the doorman's throat, while the other pulled out a sawn-off shotgun and ordered the salesmen to lie on the floor. Two more accomplices, one wearing a monkey mask, burst in and swept diamond rings, necklaces and watches from the window display into a leather briefcase. As they piled back into the car and sped off, the thieves hit several parked cars, slowing their escape. The raid was over in less than three minutes, but the staff were badly shaken.

When Jo arrived to tackle the crisis, he was flanked by his sons, rather than David, who had previously been seen as the heir apparent. It fell to Paul to raise the spirits of the rattled staff by taking them on a night out to the Hard Rock Cafe. A fashionable spot at the time, the Americana-themed diner with its leather booths, walls lined with music memorabilia and a jukebox in the corner, was a favourite haunt of Dad's. He even bought the same Wurlitzer and put it in our conservatory, proudly showing it off at parties. The Bond Street staff, including David O'Connor, who had just joined the sales team were surprised by the informal choice of venue, and the night out was long and raucous. But there was more to it than just partying at the company's expense – it was a preview of the more modern managerial style Paul would adopt when he was in charge.

As Paul's star ascended, the boys in the workshop started referring to him as 'the anointed one'. 'God's on the phone,' they'd laugh when he called for an update on an order. As David Morein was increasingly pushed out, the atmosphere in the Knightsbridge shop turned toxic. Rival camps formed and suspicions flew over which family member had taken money from the shop's cash box or borrowed jewellery for their wives to wear to a function. Lily and Paul poured poison into Jo's ear about the supposedly lavish lifestyle David was living, courtesy of the business. After all, his surname was Morein, not Kutchinsky, Paul would say pointedly, raising his bushy eyebrows to emphasise the point. Together, they orchestrated the downfall of the former crown prince, stripping away David's power and making his life a misery. Furious that his cocksure younger cousin was giving him orders, David retreated to his fiefdom in the back office and refused to engage.

Until one day, a volcanic row erupted between David and his beloved uncle Jo. Nobody can remember exactly what sparked it but Mum believes David confronted his uncle and asked for a share in the business, figuring that after decades of loyal service he should have been rewarded. Shouts were heard emanating from Jo's office, before David, red-faced and panting, came storming out. Jo followed suit, pursuing him into the back office, bellowing that he wasn't done with him. In response, David spun on his heel, his face so close to his uncle's he could feel his breath on his cheek and see the spittle forming on his moustache. So, the story goes, David then did something no other employee had ever dared. Rage flooded through him, as he snarled at Jo, 'Fuck off out of my office.'

For a second, Jo was speechless. Then disgust worked its way across his features. 'You fuck off out of my business,' he hissed. Turning his back on his nephew, he stormed off and slammed the door to his office. They never spoke again.

Once the mutiny was over, a mood of calm returned. New hires were made, and there was a sense of energy and excitement. But Jo, now a legendary figure in the jewellery trade, showed no signs of letting go. 'He was always in the centre. He was the chief, the big boss,' Mum explained. 'He lived to work.'

While Jo's hair retained a jet-black sheen (possibly from a bottle), his sideburns and moustache were flecked with grey – and nicotine stains from his incessant pipe puffing. Paul would increasingly catch his father staring at him, a pensive look on his face and was irked by his refusal to trust him. Jo would openly ask others, in Paul's presence, if they thought his son was up to the job. He would ham it up, framing it as a joke, but Dad knew it was a test.

Eventually, he passed.

At the end of 1985, Paul was formally installed at the helm of the House of Kutchinsky, with Roger running the back office. One night not long before Christmas, Paul waltzed into the kitchen of Garthside, where Brenda was making supper, with a bottle of champagne in his hand. Putting it down on the table, he swept her off her feet. Then he pulled a black ring box out of his blazer pocket and dropped to one knee, snapping it open. A crimson glow emanated from its inky black depths, where a large ruby sat enthroned on a sleek platinum band, girdled by four diamonds.

'What are you doing? you dafty,' Brenda giggled. 'We're already married!'

'We're millionaires now, though, Teddy, I thought you deserved an upgrade,' he said, sliding the ring onto her index finger and planting a sloppy kiss on her cheek. 'I couldn't have done it without yer,' he growled affectionately.

'Damn right. And don't you forget it. Now get your hands off me so I can finish making your dinner,' she teased, as he poured the fizzy gold liquid into their finest crystal flutes. As they clinked glasses and toasted their good fortune, Katrina and I slept peacefully upstairs.

It wasn't long after Dad's elevation that we moved to a house so grand it had a name rather than a street number. Looking back, I can see how gilded our lives were, but that's the trick that privilege plays on you – growing up with it, you're blind to its excesses.

The sales brochure described Hollybush House as an 'elegant country house' set in an acre of 'delightful landscaped gardens'. A wall of thick, prickly holly bushes fringed the driveway to the house, which boasted six bedrooms, a conservatory, a large kitchen, lavish dining room and a garage that future owners would make into a swimming pool. The imposing front door, which we rarely used, was framed by white stone pillars. Every spring, the garden would erupt in an electrifying blaze of pinks and purples as bluebells and rhododendron bushes bloomed, and creamy pink flowers clustered on majestic horse chestnut trees. My parents added a large playroom and a set of white electric gates that were a source of wonder to my sisters and me. We spent hours climbing on them and messing around with the remote control that made them swing open. Once my friend's little brother got his head stuck in the metal bars and screamed as our mothers smeared him with butter to wrestle him free.

The size and splendour of our new home, for which my parents paid several hundred thousand pounds, symbolised the spirit of excess that prevailed during the Eighties. For better or worse, this was Margaret Thatcher's Britain. There was a new sense of national confidence embodied in the fairy-tale wedding of Prince Charles and Diana, and the orgy of flag-waving that followed Britain's victory in the Falklands War. The first home computers were sold. The New Romantics stormed the charts. Political divides deepened. National industries were privatised. Free markets rose and trade unions were crushed in the wake of the miners' strike.

In fashion, power dressing – think shoulder pads and sharp suits – became de rigueur for women, boosted by the popularity of TV shows like *Dynasty* and *Dallas*, where oil tycoons screwed each other over in the boardroom and screwed each other's wives in the bedroom. Every week my family would sit religiously in front of 'the box' and watch the likes of Joan Collins (Alexis, bad bitch ex-wife) and Linda Evans (Krystle, goody-goody new wife) tear strips off each other while wearing high heels and fur coats and dripping in diamonds. As a child, Joan Collins was probably my first fashion icon. I would parade around in Mum's sequinned high heels, my brown curls swishing in a high ponytail, acting out scenes from the show with Katrina, who I insisted took the part of Krystle. I didn't know that our family had a real-life link to the British actress. Before landing her role in *Dynasty*, Joan Collins starred in the erotic drama *The Stud* (1978), in which

KUTCHINSKY'S EGG

Kutchinsky jewellery features prominently, including during its famous swimming pool orgy where Collins's co-star, Sue Lloyd, is naked except for a diamond necklace that sparkles above her breasts. It's an iconic image, although at the time Dad dismissed it as 'a bit low-rent'. He had bigger plans for the House of Kutchinsky. But there was still his brother to contend with.

* * *

When they first assumed control of the House of Kutchinsky, Roger and Paul tolerated each other, but their fragile truce didn't last. They were such different characters, forced together by their father's dynastic ambitions and their shared failure to imagine a different future for themselves. While Paul was seen as a bit wild but talented, his more straight-edged brother was, to quote a former staff member, thought of by some as a 'pain in the arse'. Their lack of closeness was evident to all. Around this time, the cracks in the business – and the family – began to widen. Adam, the swaggering manager of the Bond Street shop, was sacked after rumours surfaced that he'd been paying chauffeurs to steer wealthy clients through Kutchinsky's doors, taking a discreet cut of their purchases. He denied it all, threatened court and vowed to reveal 'the real story', whatever that meant.

Paul, looking for a scapegoat, turned on Roger. His loathed brother, always so self-righteous, was the company's accountant, after all. If money was leaking out, Paul reasoned, Roger had either missed it or allowed it. Roger, in turn, insisted Adam had kept everything off the books. There was no trail to follow. He was, he said, entirely innocent. Jo, weary of his sons' squabbling, told them to throw money at the problem and shut it down before it got any worse.

But it already had.

Not long after, Mira* — Adam's girlfriend, a sales assistant from the Knightsbridge shop — appeared in Paul's office. Slumping into a chair, pale-faced and tight-lipped, she placed a bundle of letters on his desk and said simply: 'You should read these.'

The letters were handwritten and painstakingly anonymised. No names, just initials. The tone was intimate, coded. Mira didn't explain why she thought Paul needed to see them but she seemed certain he'd understand.

He read just enough to sense their weight. The letters contained a secret involving someone close to the family; something so grave that, even now, nobody will tell me exactly what it was. Mum once told me she had glimpsed the first page before Paul locked them away. 'It wasn't just personal,' she said. 'It was dangerous. If it came out, it would have broken everything.'

He didn't tell anyone, not then. Instead, he took the letters and stored them in the safe in his dressing room at Hollybush, alongside his secret stash of hash and a few packets of diamonds. According to Mum, he took them with him when he left. She believes they're hidden away somewhere still, in a safe deposit box under a false name. That was how the Kutchinskys operated. Secretive. Machiavellian. Never trusting each other.

Paul never said why he kept them. But I don't think it was about hurting anyone. Not really. I think he kept them because he'd been taught by his father that power came from

---

* Name has been changed

what you didn't say. From what you held in reserve, and the possibility of leverage was something you never threw away.

This mendacious behaviour jars with the curated image of my father I hold in my memory, but it's possible I did recognise a glimmer of his narcissism even as a child. A coffee-stained Father's Day card I made when I was eight years old is decorated with 'all the things you love most, Daddy, including yourself!' Alongside crude drawings of tennis racquets and polo mallets is a man with shoulder-length brown hair, brightly coloured clothes and a blood-red gash for a mouth.

When I asked Mum why Dad kept the letters her answer was simple. 'Blackmail. What do you think? Black-fucking-mail. Do you think he wasn't the same as them? It was a horrible thing to do. That's what that family was like.'

* * *

Even after Dad took the helm, Jo was still a constant presence in the shop. He would be there at least three days a week, puffing on his cigar, dropping ash everywhere and interrogating the designers about their work. 'You don't want to make it an apology, make it big!' he'd say, scrutinising their sketches. Paul would shrug off the criticism of his more subtle style, but it still stung. Lily would soothe him, taking out her hairbrush and brushing his curls as she had done when he was a child.

'He could be vicious about his father,' Mum said, ruminating on Dad's fragility as we drove one night through the Scottish countryside. 'He would belittle Jo, calling him old-fashioned and out of touch. He was desperate to make his mark and would stop at nothing to get his father out of the picture.'

THE RISE

But the first Kutchinsky collections Paul presided over fell flat. The jewellery was delicate and romantic, and the best pieces dazzled in the windows, but it could have been made by any high-end jewellery house. It dawned on Paul that Kutchinsky was never going to upstage its European rivals, such as Cartier and Bulgari, with mere necklaces and bracelets. He needed something spectacular, on a scale the jewellery world had never seen before.

He knew the risks involved. But he felt a sense of entitlement, destiny even. There was a phrase his father was particularly fond of, which echoed in his head, as he sat in his office sifting through sketches, searching for inspiration.

'It takes a long time to build a name, and a very short time to break it.'

8

RIDING HIGH

The House of Fabergé's story is soaked in the blood of the Russian Revolution. Carl Fabergé's father, Gustav, who had French origins, founded the jewellery firm in St Petersburg in 1842, adding an accent to their name to entice the elites. When two decades later, Gustav retired to the German city of Dresden, his family went with him. His moderately successful jewellery business was left in the hands of Hiskias Pendin, Gustav's trusted manager who would later become a mentor of sorts to Carl.

Carl Fabergé was sixteen when they moved to Germany. He studied his father's trade and made regular visits to the Grünes Gewölbe (Green Vault), one of the world's largest treasure chambers, which contained various ornate eggs. He completed his apprenticeship by embarking on a grand tour of Europe's finest galleries, where he viewed many jewelled wonders. Upon his return to St Petersburg in 1870, aged twenty-four, he started working in the family business. Fabergé knew the key to success lay in winning the custom of the Russian royal family. The Romanovs were the influencers of their time; whatever fashions or jewels the tsarina wore were scrutinised and copied by the leading lights of European society. So, in his spare time he worked on restoring ancient jewels from the royal collection in the Hermitage Museum, which was right next to the tsar's official residence, the jaw-dropping Winter Palace.

The turning point in Carl Fabergé's career came when he was invited to participate in an exhibition of Russian treasures in Moscow in 1882. The Romanovs were still reeling from the assassination of Tsar Alexander II the previous year and the exhibition was intended as a display of their power and influence. A replica of an ancient gold bracelet from the royal collection, painstakingly crafted by Fabergé, caught the tsar's eye. Heaping praise on the jeweller, Tsar Alexander III said he was barely able to tell the difference between this copy and the original, which dated back 2,000 years. The tsarina then favoured the jeweller further by buying a pair of his cufflinks shaped like cicadas, a symbol of good luck. Fabergé was ecstatic. His plan had worked. Soon after, he won a contract to supply the Russian court.

By the turn of the twentieth century, the House of Fabergé employed more than 500 craftsmen and staff, making it the largest and most prestigious jeweller in Imperial Russia. Its reputation derived from turning everyday items into artworks: from cigarette cases to photo frames, umbrella handles to trinket boxes. There were even jewelled bells for dog owners to hang on their pampered pooch's collar. Among Europe's elites, Fabergé gifts became the ultimate status symbol with an estimated total of up to 200,000 objects created between 1882 and 1917. But it was the Imperial Easter Eggs that cemented his reputation as the Romanovs' favourite jeweller.

The first in the series, the Hen Egg (1885) was a gift from

the tsar to his wife, to distract her from her fears that he too would be assassinated. Its gold shell was painted milky white with enamel (a coloured powder that is melted in a kiln and then solidifies). Secreted inside was a miniature gold hen, which itself contained a replica of the imperial crown and a ruby 'egg' pendant, both of which are now lost. It was a huge success and over the following three decades, Fabergé and his team of skilled craftsmen produced about fifty of these creations, each one unique. Confining them to a string of adjectives feels reductive – they are visual, sensory objects, not to mention symbols of almost unimaginable wealth. They fell out of fashion when socialism swept across Europe but now fetch millions of pounds at auctions.

*   *   *

In a corner of Mum's overstuffed study in Scotland, squeezed between books on the history of jewellery and Jewish prayer books, I found a shrine to Fabergé, my father's hero, the Russian master's name displayed in elegant gold lettering on the spines of several illustrated tomes, which had been gathering dust for decades.

Paul enjoyed making things. He was a dreamer, who had the hustle of a top salesman but lacked the killer instinct. During his teenage beatnik years, he dabbled in art; Lily bought him oil paints and an easel, and he daubed thick, abstract streaks of black and blue paint on canvas. One of these works from his 'Black Phase' still survives. I hung it on my bedroom wall for a while in my twenties, until a boyfriend claimed it put him off while we were having sex, so I banished it and later lost it in between house moves.

RIDING HIGH

Fabergé was never far from Paul's thoughts. He felt a magnetic pull towards the Russian master, and like someone in the throes of a romantic obsession, he wanted to inhabit the object of his desire. His vision for the House of Kutchinsky was based on a grand plan to make jewelled artworks in the Fabergé mould for the oil-rich Middle East market. London in the mid-Eighties had become the global epicentre of the *objet d'art* trade. Among the extraordinary creations made in the capital's workshops was the 1983 Octopussy Egg, a Fabergé-style green and gold egg adorned with white crystals that played a starring role in the James Bond film of the same name. There were more modern pieces too, catering to the whims of the super-rich, such as gold bathroom scales coloured with semi-precious stones to match the different colours of the Sultan of Brunei's five bathrooms, brick-sized gold car phones and blinged-up models of Nintendo Game Boys, as well as a life-size gold tiger with a diamond nose, glittering eyes and fearsome claws. This was jewellery of an unprecedented size and scale, made to decorate not people but the spaces they inhabited.

But moving away from traditional jewellery was a risk. One-off pieces had the potential to bring in vast sums, but they took months to create, were labour intensive and used large amounts of expensive materials. 'There was big money to be made but you could lose your shirt on it,' a craftsman told me. While Paul craved the creative challenge of transforming everyday objects into works of art, Jo was reluctant to give the plan his blessing. As rival jewellery houses, such as Asprey, who crafted the Octopussy egg, cornered the market, Paul's impatience grew. Tempers frayed and at one point a physical fight broke out between father and son on the shop floor. As

Paul and Jo laid into each other, suit-clad limbs flailing, the staff looked on in horror. After Jo wrestled Paul into a headlock, he fought back, taking off his shoe and slapping his shiny black loafer into his father's chest. Eventually the doorman separated them but more than egos were bruised that day.

Shortly after, a blockbuster exhibition of Fabergé treasures opened in Munich in December 1986. Brenda had just given birth to their third daughter, my sister Hollie, but Paul was insistent that they had to make this pilgrimage alone, without any of us children. Ignoring her protests, he booked a weekend in the German city in late January. It was officially a work trip, so they stayed at the lavish Bayerischer Hof Hotel, located in the city centre just a short walk from the museum.

Munich was in the grip of a brutal winter, with temperatures as low as –24 degrees, and it was brain-freezingly cold. As they queued patiently to enter the city's prestigious Kunsthalle, which had drawn record-breaking crowds to this blockbuster exhibition, Paul fell into a reverential silence, his gloved hand clutching the leather-bound notebook in his pocket.

An idea began to take shape as he toured the display, transfixed by the intricacy and creativity of the Russian master's work. What if he *could* make a masterpiece to rival Fabergé's? An egg that would combine ancient techniques with state-of-the-art technology – an egg that would surpass every other in scale and wonder. Sitting in a quiet corner, he started sketching the genesis of an idea.

On the last night of the trip, he dragged Brenda to Hofbräuhaus, one of the famous beer halls associated with the rise of Adolf Hitler's Nazi Party. It was there at a rowdy meeting in 1920 that the fascist leader laid out the party's ideological foundations. Brenda shuddered. She hadn't wanted to come here. It was too linked, in her mind, to the Second World War and the horrors of the Holocaust, which she'd studied in grim detail during her conversion to Judaism. For many in the British Jewish community, the idea of even visiting Germany was still anathema. That night, the cavernous beer hall was crowded. Straining to hear as Paul laid out his big idea, Brenda felt a deep sense of unease.

He was lisping slightly, his hands flapping like windmills. Beer sloshed onto his white shirt.

'What if Kutchinsky could do what Fabergé did?' he said, slamming his tankard down on the wooden table.

'Do what, exactly? Make jewelled objects for dodgy autocrats? We already do that.'

'Ha, ha. Very funny. No. I mean, develop a gimmick. A symbol. Something that makes us famous all around the world, not just in London.'

'You've always said London is the centre of the universe,' Brenda replied drily.

'I'm being serious, Brenda! Can you just *listen* for a minute?'

His stern outburst struck her like a slap in the face.

'Please,' he said, seeing the hurt in her eyes. 'What if I make an egg bigger and better than any of Fabergé's? We could bill it as a homage to the great master but use technology to modernise it.' He stopped to draw breath, searching her face for signs of approval.

She nodded slowly.

'Come on, Bren, we can do this. Look, Fabergé's eggs sell for hundreds of thousands of pounds. They're recognised as pieces of art. This would be, too.'

KUTCHINSKY'S EGG

Paul was wired now, high on alcohol and adrenaline. He started drawing an egg shape on the napkin his beer had sat on.

'Everyone will know the Kutchinsky name.'

Brenda raised her wine glass and hid her expression behind it. She was used to Paul's crazy schemes, his need for an obsession. He always had a new hobby – skiing, painting, bridge, table tennis. He lavished thousands of pounds on gadgets and talked about nothing else for months. Then his latest fixation would suddenly fade from view, like stale bread sinking into a murky duck pond. In his work life, he was always restless, concocting new ideas, but he'd never dreamed up a project on this scale. The cost could be astronomical. She feared he wasn't thinking straight.

Later, as they struggled back to the hotel through the icy streets, the egg was all Paul could talk about. In his mind, it was already built.

*   *   *

Dad first told me of his plan to build the world's largest jewelled egg while perched in the cab of a small digger. I was nine years old, and a chunk of our garden was being ripped up to make space for a tennis court. It was early spring and the rhododendron bushes had yet to bloom. The yellow excavator had been left abandoned on the lawn, its giant muddy shovel curled inwards, and I'd persuaded Dad to lift me into its cab.

Scrambling up beside me, he imagined the news headlines that might follow if we took it on an accidental rampage around the neighbourhood. 'Kutchinsky and Daughter Cause Chaos in Richmond Park,' he joked, doing his best impression of a BBC newsreader. I giggled, enjoying the sound of us as a team, Kutchinsky and Daughter. Then he lowered his voice conspiratorially and asked if I wanted to know a secret. 'I'm going to make a giant golden egg,' he said, his eyes wide. 'The biggest in the world. Bigger than Fabergé's.'

I had no idea what he was talking about but decided to play along, nodding as Dad regaled me with the story of the Russian master, the tragic Romanovs and the missing Easter eggs. He pointed out that on Mum's bedside table there were some replicas of these porcelain eggs, which had gotten me in trouble when I was caught rolling them down the hallway. Captivated by his story, I fired off a volley of questions. How big would it be? How many diamonds would be in it?

'It will be nearly as tall and beautiful as you, with thousands of pink diamonds in it,' he said, kissing the top of my head. I looked up, surprised. I'd never heard of pink diamonds before.

Dad taught me about precious stones long before I could read or write. I knew that emeralds were green, like the jungle painting on the wall in my new bedroom; rubies were red, like Mum's lipstick; sapphires tended to be blue, like the sea. Diamonds, as far as I knew, were white. I pulled a face. I didn't like pink; it was too girly. I prided myself on being a tomboy. He stuck his tongue out at me and ruffled my tangled curls. 'Grumpy Cece,' he said. 'These diamonds are prettier than any you've ever seen, I promise.'

I must have looked sceptical because he carried on talking in that fake upbeat voice adults use when they're trying to convince you everything is fine. 'Your mother thinks I'm crazy, too, but I've told her this will make our fortune. After the egg sells, you can have anything you want.'

'Anything? Even a puppy?'

'Even a puppy,' he promised. Just then we heard Mum calling out. Sunday lunch was ready. 'Remember to keep the egg a secret,' he said. 'Just for now.'

I wriggled off the digger's seat and propelled myself forward into his arms.

*   *   *

Diamonds. No other gemstone evokes as much symbolism or emotion. They are hailed as the king of gems and the ultimate symbol of romantic love. It takes millions, even billions of years, and intense heat and pressure, for carbon to crystallise into diamonds deep within the earth.

While the desirability of white diamonds is on the wane, in part due to the rising popularity of their lab-grown counterparts, pink diamonds are increasingly seen as the gemological equivalent of Helen of Troy – so breathtakingly beautiful, they inspire envy and deceit. Few people are lucky enough to see a pink up close, and even fewer can hope to possess one. Today, these fairy-tale stones regularly fetch far higher prices than their colourless brethren. The strawberry-sized Pink Star Diamond (59 carats, 11.9 grams), dubbed a 'freak of nature' for its size and sublime hue, became the most expensive gem ever sold at auction, in 2017, when it fetched almost $71 million. In contrast, the greatest sum a white diamond has ever commanded is $21.9 million, and that was for 'The Rock', a South African whopper, roughly the size of a golf ball, weighing over 228 carats. It was sold at Christie's in Geneva in May 2022.

Pink diamonds were first discovered in the world's ancient diamond capital: India's Golconda region, which lies in the modern state of Andhra Pradesh. In 1642, French gem merchant Jean-Baptiste Tavernier travelled there in search of treasures to sell to royalty. What he discovered took his breath away – a magnificent pink stone, unlike any he had seen before. He made a sketch of his discovery, christening it the Great Table Diamond, a nod to its immense weight of about 250 carats or 50 grams (equal to a lightbulb or small chocolate bar) and distinctive flat cut.

This mythical jewel's story stretches across shifting fortunes and lost empires. It is thought to have adorned the golden Peacock Throne of the Mughal emperor, Shah Jahan, who ruled India from 1628 to 1658 and is famed for commissioning the Taj Mahal. According to legend, the diamond was later plundered, along with other treasures, when the Persian ruler, Nader Shah, captured Delhi in 1739. For many years, it was lost from sight, passing from one ruler to the next. Rumours swirled about its fate – had it been secretly traded or cut into smaller stones? But the mystery wasn't solved until centuries later. In 1958, on the day of his third wedding, the last King of Iran, Mohammad Reza Shah, wore a crown set with a stunning pink stone that was smaller but otherwise identical to the Great Table Diamond. As a symbol of his love, he had a tiara with a matching pink diamond made for his new bride.

This sighting sparked new research and in the 1960s, Canadian geologist Dr V. B. Meen and a team of researchers concluded that the original stone was split, either intentionally or by accident, to form these two smaller pink diamonds: the Darya-i-noor ('Sea of Light') and the Nur-ul-Ain ('Light of the Eye'), which remain part of the Iranian crown jewels. The prevailing belief among gemologists was that the world would never see jewels of such splendour again. Very occasionally, a bubblegum-coloured stone like the Williamson Diamond, a wedding gift to Queen Elizabeth II, would appear from a haul at a mine somewhere in Brazil or Africa but there was never a consistent supply from a location with a mythology to match that of the Golconda diamonds from India.

By the late twentieth century, pink diamonds had fallen out of fashion. The South African firm De Beers monopolised the diamond industry, and their focus was on driving up the price of white diamonds, intertwining their purity with the idea of eternal love. Their genius 1940s marketing campaign 'A Diamond Is Forever' popularised the idea of proposing with a diamond ring, a tradition that persists around the world. Back then, most of the so-called pinks in circulation were small and beige, relegated for use in industrial drills and cutting tools. But a glimmer on an anthill in the Australian outback in October 1979 changed everything. The glimmer was from diamonds, and the anthill was in the heart of a remote region known as the East Kimberley, which is encircled by the Ragged Range, a mountain cluster with jagged red peaks that resembles the knobbled spine of an ancient beast. It's one of the earliest settled parts of Australia, with humans first landing there 65,000 years ago. This starkly beautiful landscape with its dense tangle of grasslands, mangrove forests and river gorges would later reveal one of the world's greatest treasure troves, the Argyle Diamond Mine.

But this remote corner of Western Australia wasn't just rich in any old diamonds – it produced more pinks than anywhere else on the planet. To put it in perspective, only about one in a million of the diamonds that emerged from the Argyle mine were pink, but this is still disproportionately high. The question of what was so special about that particular location was another puzzle for geologists. It was near the edge of a continent, which is odd as diamonds tend to be found more towards the middle. The East Kimberley diamonds were also encased in a different type of volcanic rock – lamproite – unlike most diamonds, which are typically found in the darker, coarser kimberlite. But scientists now have a theory: around 1.8 billion years ago, tectonic plates collided to form a supercontinent called Nuna. The impact propelled these pink-bearing rocks towards the Earth's surface, where the Argyle mine now sits. Their distinctive pink hue is thought to result from the intense pressure of that geological upheaval, which distorted the diamonds' crystal structure. The window for this natural sorcery was minuscule – if the pressure had been too extreme, the diamonds would have turned brown, a colour scathingly likened by Argyle's rivals to kangaroo poo or frozen spit.[1]

There is another origin story (which personally I prefer) that derives from the traditional owners of the land. Dad told it to me when he returned from his first Australia trip in late 1989. At ten years old, I was too old for bedtime stories, so it was a rare treat to have him cuddled up next to me wearing the traditional Australian hat with corks dangling from the brim that was permanently wedged on his head at that time. As he spun his tale, he conjured the beauty of these remarkable stones, which he promised I would soon see in his egg, and shared the history of the incredible landscape he and Mum had witnessed. It goes like this:

> A great barramundi fish lived in the river near where the mine now lies. One day, a group of elderly women

spotted the fish and tried to catch her, so she swam into a cave to hide. At the cave's entrance, the women waited with their grass nets. The barramundi swam towards them and soared over their heads, scraping her glistening, colourful scales against the rock face. The scales are said to have become the diamonds that were discovered there centuries later.

The pinks that blasted out of the Argyle mine's earthy womb were a different specimen of coloured diamond. These were not mega-carat whoppers. Instead they were dainty and radiated a spectrum of such intense velvety purple through to rose pink that gem experts were left lantern-eyed, creating a new category of coloured stone just for them. But despite all the excitement surrounding the mine's opening in 1983, the snobbery around pinks endured, until another collision occurred, born out of business and creative desires, that would bring my father and his egg into Argyle's orbit.

*   *   *

The first sketch of Kutchinsky's Egg was drawn in the run-up to Easter 1989, almost by accident. Paul had hired a young, fresh-faced designer, Cheryl Prewitt, as part of his drive to bring more women into the business. With her long brown hair, chic attire and natural elegance, Cheryl's presence caused a stir, especially among the boys in the workshop, but Paul recognised her talent. Increasingly, she was tasked with designing everything from traditional jewellery to a set of gold figurines, studded with precious stones, depicting the characters in *The Simpsons*, commissioned as a gift for the Sultan of Brunei's children. Although Paul was technically breaching copyright laws by recreating popular characters such as Homer and a skateboard-riding Bart, he gambled that it was worth the risk. As soon as they were ready, they were dispatched straight to the Middle East, where they presumably still sit in splendour, viewed only by a small elite. To this day, no pictures exist on the internet of those spectacular pieces.

In a rare free moment, Cheryl had just started sketching an egg with a jewelled library inside, modelled on a bookcase in her parents' home, when Paul materialised behind her. Not daring to turn around, she nervously awaited his verdict, worried he would accuse her of time-wasting. At first, all she heard was a long drawn out 'hhhmmmm'. Then he swiped the drawing from her sketchbook and shuffled off in his Gucci loafers back to his office. 'We'll make that, Cheryl,' he called over his shoulder, a glint in his eye.

Was it pure coincidence that Cheryl's sketch chimed with the image that the Fabergé exhibition in Munich had imprinted on Paul's mind? Had she absorbed his ambition, almost by osmosis, or overheard whispered fragments of his idea to revive the tradition of creating jewelled Easter eggs? I picture him scrutinising her sketch in his office, rifling through his books for inspiration, making endless calculations about costs and measurements. The design went back and forth between them a few times, growing ever more complex until it became, in Cheryl's words, 'a monster'. As Paul's obsession with the egg deepened, so did Brenda's disquiet. Every time he drank too much wine at dinner, he would start spouting off about being the next Carl Fabergé. When he'd finished, she would roll her eyes before reminding him, in her dulcet Scottish tones, that he had a business to run and a family to provide for, before he started laying giant gold eggs. But he wouldn't listen.

The business was already on shaky ground. The million-pound deal struck to buy out Uncle Solly started the rot, and it was compounded when Jo subsequently stepped back, taking a hefty chunk of capital in exchange for his shares. But the real problem was Paul's relentless focus on outshining his father, coupled with his penchant for wild schemes.

The closest Jo had come to international success was getting Kutchinsky jewellery sold on high-end cruise ships, including the famous luxury liner the *QE2,* named after the now late queen. The description in the brochure painted a glamorous picture, describing an 'arcade of shops to rival the best in Bond Street' selling 'fashionable clothes, fine perfumes … and the cream of the current collection of jewellery by Kutchinsky: jewels to celebrate an occasion, match the magic of the moment, and capture it forever.' But when Jo and Lily set sail on the vessel, they found the clientele, at least on that voyage, wasn't quite as elegant as they imagined. Every night at dinner, Lily would waft to their table in a designer gown and high heels – she loved lace and black velvet – only to find herself encircled by a forest of tracksuited pensioners. Paul was determined to do better. If Fabergé had managed to get his family name known as far away as Thailand (the King of Siam was a regular client), surely he could at least manage Europe. Once in charge, he focused his energy on finding the perfect location for an overseas branch. The Bond Street shop, which had opened to such fanfare in 1965, was to be sold to raise the necessary funds.

I can understand why he chose Geneva – the watch capital

of the world. Set on the shores of a crystal-clear lake, snow-capped mountains looming in the distance, the picturesque city is awash with billionaires and diplomats. Home to global agencies like the United Nations and the Red Cross, even its crisp Alpine air smells expensive. It is also a handy pitstop for the European jet set travelling to skiing holidays in the Alps, a route we started following in the mid-Eighties.

From the start, Paul's Swiss adventure was dogged by problems. It opened behind schedule in September 1987, missing the peak season for Middle East trade over the summer, when the region's wealthiest people retreated to cooler climes overseas. Then there was the fact that as a small outlet in Geneva's Passage Malbuisson – an arcade in the city's fanciest shopping district – it faced stiff competition from more than a hundred other jewellers better established within the local market. Money was splurged on a champagne-fuelled launch party which Mum and Dad flew over for. I remember them bickering as they left for the airport, but unbeknown to me there was an extra layer of angst beneath the surface. The night before, Lily had received a sinister crank call. There was a bomb in the Swiss shop, the muffled caller claimed. If the opening went ahead it would detonate. Terrified, my grandmother called the police who sent sniffer dogs to search for explosives but found nothing. Jealous rivals, the police concluded, trying to warn them off.

Whatever pressure Paul was under, he shrugged it off. In the afternoon, while Brenda fussed over the flower arrangements and guest list, he slunk off to buy her a new dress with her best friend Philippa, an elegant brunette with a devilish sense of humour. Paul's insistence on choosing his wife's clothes had intensified since he took over the business, verging on bullying masquerading as love. If she dared defy him, he sulked and withheld affection until she caved. Mum remembers an argument over a dress she wanted to wear to one of our birthday parties. 'He didn't think it was suitable so I couldn't wear it,' she explained, matter-of-factly. 'I could only wear what he thought was right. You had to be who he wanted you to be, otherwise there'd be a huge row.'

Her memory is blurry as to which year that particular argument took place. 'He chose all my clothes, so it could have been any year,' she sighed. But watching the video of my sixth birthday, my instincts tell me I'm witnessing the aftermath of that stand-off. In the video, she looks awkward, aware perhaps that she is dressed more for a night out in St Tropez than a children's party. Her dress is eye-catching with colourful swirls of tropical fruit printed on pink silk and flatters her figure with spaghetti straps and a knee-length hem. But the weather is gloomy, despite it being the height of summer, and she sits alone on a white sun lounger hugging her arms across her chest. Crossing the lawn to rejoin the other parents, she wobbles slightly on her strappy black high heels. Later, Dad lets the camera linger on her receding figure as she picks up my fairy castle cake, steadies herself and struts defiantly back to the house. If she feels his eyes on her, she doesn't look back.

Geneva wasn't the first time Philippa had accompanied Paul shopping. They came from similar Jewish backgrounds and got on well, sparring with each other over their different fashion sense. Philippa's style was classic with clean lines, whereas Paul liked the Debbie Harry look of big hair, short skirts, frills and shoulder pads. But on this trip his behaviour was notably erratic. A particular dress caught Philippa's eye and she tried to persuade him to buy it, teasing him until he broke.

'Are you mad?' he shouted, angrily throwing the dress at her. 'If it's so amazing, you have it. I'll buy it for you.' The sales assistant watched open-mouthed as this irate customer threw the expensive garment on the counter and insisted on buying it for Philippa, who was caught between gratitude and horror.

She often felt that way in Paul's presence. Once, during a cosy dinner in a fancy restaurant, her husband, Nick, had complimented Paul's French silk Hermès tie. In response, he'd whipped it off and insisted his friend have it. Aware the tie had cost hundreds of pounds, Nick demurred. But Paul wouldn't let it go; in the end, he got his way.

Much to everyone's relief, the Swiss shop's opening night was a success. Guests spilled out into the arcade's tiled passageway, drinking, smoking and gossiping under the starstrewn sky. Every hour, the musical chimes of an elaborate wall clock, a tourist attraction in its own right, made Brenda jump. Breaking away from the crowd briefly to get some air, she stared at the bronze figures parading under the clock's sixteen bells and shivered. Clearly the bomb threat had been a hoax, but it still made her feel they weren't welcome here. Jo and Lily were putting on a front and smiling, but in private they shared her reservations. It was the first time she'd seen Paul make a business decision that was more about ego than common sense.

My recollections of Geneva are fragments. Being dragged around the glossy boutiques of the Rue du Rhône (the Swiss city's equivalent of Bond Street), where the names of famous watchmakers were lit up; watching the Jet d'Eau fountain shoot a plume of water high into the sky; gazing greedily into the windows of Swiss chocolatiers. But the abiding memory is far less rose-tinted. It was 1988, about six months after the Geneva shop opened, and we were spending a night there so Dad could do some business before switching off on the ski slopes. Everything was the same as normal, but it felt different. He was irritable and distracted. Mum was exhausted and smoking more than usual. There was chaos in our large hotel room. Nobody noticed my baby sister, Hollie, crawling off into a corner and discovering a foil tray of pink pellets that looked deceptively like sweets but turned out to be rat poison. I will never forget the fear on Mum's face as she rushed Hollie to hospital to have her stomach pumped, or the lonely sight of her limping back into the hotel room hours later, carrying my sister in her arms, flecks of vomit clinging to her mink fur coat. Dad was nowhere to be seen.

The Geneva shop lost around a million pounds in its first year – equivalent to about three times that today. Some of the losses were due to stock worth almost £100,000 being stolen while en route from London in what was presumed to be an inside job. Mary Turner, a robust septuagenarian with a gung-ho attitude, filled me in on the details. Her husband, Barry, was a police officer who worked in the West End and had grown close to the family. Over the years, he advised first Jo, then Paul, on security and even helped them obtain a gun licence when Paul hit on the idea of selling a golden pistol to a Middle East sultan.

Following the theft, Mary, accompanied by a French-speaking friend, was sent to Switzerland to try to reclaim the jewellery in a covert mission. Paul had paid an agent to transport it from London to Switzerland, wrapped in newspaper and hidden in luggage, to avoid paying insurance and customs duty. This was nothing new; he regularly travelled around the Middle East with far more jewellery than he declared, but where he went wrong this time was involving a third party. The agent absconded with the goods, calculating he could make far more from selling them on the black market. With Barry's help, Mary managed to track the agent to a small jewellery outlet in a run-down part of Geneva. The way she described it sounds like an indoor market with retailers of all varieties squeezed into narrow units. A far cry from the renaissance grandeur of a Kutchinsky salon.

'I was dubious about going inside when I saw how small a place it was,' she recalled. 'It was like going to the East End where you go into a block and Joe Bloggs is doing leatherwork and Fanny Smith is doing jewellery.'

Assuming a composure she didn't feel, Mary pushed through the flimsy double doors. Inside, the agent stood behind the counter of a cramped first-floor unit. Wiry and in his late twenties, he looked visibly agitated – shifting from foot to foot, casting anxious glances over his shoulder. When she explained who she was and why she'd come, he blanched and hurried to confer with an older colleague.

Moments later, he beckoned her into a back office and laid out the stolen jewellery – an exact match to Paul's description. Hoping to broker its return, she called Paul, but the negotiations quickly faltered. The price the criminals were demanding was far too high.

In a moment of despair, he suggested Mary grab the goods and run for it. 'I said, "Are you kidding me! I don't want to end up in the river,'" she exclaimed, shaking her head. The problem for Paul, she explained, was that the jewellery hadn't been declared at customs. If he went to the police, he'd have to confess his own wrongdoing, which he wasn't prepared to do. The thieves knew that and so weren't inclined to give it back.

In the end, Paul had to concede defeat and the business took a huge financial hit. 'The person your dad trusted to take it over really shafted him,' Mary said to me, sounding almost saddened by his naivety.

The Geneva shop didn't last long after that, shutting its doors a mere eighteen months after it had opened. Paul brushed it off, determined not to let its failure dent his self-belief. But beneath the showman exterior, his pride was bruised. Dark thoughts about the future swirled around his brain when he lay restless next to Brenda in their big brass bed. He started nervously picking his right thumb until it was red and raw, with yellow flakes of skin hanging loose. At night, he would make himself a screwdriver (vodka and orange), roll a joint and lock himself in his bathroom, seeking oblivion in the tub.

During the day, the shop's doormen were sent out to buy endless bottles of Benylin, a popular cough syrup that came in a glass bottle with a dark aubergine hue. His throat was playing up, he would say, with a slight hack. Empty bottles would pile up around his desk and rattle suspiciously in his leather briefcase. The sticky reddish syrup he favoured was one laced with codeine, a highly addictive opiate. Staff whispered about how much he was taking, especially when he was spotted looking glazed and stumbling on the shop floor. He would lock himself away in his office and stare at Cheryl's sketch of the egg, pondering how to make his masterpiece a reality. Making a multi-million-pound Fabergé-style piece was a huge gamble but if he pulled it off, his financial woes would be over for good.

When his Swiss dream began to crumble, Paul moved on to his next big idea. Looking back now, I can almost feel the frenetic energy pumping through his veins. Polo, the sport of kings, would be his new way into the English market of aristocrats and wealthy entrepreneurs born out of the 'greed is good' spirit of the Thatcher years. The idea was conceived from a chance meeting on a skiing holiday. My parents had become regulars at the Annapurna, a family-owned hotel high in the French Alps which was always buzzing at Easter. Dad never fully relaxed on his holidays. Schooled by his father in the art of spotting a potential client in the lobby or bar of a luxury hotel, he was always on the alert. If a man was wearing an expensive-looking watch or a woman was dripping in jewels, Dad would befriend them and persuade them to make their next purchase from the House of Kutchinsky. That was how he met Jimmy Thomas, a British gambling king in his fifties who'd made millions buying bingo halls across England and who with his son Simon would later open the iconic Hippodrome Casino in London's Leicester Square.

Like Dad, Jimmy was larger than life with a big laugh, perma-tanned skin and dark brown hair that was peppered with grey. His eldest daughter, Lisa, who was in her early twenties, was involved with William, a tall, handsome polo player who looked like a character out of a Jilly Cooper novel. Memories are blurry as to how the initial connection came about but our stay coincided with a dinner and dance in the hotel restaurant where prizes were given out for various ski competitions. I was unusually subdued, having fallen over during my race and disappointed Dad, who was my biggest champion. He'd consoled me with a big hug and didn't seem overly concerned about the prizegiving. Instead, he disappeared to chat with the Thomas family and was sitting on their table when my name was read out as the silver medal-winner. I skipped up onto the stage, waving proudly in his direction. When he finally returned to our table, fired up on alcohol and the excitement of a new friendship, he berated the waiter for serving him fries that weren't perfectly thin and crispy. He could be obsessive over small details, imagined slights that triggered his insecurities. Later, he and Mum slow-danced together to 'their song' – Chris de Burgh's pop ballad 'Lady in Red'. After she took us off to bed, Dad stayed up in the bar chatting and drinking into the night.

Paul and William, who was about a decade younger, forged a close bond and would often meet up in London at Annabel's nightclub, once dubbed the poshest basement on the planet. Inside, it resembled a psychedelic country house with mirrored pillars, swirling purple carpets and portraits adorning labyrinth-like corridors. A towering Buddha sat in an alcove overlooking the wooden dancefloor where the likes of Mick Jagger, Frank Sinatra and Princess Diana all strutted their stuff. Membership was notoriously difficult to obtain but, magician-like, Paul could always conjure it for close friends and clients, and he fast-tracked William. Behind the scenes, it was actually Brenda pulling the strings. She'd befriended Lady Annabel, after whom the club was named, as her son was at nursery school with my sister Katrina. Together, Paul and Brenda were becoming a power couple of Eighties London.

It was likely in Annabel's, sprawled on a red velvet sofa, that the idea of a Kutchinsky polo team was born. Their big rivals Cartier had got into the sport first, sponsoring competitions, but Paul wasn't far behind. How much, he asked William, would it cost to put the Kutchinsky name on a polo shirt? The answer was about £25,000 (almost £40,000 today) for two years' sponsorship, starting in the summer of 1988. In retrospect, it was money the House of Kutchinsky could ill afford. But to Paul, it was an adventure, a chance to have fun with his friends and forge new connections. The business had been there all his life, such a constant that I don't think he ever entertained the idea that it might be under threat.

I still have a Kutchinsky polo shirt. It is a relic that hangs on my living room wall. The black and gold design is eye-catching, with our surname squished to fit across the middle. Yellow and black caps made from plastic and foam were also made. The team included William, his friend and fellow amateur Christopher Courage (scion of the famous brewing family), an occasional celebrity player – Stewart Copeland – the drummer from rock band The Police and a sole professional, Earl Herbert. In photographs, these muscular demi-gods tower over my father in their white trousers and brown leather boots. He is the odd one out in his suit and tie and looks diminutive in a way that is alien to me.

In my memories, the polo stands out as a pinnacle moment. 'Paul was riding high,' a family friend once told me, unaware of her pun. Weekends were spent driving around the English countryside to watch the team compete. I loved horses and had been riding since I was about five years old. While the adults drank Pimm's, Katrina and I would sneak off to get a glimpse of the glossy thoroughbreds with their stumpy manes and tightly braided tails. It was a thrill seeing our name emblazoned on the riders' chests during matches as they teetered in their saddles, the green grass blurring beneath them as they galloped at lightning speeds, brandishing what looked like elongated croquet mallets. The highlight was always treading the divots – the ritual in between play that sees the well-groomed crowd parade onto the pitch and stamp on the turf in a bid to flatten it. Women who made the mistake of wearing stiletto heels would often find themselves stuck and in need of rescue.

This was how in summer 1988, the fabled encounter with the sport's most famous English player of the time, King Charles (then Prince Charles), occurred. Paul had paid for a marquee at Kirtlington Park, a historic polo club in Oxfordshire which adjoins a spectacular manor house. Black and gold Kutchinsky flags fluttered in the late spring breeze and glass cases of jewellery stood at the entrance. A long, rectangular cake covered in black icing with our name in gold formed the centrepiece of the buffet lunch. Using their shared passion for Aston Martins, the vintage sports car made famous by James Bond, as an icebreaker, Paul captured Charles in conversation long enough to pass him a Kutchinsky cap, which the prince was later photographed holding. The money shot.

Caught up in the refined hedonism of the polo scene, Paul decided to raise the stakes. Ignoring his father's concern that he was stretching the company's finances too thin, he bought a thoroughbred polo pony worth a quarter of a million and for two successive summers staged lavish events at a polo club not far from our house. It was almost as if my parents were putting on the traditional wedding they never had. About 250 of their closest friends and clients crowded into a sumptuous marquee for a luncheon. While the horses churned up the manicured lawn, the champagne flowed and a steel pan band tinkled away, adding a tropical feel, while happily lubricated guests spent thousands of pounds on charity raffle tickets. Among the famous faces were legendary game show host Bruce Forsyth, who had to deal with endless repetitions of his catchphrase: 'Nice to see you, to see you nice ...', British actress and Bond girl Fiona Fullerton, Richard Burton's widow Sally and then *Sunday Times* editor Andrew Neil. When the Kutchinsky team emerged triumphant, there was much back-slapping and cheering inside the marquee.

Photographers snapped away, capturing images that would be printed in the society pages of glossy magazines like *Tatler* and *Harpers & Queen*, and several national newspapers. In 1988, *Tatler* ran a side-profile of Mum, her tousled blonde hair blowing in the wind, diamond earrings glittering in the sunlight. The photographer captured her unawares, and she looked natural and at ease. Paul was so enamoured with it, he proudly displayed it on his desk, pointing it out to anyone who strayed into his office. His beautiful wife, in *Tatler* no less. Finally, the upper classes were treating the House of Kutchinsky like one of their own.

But did it secretly jar that the society bible chose to feature Mum instead of him? Did envy start to gnaw away at him as he found himself in the shadow of his once-shy Scottish girl? During their bitterest rows, he would remind her that she should be grateful to him for the life he'd given her. Was this need to reinstate himself as the family figurehead part of what motivated him to build his egg?

There's a particular photograph that I keep being drawn back to. Dad, who looked deeply suspicious whenever he sat on a horse, once gamely tried his hand at bicycle polo during a polo day. He is playing the fool, grabbing the spotlight at his own expense. His mouth is wide open and his arms are splayed, the sinews taut and twisted under his tanned skin. A Kutchinsky polo shirt flops untucked over jeans and a yellow cap is crammed askew on his wild hair. His left hand grasps a mallet and there's a flash of a gold wristwatch on his arm. He looks ecstatic but also vulnerable.

Among the crowds at the polo were two guests who would flatter my father, befriend him and fatally divide him from Mum. This is where the Vainer brothers enter the scene. Dad's relationship with these diamond dealers from Hatton Garden lit the fuse of his downfall. Without them, Kutchinsky's egg would never have been made.

9

The Deal

Paul loved flattery. A lifetime of spoiling by Lily had bred in him an unguarded innocence, a belief that everyone was naturally on his side. Normally, Mum was on hand to help filter out the fake platitudes from chancers in the jewellery trade who buzzed around him because his name was Kutchinsky. But by the late Eighties, she was increasingly busy with three young children – Hollie was barely a year old and, as before, it fell to Mum to do all the late nights. In the morning, Dad would sometimes wake to find her fast asleep, curled up in bed with my baby sister.

She was also getting more involved with high-profile charities like Help the Aged, of which Princess Diana was a patron, and the Queen Charlotte's Ball, a historic highlight of London's social season. The committees for these events were highly exclusive: members were invited to join, normally by someone called Bunty, and were expected to dedicate their time for free. Dad boosted Mum's credentials by offering up Kutchinsky jewellery to be auctioned off to wealthy philanthropic types, bringing publicity on a scale the business had never seen before.

KUTCHINSKY'S EGG

In December 1987, a Kutchinsky watch graced the cover of the *News of the World*'s Sunday magazine, next to a close-up of a smiling Princess Diana, with the headline 'World exclusive: Win Di's jewels!' Finally, the House of Kutchinsky had the royal seal of approval. Jo was delighted. His investment in his son was paying off and he resolved to give Paul more space to pursue his own ideas.

*   *   *

Most of the adults who circled around my parents are imprinted on my memory, but when I search for traces of Richard and Martin Vainer, there are just waves of static. Standing on the precipice of mid-life, Paul could feel his rebellious spirit stirring. In these diamond dealer brothers, who were both bachelors in their early thirties, he found drinking partners who were more carefree than his married friends. Mum still utters the name 'Vainer' as if it were a swear word. The hatred is mutual; Richard Vainer claims Brenda represents 'intrinsic evil' to him. Until I started my quest, I avoided prying into the reasons behind this enduring malignancy between our families, although I knew it was wrapped up with the egg. In some ways Mum is very open – she doesn't hold back with her emotions or political opinions – but she is also deeply protective of me and my sisters, and much of what happened after Dad's departure she hid from me. Until now.

Unlike Dad and Roger, the Vainers came as a pair, despite striking differences in their looks and personalities. Richard, or 'Dirty Dick the Diamond Dealer' to his friends, was a charismatic bulldog – attractive and arrogant with broad shoulders and a wide, ruddy face with piercing brown eyes, framed by thick brown hair. He exuded an unshakeable magnetism and revelled in his roguish nickname, even keeping a sign with it printed on in his office. To his friends, he was a bon vivant, fun-loving and generous. To his critics, he was a caddish playboy who despised the idea of settling down and was an irrepressible flirt.

While Richard enjoyed a jet-set lifestyle, travelling around the world and networking with clients, his brother preferred to stay in London, basing himself primarily in the office. Younger by four years, Martin was blond and lean with a whippet-like physique and a whimsical, at times earnest, air. He would go on to marry Brenda's former manicurist Jilly, who he met at a Kutchinsky polo day. Mum saw this as a betrayal, cursing Jilly with the *EastEnders*-style insult of 'two-faced cow'.

Like Jo Kutchinsky, the Vainers' father, Milos, was a powerful figure with whom Paul developed a close, almost parental, bond. A Czech wartime refugee who had previously been a successful lawyer, he fell into the diamond trade after a chance meeting over a game of bridge with Harry Oppenheimer, the chairman of De Beers. Unlike many of their fellow Hatton Garden diamond dealers, the Vainers weren't Jewish, but Milos's ambition and passion won him respect within the otherwise closed ranks. He rebuilt his family's fortune, giving advice on how to value diamonds to the governments of nations like Botswana, Russia and, later, Australia. He also worked with countries like Sierra Leone, which were plagued with corruption, to help them clamp down on diamond smuggling.

When Milos wasn't travelling, he was searching for new ways to make diamonds sparkle. Like the Willy Wonka of the gem world, he filled their premises in Hatton Garden with cutting-edge machinery and hired 'crazy geniuses' to devise new cutting and polishing techniques. Once, they succeeded in repolishing a huge 13-carat pink diamond with a deep fissure which nobody else dared touch. But it was the search for beauty, rather than cold, hard cash, that motivated him. He had a reputation as a serial philanderer but in business, his sons say, he understood the value of being true to your word. At a certain point in the late Eighties, Milos retired to spend more time pursuing his other passions – tennis and women, leaving his sons to get on with it.

I suspect Paul saw Richard as a kindred spirit; a rising star in the jewellery trade who also felt pressure to step out of his father's shadow. Today, the man Mum calls her 'nemesis' is in his late sixties and has the broad girth of someone who enjoys the finer things in life. Richard's attitude towards Paul now is, at best, disparaging. But it's clear that at first there was a bromance of sorts between them. Lurking in Mum's attic in a folder, among faxes, cheque book stubs and hand-written receipts, I found a letter recommending Richard for membership of Annabel's, where Paul described him as a 'successful business owner and man of upstanding character'. When Mum found out about the membership bid, she was furious with Paul. Over the years he'd stubbornly refused to recommend some of their closest friends, including Philippa and Nick. They're not the right kind of people, he'd say with a shrug when she pressed him. Bewildered, she stared at him openmouthed. He could be moronic, at times, but he was rarely mean. Paul's lack of snobbishness was one of the reasons she fell in love with him. What was happening to her husband?

THE DEAL

He started making excuses not to see their old friends. They were too old. Too boring. Too weighed down by the baggage of family life. Instead, he threw himself into a more youthful, fast-living scene. He bought a share in a riverboat with the Vainers. There were lively summer parties at their riverside home which he insisted on attending, ignoring his wife's reluctance. The way Brenda saw it, Paul was almost forty – when was he going to grow up and stop acting like Peter Pan? But if she was hoping that, as in the old days, her disapproval might have an impact on her husband, she was bitterly disappointed.

*   *   *

As a child, I sensed the fracturing between my parents. There were money worries. Their bickering turned from affectionate to bitter, and holidays were either scaled back or cancelled. I'd always felt secure in our family unit, proud of my parents' happy, tactile relationship. Their arguments could be explosive, sometimes involving Dad smashing plates, but they would always kiss and make up. Until they didn't.

Creeping down the stairs one night when Dad was out, I overheard Mum in the kitchen complaining to her neighbour Zeina that he had dumped all their friends for the Vainers. They were going to destroy him, she muttered, draining her wine glass. Zeina, who had her own marital woes, nodded sagely, knowing better than to contradict Brenda when she was in this mood. Instead, she topped up both their glasses with the Chardonnay she'd brought over. 'I just have this terrible premonition of disaster,' Mum said quietly, clinking her ruby ring against the stem of her glass, almost as if to ward off bad spirits.

There was no corner of our lives that Dad's infatuation with the Vainers didn't touch. He even invited them to visit our fisherman's cottage in Pennan, a picturesque coastal village outside Aberdeen, not far from where Brenda grew up and where they first met. It was our family's haven, a retreat from the pressures of London life.

But the Vainers' visit wasn't purely social. A property deal was on the table. Brenda's sister, Anne, was an estate agent and had alerted her to the existence of 30 acres of prime land just outside Aberdeen that was ripe for development. The region was still in the grip of the oil boom and the housing market was lucrative. My parents' proposal for the Vainers was that they jointly buy the land, plus an adjoining mansion block, and turn the latter into flats which they could then sell to fund further development. It seemed an opportunity that was too good to miss, from which everyone would walk away richer.

The brothers arrived on a blustery day in 1989, around Easter time. The plan was for them to spend the night in Pennan before visiting the proposed development site the next day. After nursing pints of Scottish stout on the seafront, Paul announced they were going on a hike to a nearby sandy bay and set about grabbing flat caps, walking sticks and a hip flask. He led the way, trampling through muddy brambles and thick yellow gorse bushes, his booming laugh carrying on the wind. As they strolled briskly across the clifftops, Richard fell into step with Mum. 'It's you who's the clever one,' he muttered conspiratorially. 'Paul's weak. We think he's a joke.'

Frustrated as she was with her husband, Brenda was fiercely loyal. She tried to brush it off as a joke, tittering nervously, before stopping to tie her shoelace in a bid to shake him off.

THE DEAL

Later, when she tried to warn Paul about what his new friends really thought of him, she was accused of being jealous.

'He wouldn't listen, he was obsessed with them,' Mum recalled. 'He was like a lamb to the slaughter.'

This is how Mum tells the story, and it's important to say that recollections aren't hard facts. It's possible Richard's words were a joke she misconstrued and that her memory is coloured by the bitterness of subsequent events. Perhaps this exchange took place somewhere else entirely. Perhaps it was even a figment of her imagination. What I do know for certain is that in the late 1980s, our family's fortunes became entangled with the Vainers', the consequences of which we are still living with today.

By this time, my father was harbouring another new infatuation. Anna Powell was an attractive 22-year-old Londoner with a sharp brain, piercing blue eyes and long, lustrous blonde hair, who wore stiletto heels to boost her already above average height. The eldest of four siblings, she had a maturity and a presence that belied her youth. Her boyfriend was a charismatic nightclub impresario, James 'Jimbo' Johnston*, a big, hairy man with a thick beard, a slovenly manner and a fondness for partying who also dabbled in what Anna called 'tits and arse photography' for magazines like *Playboy* and *Penthouse*. A former private schoolgirl from a middle-class family whose parents had split up in her late teens, Anna was nineteen when they first met. Jimbo was twenty years older than her. It wasn't immediately clear what Anna saw in him, aside from the excitement and glamour of the club scene. They

---

* Name has been changed

lived together in a small flat in the West End, just behind Selfridges.[1]

In early 1989, Anna got a job through a contact of Jimbo's as a sales assistant in an antique jewellery shop based in the Vainers' Hatton Garden premises. She didn't have any real interest in either antiques or jewels but was keen for a change of pace. The instability of life with Jimbo was wearing her down. He would pick up cheques from Fleet Street for freelance journalism jobs, cash them straight away in the pub and drink away the proceeds. The Hatton Garden job opportunity came through a friend of his, Carol, a TV game show hostess, who played tennis with the shop's owner, and Anna jumped at the chance to earn a steady wage. 'I had no bloody money. Jimbo and I were all about nightclubs. I didn't even have a suit,' Anna recalled. 'I just toddled along in the best skirt I could find.'

Anna was one of three female sales assistants and the atmosphere was lively. When important clients dropped in on their way upstairs to see the Vainers, the shop manager, Seima, would bat her eyelashes and suggest they take the girls for a bottle of champagne. 'She was like a tornado,' Anna recalled. 'It was always: "Darling, when are you taking us for champagne, darling?" Whatever hapless dealer came in at 5.30 p.m. on a Friday night would be hauled round to the Bleeding Heart tavern in Farringdon to buy a bottle of champagne, then they could bugger off.'

Suddenly, Anna found herself surrounded by wealthy men who wore suits, drove expensive cars and ordered bottles of the finest fizz without blinking. Jimbo, by contrast, didn't even have the right credentials to open a bank account. 'I was just the shop girl, lost in this extraordinary Hatton Garden world. It was alien to me.'

Despite Jo being sniffy about Hatton Garden, calling it the 'dregs of the jewellery trade', Paul became a familiar face in the shop as he got in deeper with the Vainers. It wasn't long before he started finding excuses to be there on Friday afternoons, happily succumbing to Seima's demands for champagne. He even started bringing a bottle with him and drinking it in the shop. But it wasn't Seima's company, or even the Vainers, he was seeking.

It was Anna.

* * *

After the Argyle Diamond Mine opened in 1983, Milos Vainer was one of the first experts to visit the site. Richard followed in his footsteps, making regular trips to advise the Australians on how best to cut and polish their diamonds. By 1989, this remote red pit had become the world's largest diamond producer by volume, though most of its output was dominated by low value stones with just a sprinkling of its mystical pinks. Aware of Argyle's wish to raise its profile with a hero piece of jewelled art, the Vainer brothers sensed an opportunity: connecting the House of Kutchinsky to Argyle, whose owners had deep pockets and big ambitions, seemed the perfect match.

Work had already begun on the Library Egg before Argyle came on board in summer 1989. There was much excitement in Argyle's headquarters in Western Australia at the idea of working with the son of the legendary jeweller Jo Kutchinsky. Perth was booming in the 1980s, with millions of dollars flowing through it, partly due to the growth of frontier industries like gold and diamond mining, and there was cash to splash on wild schemes. A visit was planned for early November, with a tour of the diamond mine in East Kimberley and a VIP trip to the Melbourne Cup, a four-day horse racing carnival which was Australia's most high-profile sporting event. Paul and Brenda made the trip solo. Paul took photographs of the work in progress to show the firm's executives, who were impressed by the scale of his vision and his determination to be faithful to the Fabergé myth.

While Paul bonded over beers with the Argyle executives assigned to the egg project, Brenda bristled against the blokeish culture she encountered. In London, she played a central role in the business, but here she was sidelined – left out of meetings, referred to as a 'sheila' by the worst offenders. When it was suggested she leave the room during a critical point in negotiations, she was furious and refused to budge. Paul was too easily swayed. His naivety was part of his charm, but it functioned best when offset by Brenda's canny scepticism. Her instincts told her the business needed a period of stability but Kutchinsky's egg represented the opposite. The sense of storm clouds gathering in the distance grew ever stronger.

Paul proudly kept his copy of the contract with Argyle. It reads: 'The parties have agreed to manufacture and design a Library Egg approximately 63 cm tall, comprising 17,650 grams of 18 carat gold and 700 carats (140 grams) of diamonds.' Argyle agreed to pay Kutchinsky A$870,000 (about £444,000 in 1989) to cover half of the materials and other manufacturing costs, as well as supplying more than 2 million Australian dollars' worth of predominantly pink diamonds. The sale price was set at 'no less than $5 million' and the profits were

THE DEAL

to be split 60/40 in Argyle's favour if a buyer could be found. That was the easy part, Paul assured them. He had the Midas touch where sales were concerned, especially in the Middle East. And if the Sultan of Brunei wasn't interested, there was always Donald Trump, the American multi-millionaire famed for his love of golden trinkets, or a corporate collector who might want to display it as a 'wow piece' in their offices. He wasn't worried about that part. For now, his focus was entirely on 'making the bloody thing'.

After Perth, they headed into the wilds of the outback to tour the diamond mine. First, they flew to the remote town of Kununurra that sprouts on the banks of the River Ord like a mighty boab tree, the region's unofficial emblem, with its swollen trunk and spindly branches. Founded in 1961, the town's name comes from an indigenous phrase meaning 'big water'. It's a place where crocodiles outnumber humans, rare birds whistle overhead and sunsets sear themselves into your brain. In the wet season, electrical storms split the sky asunder, turning the arid surface of this sacred land – which native Australians had inhabited, undisturbed for centuries – into a gushing sea of blood-red mud.

When my parents passed through, the skies were calm but the sun was hot and the humidity intense. Paul barely seemed to notice the oppressive heat. He'd always been a sun worshipper, his olive skin a protective cloak shielding him from sunburn. But Brenda's Scottish skin itched as if her blood was boiling from the inside. Her mood took a further nosedive when she saw the small propeller plane that was scheduled to take them to the mine.

'I'm not getting in that. No way. It's a deathtrap!'

Somehow, Paul cajoled her off the tarmac and into the tiny aircraft which could fit a maximum of about twelve people. This was the route the mine's 800 workers took on a regular basis, flying in and out for two-week shifts from their homes, which were often thousands of kilometres away in cities like Perth. As the plane pitched high into the sky, Paul pressed his face excitedly to the window and Brenda's stomach heaved. Petrified, she was numb to the beauty of the wilderness below. A single thought flashed through her brain like a record stuck in a groove: if this plane goes down, we are finished and the girls will be all alone. Glancing at her husband, she wondered how he could seem so immune to fear, so oblivious to the risk this posed to their daughters. Instead, he was grinning, basking in the aura of invincibility that striking the egg deal had given him.

Their journey took them over ancient gorges that sliced through red cliffs and across the vast, glistening waters of Lake Argyle. After about ninety minutes in the air, they had their first glimpse of their destination. Burrowed into a gully called Barramundi Gap, named after that mythical fish from the Aboriginal tale, this natural jewel box was an industrial stain on the landscape[2].

As the pilot swooped down towards the private airstrip, where wandering cattle and wallabies grazed, Brenda clenched her fists, her red nails digging like talons into her skin. She closed her eyes. *Thump. Thwack.* The jet slammed down onto the tarmac, the force of the impact making the passengers' bodies shake like blancmange. Even Paul paled under his tan.

Security at the mine was tight, with a set of radio-controlled gates guarding the entrance. Paul complied with

The Argyle Library Egg by Kutchinsky was first unveiled to the public in April 1990.

Dad with the miniature jewelled library that fit inside his giant, gold Easter egg.

The Kutchinsky family c.1910. From top left: Moshe Aaron Kutchinsky, Nathan Williams, Fanny Williams (née Kutchinsky), Leah Kuchinsky, Hannah Kutchinsky.

Dad, aged fifteen, looking dapper in his school uniform, autumn 1965.

Dad inherited his looks and sense of style from his mother, who adored him.

Grandpa Jo at work in the Knightsbridge store, charming a client, c.1978–81.

Grandma Lily striking a pose at a society event, wearing Kutchinsky jewels, 1963. Inset: a Kutchinsky diamond bracelet, later sold at Bonhams.

Event photo – Courtesy of the Kutchinsky family archive; Bracelet photo – © Bonhams, reproduced with permission
Overall Bonhams: The Kutchinsky Collection, The Personal Collection of the late Jo Kutchinsky, 27th April, 2001

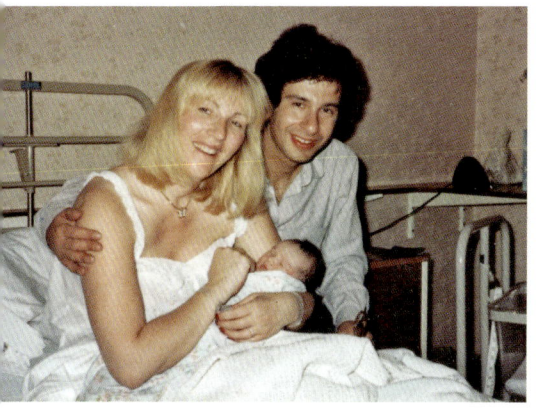

Mum and Dad were all smiles when I was born on a summer night in 1979.

My birth brought Mum and Grandma Lily closer than ever before.

Mum and Dad were a power couple during the House of Kutchinsky's heyday, in 1980s London.

On family holidays, Dad was always behind the camera – an absent presence in our midst.

I loved stealing moments with Dad on the slopes. He took this photograph while coaching me for a ski slalom race.

Dad loved messing about in boats. On a family holiday to Disney World, Florida, he taught me and Katrina how to take the wheel.

Mum and Dad captured looking happy and relaxed during a night out – before the egg.

The Kutchinsky polo team scored a memorable victory over the sport's most famous player; King Charles c.1988–89.

Dad didn't like horses but he loved winning. Here we are celebrating a Kutchinsky polo team victory, c.1988.

Beneath the smiles a bitter family feud was brewing when Jo was quizzed on the future of the business in a luxury magazine interview. From left: Paul Kutchinsky, Solomon Kutchinsky, Stanley Dessar, David Morein, Roger Kutchinsky, Jo Kutchinsky.

Mum was excited to meet Princess Diana at a charity ball in October 1987.

Grandpa Jo threw a glittering party at the Dorchester Hotel for his seventieth birthday. From left: Jo, Lily, Roger (in shadow), Paul, Brenda, Katrina, me, my cousins Natasha and Tanya.

I was allowed to stay up late to attend the egg's launch at the Victoria & Albert Museum, London, May 1990.

Courtesy of the Kutchinsky family archive

Mum and Dad shared a joke with the Duchess of Norfolk at the Chopard and Kutchinsky exhibition in October 1987. Mum turned heads, wearing her favourite diamond bow earrings.

Courtesy of the Kutchinsky family archive

I felt a strong connection with the egg's new owners, Reiko (left) and Takashi Mabuchi.

After so many false starts, I was finally reunited with dad's egg in its new home: The National Museum of Nature and Science, Tokyo, October 2023.

The sight of the Kutchinsky name imprinted on the egg's golden shell filmed me with huge pride.

THE DEAL

the various checks, fizzing with enthusiasm. 'Fair dinkum,' he quipped when warned that picking up anything off the ground would trigger a robust body search. Brenda cringed next to him, but he remained unperturbed. All that mattered was absorbing every last morsel of information about these fairy-tale gems. When he lasered in on a subject, it was as if nothing else existed. He'd been like that about Mum when they first met. About the business before he took over. About me when I was first born, proudly writing down my milestones (crawling, walking, standing) in his work diary. And now about his egg.

As they drove along the mine's dusty track, huge dump trucks rumbled past. Occasionally, the earth would shake as controlled explosions echoed around the mine. The sheer scale of the operation took Paul's breath away. This wasn't mining as he'd imagined it from the old days, when workers wielded pickaxes in intense heat, scavenging for diamonds with their bare hands. Argyle was already producing diamonds on an unprecedented scale – about 35 million carats a year – and the technology used was cutting edge. Still, the pink diamonds were the rarest of them all: for every million carats of diamonds, Argyle produced just 2 carats of the finest pinks. The bulk of the heavy lifting was done by machines while workers sheltered in air-conditioned trucks and control rooms. Muddy rocks, of which just one in a thousand had a sparkler buried inside, chugged along on conveyor belts until they were spat out, the rhythmic clatter of their fall echoing off the cliff face.

Their next stop was the vantage point at the top of the mine, which offered a gut-punching view. The mine sprawled before them with its spider's web of rollercoaster-like structures merging with the rocky red earth, scorched bushland and Lake Argyle shimmering in the distance.

After beauty came danger. Their tour took them to the open pit face where the mercury could at times creep towards 50 degrees centigrade. Setting foot outside for more than thirty minutes could pose a genuine risk to life. At times, Paul felt like he was having an out of body experience or was an actor in a movie about his life. Peering inside the sci-fi-esque control room, which resembled the bridge of a spaceship, with rows of monitors and flashing buttons, that feeling intensified. He glanced at Brenda – did she feel this sense of dislocation too?

Their final stop was the diamond viewing room which housed some of the most valuable rocks on the planet. Paul had seen thousands of polished diamonds in his life but roughs still held some mystery for him – frosted pyramids that belied the fire within them. This is what he'd come for – to feel a connection to the stones that would encrust Kutchinsky's egg.

Their evening was spent relaxing over dinner and drinks in the workers' village, which was a short drive from the main site. The staff nicknamed it Club Argyle, due to its country club atmosphere and high-end package holiday-style facilities. In the centre of the village was a large swimming pool, cloaked by trees and shaded from the sun by teal-coloured cloth sails, miniatures of those which festoon Sydney Opera House.

Back then, Argyle village was probably the most comfortable accommodation in the region. The mine's Australian directors faced criticism from their London shareholders over the perceived extravagance of it. Now, there are five-star resorts and luxurious lodges where travellers can stay, disrupting nature while trying to connect with it. Brenda remembers their lodgings as being fairly 'basic' but nothing could dent Paul's good mood. He was in his element, holding court in the bar and later sitting out on the terrace, watching the sun melt into a watercolour sky, its purplish-red hues conjuring the colour of Argyle's finest diamonds. The scenery was so stunning, all that was missing was a spliff to help him sink into it. He always had a supply of weed at home, stashed in the safe alongside Mum's jewellery and packets of diamonds (for emergencies) and other assorted items. Now, he was regretting not taking the risk and hiding a few joints in his luggage, like he often did on a long trip. He had even considered asking one of their Argyle contacts if they could source him some, but had dismissed the idea, sensing Brenda would disapprove. It probably wasn't a good look, he admitted, sighing reluctantly to himself. I suspect I would have had the same instinct as Dad, tantalised by the thought of enhancing the beauty of the landscape with that particular intoxicant.

Even without the weed, Paul's mood was buoyant. Kutchinsky's egg would be made. The business's future was almost secure. Nothing could ruin this moment. Nightfall brought a stillness to the East Kimberley but with it came a new wonder. The pristine sky was studded with more diamonds than could ever be extracted from the ground. Billions of stars and planets cast an ethereal glow on the rocks, lakes and trees below, as the Milky Way swirled above my parents' slumbering heads.

10

THE CREATION

As a child, I was blissfully ignorant of the tensions around the egg's creation. It was only when I started trying to trace the goldsmiths who had soldered, sawed and spun Dad's masterpiece into existence that I first heard the name Leo de Vroomen. I had always assumed that like all the other beautiful things that filled the House of Kutchinsky's windows, the egg had emerged from our workshop. When it came to tracing the craftsmen who worked there, my memories were blurry. I recalled their cockney-tinged accents and casual attire of jeans, trainers and polo shirts. Occasionally, Dad would swing by the workshop to collect some jewellery with me in tow, and I'd peer round the big metal doors with a mix of awe and trepidation.

At the outset of my search, I floundered. I was a journalist, not a jeweller. My link to the world of gold and gems was severed when Dad died. My focus had always been the 'why' of the egg; obsessing over his motives for risking everything to build his golden ego. But as I followed its trail, I started to see that he designed it, in part, as a love letter to an industry on the brink of extinction. Many of the techniques used to

THE CREATION

make it have vanished, a result of automation and changing tastes, and hardly any craftsmen are emerging to take the place of those who have retired or died. Kutchinsky's egg belongs to a specific moment in time. It could never be made again.

Rummaging for clues in Mum's attic one weekend, nearly a year into my investigations, I struck gold. First, there was a sketch of Dad's creation, printed in the glossy brochure that accompanied its launch at the Victoria and Albert Museum. Back then, I'd paid scant attention to it. But now I wondered how this sketch, Dad's dream, had become reality. Who were the people who had toiled so hard to make this extraordinary object? The egg's vital statistics were imprinted on my mind: 7,000 hours, 15 kg of gold, 24,000 diamonds. But beyond what was printed in the brochure, how the egg was made remained a mystery to me.

Next, I unearthed a battered leather Filofax containing a number for Peter Stein, son of Nat, one of the Kutchinsky workshop's original founders. When Len and Nat retired, Peter took over alongside Gerald Earle, who'd worked for the firm since the Commercial Road days. But Mum was dismissive when I suggested he might help with my enquiries. Why couldn't I just let 'that stupid egg' go, she asked, rolling her eyes.

Peter wasn't in the inner circle, she said tersely, refusing to name who was. Intrigued, I saved his number in my phone and resolved to call him when I got back to London.

But the right time never came. Weeks passed, then months. I kept putting it off, plagued by a growing sense there were truths about my father, and his egg, that I might not want to face. It wasn't just Dad's flaws I was hiding from; it was also a lingering fear of what it might mean for me. I had always worried that somehow I was destined to repeat his mistakes. I enjoyed pushing my boundaries, just like him. I enjoyed a party, just like him. I believed in saying 'fuck it' and shooting for the moon, just like him.

Every time I thought about calling Peter, dark clouds of grief and inertia gathered in my mind. I could hear my family's voices laced with a sharp, defensive dread. *Forget about the egg. It was a failure. A fuck-up. Like your father. Like you.* It wasn't that they wanted to hurt me — they wanted to stop me from reopening old wounds that had never really healed, especially for Mum. The possibility of causing them more pain made my chest tighten. Was I wasting my time dredging up the ghosts of my past? I'd just turned thirty-five, should I be focusing instead on making decisions about my biological eggs?

Finally, after another heated conversation with Mum about the egg, with her telling me I didn't have a hope of ever finding it, I cracked and nervously dialled Peter's number. I needed to prove to myself that I wouldn't give up.

The goldsmith's voice sounded familiar, an echo from a long-buried past. A decade younger than Dad, their paths had mirrored each other to some degree, both rising up to take over their family business, and he spoke admiringly of Paul's passion for the craft of jewellery. 'He loved his time in the workshop, your dad. He enjoyed the fact that you actually produced, or were part of, a piece of work.'

Peter suggested we meet for lunch at a Central London pub the next day. Just before he hung up, his tone darkened. 'Paul made some bad decisions,' he said ominously. 'I can't say anymore now. It's better in person.'

THE CREATION

Staring at my phone, I wondered what had gone so horribly wrong that Peter had to steel himself to talk about it.

*   *   *

Conversation flowed easily over lunch – until I brought up the subject of Kutchinsky's egg.

'I still can't understand it,' said Peter, who was then in his mid-fifties, taking a sip of his pint. 'We didn't know about it at first,' he added, his grip on his glass tightening.

I stared back, confused. If their workshop didn't make it, then who did? Sanitt and Stein, his father and Len's company, had manufactured jewellery exclusively for the House of Kutchinsky for fifty years. Why, on his biggest project, would Dad cut them out?

'Your dad took the design to Leo de Vroomen. Make no mistake, Leo was good,' Peter muttered, blinking behind his glasses as if batting away bad memories. De Vroomen Alexander, he explained, was a London-based manufacturing firm founded in 1984 by Leo, an ambitious Dutch jeweller, and his partner, Alexander Parkes, a top goldsmith who had previously worked for Cartier. While Leo was the frontman, socialising with clients and winning new business, Alex disliked small talk and was happiest in the workshop. Specialising in *objet d'arts*, the firm had won acclaim for their creativity and were seen as an alternative to some of the bigger workshops operating in the capital at that time.

'I won't pretend we weren't upset that they took the egg elsewhere,' Peter said, as he took a bite of his sandwich. Historically, the relationship between the workshop and the House of Kutchinsky was based on trust, success, even love.

Together, Jo and Len had escaped the East End, become wealthy and lived the good life. But just before they both retired, their bond was broken when Jo accused Len of stealing diamonds from him.

The trouble started at a charity ball where Lily spied Len's wife, Sonia, brandishing a diamond ring, larger than any she owned. When Lily coyly enquired about the origins of the glittering stone, Sonia proudly said Len had made it for her as a gift. When Lily reported this back to her husband, he was furious. Only Jo Kutchinsky had access to stones of that quality, he raged, and only his wife deserved to wear such magnificent jewellery. Wrongly, he concluded that Len must have robbed him. Lily, who had never liked Sonia, purred her agreement. The truth was that Len had bought the stone himself from a dealer who visited the workshop every Christmas, selling exceptional gems at trade prices. But Jo refused to listen and never spoke to Len again, abruptly ending their decades-long friendship. Once the rot set in, the workshop dwindled in size from forty craftsmen to eighteen and both sides started doing the dirty on each other.

In the run-up to the egg, Paul got 'the needle' with the workshop, said Peter. He accused them of inflating the manufacturing cost of a jewelled shaving column, made from rich green malachite which contained a small gold brush, and siphoning off their own profit at the shop's expense. It's possible Paul saw cutting Sanitt and Stein out of the egg as a form of revenge. 'But you have to know the pool you're swimming in,' Peter reflected, ruefully. 'We were goldsmiths – we knew how to deal with the trade.'

It was hard to peel myself away from lunch. I felt I'd found a genuine ally in tracking down the missing egg. But when it came to seeking out Leo de Vroomen, Peter was circumspect. There was bad blood there, he said, warning me to steer clear. As I walked back to the Tube, I recalled hearing de Vroomen's name come up during a visit to Goldsmiths' Hall. In my memory, the receptionist had looked sceptical when I asked for information on the Argyle Library Egg made by Paul Kutchinsky. Slicing through my enthusiasm with a frosty stare, she said: 'It was Leo who made it. Leo de Vroomen.' Confused, I smiled and corrected her that my father was in fact its creator. 'It was trouble that's for sure, whoever was behind it,' she said, motioning for me to go upstairs into an ornate reading room. I'd dismissed it at the time but now the memory niggled. In the eyes of the jewellery trade, did the egg belong to Leo de Vroomen?

Taking the egg to de Vroomen was a terrible decision, Mum said when I brought it up, his name sticking in her throat. 'Leo was all over your father like a rash at first,' she divulged. 'Egos got involved. Leo threatened to put his hallmark inside the egg. Your father was furious but I never imagined the hatred would be so bitter.'

Hallmarking is like a secret jeweller's code that tells the creation story of every piece made in Britain. It isn't something a jeweller can just add themselves. The piece has to be taken to one of four assay offices in the UK, where the purity of the gold is tested and then stamped by experts. Look closely at any item and you'll see a series of four or five tiny marks. On rings, they're on the inside of the band; on necklaces, they're hidden on the clasp. On the egg, they are proudly imprinted on top of the shell. The first of these marks is always the creator's: the stamp of ownership that records who conceived and created it.

KUTCHINSKY'S EGG

The relationship between craftsman and retailer has always been a delicate balance, with power typically vested in the high-end jewellery houses. Often craftsmen labour tirelessly, pouring their heart and soul into a piece, knowing the spotlight will never fall on them. Even Fabergé faced criticism for not giving enough credit to the hundreds of highly skilled goldsmiths and artisans employed in his workshops.

* * *

Mum repeated Peter's warning to stay away from de Vroomen. But the more people tried to deter me, the more determined I became to find him and hear his story. His email was easy to locate. It was there on his website, which proudly displayed his jewellery but made no mention of the egg. It would have been so easy to reach out and introduce myself, but something made me hesitate. I spent ages drafting an email but left it unsent, indecision nagging away at me.

Then in early 2016, I mentioned the unsent email to my best friend, Fran, an artist, who often helped me make sense of difficult situations. 'What are you scared of?' she asked. 'I'm sure he'd be happy to celebrate his work, and whatever happened, it was a long time ago. Don't let your mother get in your head.'

I took her advice and pressed send.

That was how I found myself standing in an elegant part of London outside a showroom with a glass front and shiny black door, on a dull March morning. The name de Vroomen hovered above the window; gold letters on thick black paint. I was early, so I strolled around the empty streets, running through my questions in my head. There was so much I wanted to ask. Not just about what had happened to the egg but about how it was made, the ancient techniques involved, the personalities who toiled to make it. The egg meant so much to me, and I imagined that would give us an instant connection.

De Vroomen's reply to my email had been short but polite. He sounded happy to meet me, and I felt vindicated in reaching out. As I entered the brightly lit space, a tall, imposing figure with a broad forehead and greying, sandy hair greeted me. As he shook my hand, ushering me into his basement office, I detected a menacing note in his softly accented voice that made me uneasy. The buzzer rang and he jumped up, seemingly expecting it. A friend of his, Joanna, a jewellery historian, had arrived and she would apparently help set the record straight on the egg. It was fast becoming apparent that this wouldn't be the cosy, nostalgic chat I had envisaged.

'I've got some bad news for you,' de Vroomen said abruptly, seeming to relish my discomfort. 'My workshop designed the egg. It had nothing to do with anybody else.' His tone was blunt and matter-of-fact.

'We've never been given any credit,' he added bitterly. He went on to accuse Dad of lying and pretending that Cheryl, 'a little girl, who knew nothing about anything', designed the egg. Later, he admitted that she did do the initial drawing, but derided it as 'diabolical'.

But his main complaint was about money.

'We made the egg and got into big trouble with your family,' he said, raising his voice above the inopportune drilling that was filtering in from outside. 'We never got paid,' he added huffily, spitting out each word for emphasis, before clarifying that they were 'partly' paid.

I nodded, fighting the urge to run. As my attempts at

friendly chit-chat dwindled to a tight-lipped 'Oh dear', Joanna chipped in, implying that if I told a story that deviated from de Vroomen's narrative, she would discredit me.

'It's difficult to talk about the egg with any authenticity if the world doesn't know there is this horrible history behind it,' de Vroomen added. 'The trade knows that egg was the demise of De Vroomen Alexander.'

With a dramatic flourish, he produced legal papers which showed that De Vroomen Alexander had tried to sue the House of Kutchinsky over alleged unpaid costs.

'The Kutchinsky family or Argyle owes us a huge amount of money,' he claimed, adding that in his view, it amounted to an outstanding debt of £750,000.

'I don't feel terribly fond of the Kutchinsky name,' he added petulantly. 'I don't want to talk about [the egg] and I don't want my name attached to it ... We spent a huge amount of time and money on the litigation and had nothing to show for it. Consequently, my company had to be closed down ... and we've never made another *objet d'art* since.'

'Really? Oh dear,' I mumbled, rubbing my temples as the industrial drill noise outside intensified. Not even my father's untimely death had blunted Leo's anger. His next question revealed his true reason for meeting me. Would someone in 'my organisation' be able to stump up the cash? he asked.

'Sorry, it's just me,' I replied, feeling nauseous. At a loss for what to say, I blurted out that I was sorry without really knowing what for. Realising that I was unable to pay him and hadn't come for a fight, he softened. 'You were a little girl at the time, you don't need to apologise. It brings only bad memories back.'

THE CREATION

Transported back to a more carefree time, his voice shifted, taking on a dreamy tone, as if he was once again watching the egg take shape. 'It was a fantastic piece of craftsmanship; some of the best craftsmen in the country worked on it,' he said, a flash of suppressed pride drifting to the surface. 'It was a fantastic thing with a remote control! This was before everybody was walking around with mobile phones.'

For a moment, I dared hope that de Vroomen might open up about its creation, if I could keep him talking about the artistry that went into the egg, rather than the 'aggro' it caused. But that was short-lived. The glint in his eye was extinguished by another memory. 'The joke is Leo got egg on his face,' he brooded, sounding hostile but detached, referring to himself in the third person, almost as if it hadn't happened to him. 'Trust was broken and that's the worst thing that can happen in this industry ... a lot of misery is attached to that egg.'

An awkward silence descended. 'Well, I don't want to prolong the agony,' he said, giving me my cue to make a polite getaway. As I emerged from the showroom, back into the gloom, I realised my legs were shaking. I walked until I was out of sight, trying to make sense of what I'd just heard, before collapsing on a bench. What now? I hadn't told Mum I was going to see him, so I couldn't call her for reassurance. Whether the egg was entirely to blame for the loss of Leo de Vroomen's business, I didn't know, but it was clear that the sphere of destruction of Kutchinsky's egg extended further than I ever imagined.

Maybe it was cursed after all.

*   *   *

As with Richard Vainer, Paul saw in Leo de Vroomen a kindred spirit of sorts. They were of a similar age, sociable, ambitious and inclined to break the mould. While manufacturing *objets d'art* was a lucrative sideline, Leo's real love was jewellery. His ambition was to become an international brand in his own right. But while his bold, sculptural designs had captivated the American market, in Europe he had enjoyed less success.

The introduction came through mutual friends, and soon Paul was inviting him and his artist wife, Ginny, out for dinner to share their love of making jewelled treasures. Mum remembers those evenings as pleasant but something about the couple unsettled her. They'd suffered a terrible tragedy some years before when their young son had drowned, and she sensed their loss weighed heavily on them. The whispers in the jewellery trade were that grief warped Leo's character, imbuing him with a sense that the world was against him.

In late February 1989, Paul called Leo and asked him to come to the shop for a secret meeting. He had a plan to make the ultimate *objet d'art*, he lisped excitedly. He'd already shown Cheryl's design to a handful of other skilled craftsmen, who all begged to have the chance to make it, but he wanted de Vroomen. Both Jo and Brenda disagreed with him, for different reasons. 'He's not an *objet* man,' Jo croaked, shaking his head. 'He won't understand it.' Whereas Brenda could sense that, unlike other craftsmen who respected the hierarchy between the workshops and the jewellery houses, Leo, with his thrusting ambition, wouldn't be happy being in Paul's shadow. But her husband wouldn't listen. In his eyes, only the Dutch designer, who was known for his enamel-work, could execute

THE CREATION

his vision to the highest artistic standards and be faithful to Fabergé.

Back then, de Vroomen's workshop was based in a red-brick Victorian warehouse in Clerkenwell, an East London district that was home to some of the world's best *objet d'art* makers. His design studio was on the third floor, and the workshop, run by Alexander Parkes, the other half of De Vroomen Alexander, was downstairs on the second. Its large windows were framed by hanging plants, their leafy tendrils trailing down the off-white walls. Five jewellery benches, strewn with wood tools, chisels and blow torches, filled the space. Bright halogen lights hung low over the craftsmens' heads as they sat absorbed in the intricacies of their tasks. After work, they would congregate in one of the local pubs, sinking pints and swapping stories about the extravagant items they were tasked with making.

Originally a student of Leo's in the Seventies, when he taught at London's Central School of Art and Design (now Central St Martins), Giselle Moore worked with the Dutchman for over twenty years. When I tracked her down, after being ghosted by several craftsmen who had worked on the egg and still bore a grudge against the Kutchinsky name, I was surprised by how candidly she spoke about her old boss, describing him as 'autocratic' and inspiring in equal measure. 'He was passionate about jewellery,' Gisele explained. 'He could be infuriating but he had a vision ... We made beautiful things, beautifully.'

The egg project was cloaked in secrecy from the start. In Clerkenwell, all they knew was that Leo kept disappearing for meetings and coming back hours later, bubbling with excitement. Then one day, he returned with a sketch of a giant egg in purple pencil on dark paper and plonked it on Giselle's desk. 'We're going to make this in the finest, eighteen carat gold,' he said with a grin as he instructed her to improve the design.

'I went more or less by Cheryl's drawing in terms of it had an opening and furniture, but it didn't hang together,' Giselle recalled. 'She hadn't put it on anything and it needed a stand otherwise it would just roll over.'

Once Giselle started sketching and doing the measurements, the design, over which my father had final sign-off, came together fairly quickly. 'I ended up with a file that was about an inch thick,' Giselle told me. 'I had to do a technical drawing for every single little piece, all the different flower sizes, all the stone sizes ... I spent huge amounts of time trying to make it perfect because the craftsmen were using [my drawings] to make it fit together.'

By the time Leo finalised his quote, with the total cost to make the egg estimated at £260,000, the ambition for the project had evolved. The shell, which was composed of sixty identical gold panels, would slide open to reveal the jewelled library inside, which in turn would rotate to reveal the portrait gallery decorated in a rich cornflower blue hue associated with Fabergé. 'It seemed daft to have one scene inside because it would be too deep,' Giselle explained. 'We thought two scenes that turned around would be better.'

The two-page plan that was faxed over to Paul by De Vroomen Alexander is recognisable as the blueprint of the egg, including everything from the gem-encrusted drawer handles to the tiny diamond-studded ink blotter that sits in

THE CREATION

the library. But there was one notable exception from Leo's initial outline: no pink diamonds. It wasn't until six months later that the Australians got involved, further evolving the design and sending the value of the piece skyrocketing with their rare stones.

From the start, the biggest technical challenge was how to make the egg's heavy gold shell open. Making the doors from brass, which was much lighter and could be polished to a golden glow, wasn't an option because it would destroy their ability to market it as a pure gold product.

'The weight of it was astonishing,' Giselle recalled. 'You couldn't hinge the doors because there was no way they could hold it. It was always a problem.' Alex Parkes enlisted the help of an engineer who specialised in making motors for music boxes and other automated pieces. Their initial solution was for a secret button on the egg's summit called a 'pusher', which when pressed would power up the mechanism that opened the doors. It was an electronic version of the clockwork mechanisms used in Fabergé's most elaborate eggs and was expertly camouflaged with a band of bright coral enamel and layers of diamonds.

Dad would fill me in on the progress of his mystical egg during our drives to school, rhapsodising about how gold 'sung' when it was used to make the shell. I always thought that was made up to capture my imagination, but during my hunt, I spent hours watching YouTube videos of artisans manipulating thin sheets of the precious metal, until it vibrated and emitted a climactic whine, like wind chimes whistling eerily in the breeze.

In the egg's case, this stage of the metalwork was done at

a large, brick-walled factory in the Kent countryside. The short film that Argyle made to document its creation shows a nameless boiler-suited worker with gnarled hands hunched over a hulking metal lathe that resembled a relic from the industrial revolution – like a giant metal sewing machine with a steering wheel. Holding a spear-like wooden tool with a blunt steel blade, called a spoon, he teased the metal (which was actually brass since this was a re-creation) over the mould. As concentric curves rippled across its surface, the undulating metal contorted into a shimmering cyclone before emitting a high-pitched whine.

Once the two halves of the egg's shell had been formed, de Vroomen's team took over. 'Everybody was working on it because it was such a massive, scary thing to do,' Giselle recalled. 'There was an atmosphere of organised chaos.' The egg dominated the entire workshop, with Alex hiring several massive machines to create its hundreds of gold components. The first morning that he wrestled the top of the shell onto the lathe and turned on a large blow torch to begin soldering it, a ceremonial silence descended on the room. One wrong move or if the gold warped, it could cost them hundreds, even thousands, of pounds.

Alex spent weeks standing, statue-like, piecing it together like a brain-bending jigsaw. When there were gaps in his team's expertise, he filled them with freelance workers skilled in ancient techniques like the spiralling 'guilloche' engraving, also known as engine turning, another intrinsic aspect of Fabergé's signature style.

In the early stages of the egg's creation, Paul was often found hovering excitedly around the De Vroomen Alexander workshop, checking on progress. The craftsmen tolerated his presence, even laughing at his bad jokes, but tempers frayed when Jo started muscling in. Eager to show this future masterpiece off to friends and clients, he would turn up with an entourage after giving just a few hours' notice and expect VIP treatment. When the call came that the old man was on his way, most of the workers would start frantically cleaning their benches and sweeping the floor, while Alex stood grinding his teeth, rolling his eyes and muttering profanities: 'For God's sake, can't we just get on with it?'

But even that irritation wasn't enough to break the bonhomie among those involved. Everyone sensed they were part of something special, which would burnish their reputation. The creation of this 'wonderful article', as Paul termed it, was no longer just another job. I imagine Leo and Alex saw it as a defining moment for their company, never imagining it would trigger its demise.

The first signs of a clash came during the long, hot summer of 1989. I picture Alex's team toiling away in the workshop, wiping sweaty palms on denim-clad legs, pausing to dab their brows with hankies and swig water; the rhythmic chug of an electric fan splitting the air as machinery clanks, metal saws scrape, blow torches hiss and a small radio plays Eighties pop hits. It was during this time that the first row over hallmarking erupted.

One day, so the story goes, Paul drove to the Clerkenwell workshop in a fury, having heard a rumour that the Dutch jeweller intended to put his mark on the egg. No one in the trade could say whether it was anything more than an empty threat, but Paul, driven by ambition, was determined to find out.

KUTCHINSKY'S EGG

It later emerged that De Vroomen was not alone: every craftsperson who worked on the egg engraved their name on the back of its largest drawer and hid it beneath the velvet lining, a quiet act of collective authorship. Whether the list still survives, buried under felt or erased at Paul's insistence, the sheer hint of its existence was enough to enrage him.

There had been disputes over hallmarking in the past with other firms but typically an agreement was reached whereby the manufacturer could place their stamp somewhere discreet, as long as the Kutchinsky hallmark took prominence. Paul had good relations with most workshops and saw the benefit of keeping it that way. But he liked to be asked first.

Tony Bellingham, an award-winning goldsmith, who had made the Simpsons characters, some brooches in the shape of Tinkerbell, and the fairy from Disney's *Peter Pan* for the House of Kutchinsky, spoke about Dad with genuine affection. 'Paul was an odd character but I really enjoyed him,' he said with genuine warmth. 'He was mad as a box of frogs but he had quite a slice of style.'

Tony also knew Leo de Vroomen, and the way that he remembers the row chimes with the story Dad always told. 'It all kicked off because Leo put his mark on the egg. Paul was very upset ... Leo was trying to put hallmarks on things and steal other people's thunder ... He wanted to be recognised as being as big as Asprey and Cartier but he simply wasn't.'

In July 1989, Paul sent a sternly worded letter to Leo de Vroomen, stating that any pieces designated as 'special orders' i.e. those 'specifically ordered by [Kutchinsky], must be hallmarked with the "Kutchinsky" hallmark, not your own.' Whether this applied to the egg or another of the smaller pieces that Paul ordered from De Vroomen Alexander around this time is unknown, but his overall message was clear: any piece he commissioned should bear the House of Kutchinsky's stamp. On the surface, this seems to have diffused tensions, and the production of the egg progressed, but it was a harbinger of things to come.

When Argyle Diamonds came on board in late summer, taking centre stage alongside the House of Kutchinsky, Paul's focus shifted to Hatton Garden. He spent hours holed up in Richard Vainer's office with the egg's designs spread in front of them, sorting through thousands of pink diamonds. Paul approached his task with a mixture of passion and obsession, scrunching his monogrammed gold jeweller's loupe into his eye socket, squeezing each stone between long, thin tweezers and tilting it to assess the evenness of its hue. After selecting the pick of that day's crop, he would stash the precious cargo in his suit pocket and make the short drive to Clerkenwell, where the diamond setter was waiting to enact the production's grand finale: teasing thousands of gems into the tiny holes he had painstakingly drilled into the egg's surface.

The addition of vast swathes of pink diamonds, then valued at £1.1 million, necessitated tweaks in the design, making it ever more elaborate. In October 1989, an estimate of an extra £115,000 for manufacturing costs was agreed between Dad and de Vroomen. When Paul started swanning around with the film crew sent by Argyle in tow, it exacerbated tensions with the workshop, not least because they had to waste time recreating past stages of the egg's creation. Time was running out and the mechanism to power the doors still wasn't working. The problem with building something on such an unprecedented scale was that there was no blueprint. The way the doors were designed, the top of the egg had to lift up to create enough space for them to slide up and around. This placed a huge strain on the motor. Sometimes it burned right out, closing the doors. On good days, the shell would judder open, making a rattling sound, then stutter to a halt. To get to this point had taken almost a year, and both sides had incurred crippling costs. Failure was not an option.

The 1 April 1990 deadline came and went, and Paul started to panic. The film crew returned from Perth to shoot their final scenes, only to be told that the egg wasn't ready. 'Any day now,' Paul assured his Australian business partners. Desperate to keep up appearances, he offered to pay for the crew to stay in a luxury hotel for as long as it took.

The egg's publicity schedule was already packed, with its first public appearance scheduled for 17 April at the Basel Fair, the most prestigious event in the jewellery calendar. From there, it would go on show at the V&A museum in London, then head to Tokyo and New York, before being sent to Brunei where Paul was hoping to secure the sale that would save the House of Kutchinsky. But the problem with the motor, the extent of which he had so far hidden from his Australian partners, urgently needed fixing.

The strain was building, and he finally erupted when a vastly inflated invoice from de Vroomen landed on his desk. The final bill was about £850,000 — more than double the original quote. Shaking with anger, Paul grabbed the fax and ran out of his office, shouting and swearing so loudly that his tirade filtered down to the shop floor. 'Paul was going potty!' said Tony Bellingham, who happened to be dropping some

THE CREATION

jewellery off in Knightsbridge that day. 'Steam was coming out of his ears. I sat with him while he ranted about it.' If any of the other independent workshops had pulled a stunt like that with a jewellery house of Kutchinsky's status, they would never have worked again, he added.

But Leo was clear – unless Paul paid up, the egg stayed put.

Originally, Paul had planned to sell his record-breaking *objet* for £3 million. But reports in the press, ahead of the egg's unofficial unveiling, priced it at £7 million. Furious, de Vroomen accused Paul of double-crossing him, lying about the sale price in order to pay him less. Relations soured irrevocably. Amid Dad's papers, I found bitter legal letters, dating from May 1990, laying out the grievances on both sides. The inflated invoice stemmed from the Dutch jeweller's belief that he was due a 'reasonable' share of the profits and that his final bill with Kutchinsky would be worked out based on the sale value of the egg. The £375,000 previously agreed, it was claimed, wouldn't even cover the costs his firm had incurred in labour and materials, which he estimated at £400,000. Paul's solicitor vehemently denied the existence of a sliding scale contract, explaining it wouldn't have been 'practical' because the House of Kutchinsky needed to know from the outset what the total bill from De Vroomen Alexander would be to 'satisfy itself it could make a profit'. So the story goes, Leo then tried to scupper Paul's plans by taking out an injunction to prevent the egg leaving the country.

The £7 million was a line Dad threw out to get the media excited, Mum says. He expected to get less but was trying his luck. It all started when a TV reporter, who'd heard a rumour that the House of Kutchinsky was making a giant gold egg, assailed them outside the shop a few weeks before it was finished. Caught off guard, Dad lapped up the attention, Mum tugging his shirt sleeve whenever he threatened to reveal too much. When the reporter started trying to guess the value of the egg, the tugging intensified. 'He plucked that figure out of the air,' she said, rolling her eyes.

It's possible Dad decided this was the best way to ensure a sale. Or maybe it was a sign of his growing desperation, as the financial pressure on the business deepened. Another secret he was hiding, even from Brenda, was that he'd raided their emergency stash of gems to buy extra diamonds for the egg. This was their insurance, their buffer to see them through the bad times, but now that too was gone. Like a poker player down to his last chips, he had steeled himself and gone all in.

The story of the £7 million egg ran on a TV news bulletin and from there it spiralled. Newspaper reports and TV interviews followed, and it was even featured in the *Sunday Times Magazine*, where two decades later my first article would appear.

With the egg held hostage in Clerkenwell and the clock ticking down to the Basel Fair, Paul called an emergency summit of his inner circle at Hollybush House. Huddled conspiratorially in the conservatory on a Saturday afternoon, he sat on the rattan sofa anxiously shelling fistfuls of pistachio nuts.

After much heated debate, punctuated by Paul railing against Leo and Brenda trying to stop herself from saying 'I told you so', a plan was made to extract the egg from the Dutch jeweller's grasp. Dad had a crucial advantage: he'd kept a key to de Vroomen's workshop. Among the plotters was

Barry Turner, the police officer. Barry towered over Paul, a mountainous man with grey flecked hair, a softly-spoken Midlands twang and an infectious, throaty chuckle – and he was fiercely loyal. It was agreed that Dad and Barry, in his full police uniform, would drive to the workshop just before dawn on Monday morning, grab the egg and scarper as the sun rose across London.

On the day, everything was going smoothly until they entered the workshop and found a few early bird workers already at their benches. Trying not to panic, Dad signalled to Barry to grab the 'Big E'.

Fixing the craftsmen with his best arresting officer gaze, Barry simply said: 'I've come for the egg.' With Paul's help, he eased a Harrods carrier bag over the shell, before grappling with its unwieldy stand. Throwing backwards glances over their shoulders, they hurried out of the building and towards Barry's police car, grunting and sweating under the weight, before the craftsmen realised what was happening. Placing the egg gently on the back seat, Paul clambered in next to it, cradling it in his arms while trying to lie as flat as possible to avoid detection.

'I turned on the siren, and off we went,' Barry recalled. 'Your dad kept telling me to hurry. He was worried they were coming after us.'

I can only imagine the eruption that followed when Leo de Vroomen realised the egg was gone. It was becoming painfully clear that this giant gold creation wasn't going to enrich his firm in the way he might have dreamed.

*   *   *

High on success, Dad wanted to celebrate. In the past, he'd always turned to Brenda but now it was someone else's company he craved. Since the task of choosing the egg's diamonds was over, he had no official reason to visit the Vainers' Hatton Garden premises. But still he kept drifting there after work, armed with bottles of champagne, hoping for a glimpse of Anna Powell. A hopeless romantic, he'd been with Brenda, his Teddy, for nearly twenty years, and while he was happy to chat, and even flirt, with other women at parties, the thought of being unfaithful had never crossed his mind — until now.

Anna had become a bit of a local celebrity in Hatton Garden for being not just beautiful but also talented, having briefly played keyboards for the American disco group Odyssey on a UK tour. When the sound of her stilettos echoed through the narrow streets, workshop windows would crack open and craftsmen would hang their heads out, straining to catch a glimpse of her long blonde hair as it swished behind her, tied up in a polka dot scrunchie. She wore just a dash of make-up, a flash of pinky-red lipstick lighting up her heart-shaped face. Anna could have had her pick of the men in Hatton Garden, and Dad couldn't quite believe he was the lucky one to receive her attention. Staring into her blue eyes, sparkling with wonder at the glamour of the jewellery world, Paul felt his worries melt away.

Recently, they'd started going for drinks on their own. Paul found himself looking forward to these interludes with an intensity that surprised him. He started counting the days until he could casually stroll over to Hatton Garden and offer her a lift somewhere in his Aston Martin. It wasn't long before he confessed to being unhappy at home. His wife didn't understand him or make him feel loved anymore, he whined, looking doe-eyed at Anna from behind his spectacles, his bottom lip protruding like a petulant child. As she shared her own frustrations with Jimbo, he sipped his wine and nodded, while trying to fix his gaze somewhere other than her breasts. The more time he spent with her, the more he felt he was falling for her.

Trying to justify his desire, and win her sympathy, he reeled off all his frustrations with Brenda, from her annoyance at him adding his Argyle buddies, Ray and Ron, to his fortieth birthday party guest list at the last minute to threatening to tell Jo about his plan for a range of jewellery under his own name. Brenda had caved on the party invite but, weary of his wild schemes, she stood firm on revealing his side-hustle to his father. The resentment over this lingered, like a stubborn frost.

Perhaps Anna convinced herself that their flirty, champagne-fuelled chats where she provided Paul with a sympathetic ear were safe because they were both in relationships. Her own parents had broken up acrimoniously when she was seventeen, and she didn't want to inflict that hurt on others. A chameleonic figure who exuded a calm confidence, she was skilled at adapting to look and sound like those around her. For her part, here was this wealthy man, one of the Vainers' biggest clients, treating her like an equal, driving her around in his sports car and beguiling her with tales of gold eggs and polo teams. When he wasn't complaining about his wife or parents, she found him funny, endearing and, in his smart suits and Gucci loafers, a total antithesis to Jimbo.

Over a period of about six months, Dad started confiding in Anna and they grew closer but, wanting to play the successful businessman, he hid the true extent of his financial woes from her. It was around the time of Dad's appearance on *Wogan*, when he seemed to Anna almost like a celebrity, that their friendship crossed the line. One night, after drinks in a discreet wine bar in Chelsea, he offered to drive her home and pulled up a few streets from Jimbo's flat. His inhibitions loosened, and desperate to find out if his desire was reciprocated, he leaned over as she was undoing her seat belt and kissed her.

11

THE MISSION

'Don't talk to me about that bloody egg!' Gerald Earle, now in his eighties, sputtered. His voice was familiar from my childhood, a distinctive blend of cockney growl and Yiddish lilt. I had come to visit Gerald to get the details of the egg's next chapter, after it left de Vroomen's workshop so unceremoniously. He took a sip of Scotch, slowly swirling the honey-coloured liquid in his crystal glass. I noticed a slight tremble in his hands. Gerald had worked for the House of Kutchinsky for almost half a century. He started out, aged fourteen, as an apprentice in the East End and rose to become the foreman of the Sanitt and Stein workshop in the late 1980s.

'Listen, sweetheart, your dad was a poser.' Gerald pushed his glasses back up his bulbous nose before continuing. 'A total poser. But we got on well. It was difficult for him, he had aggravation from his dad, aggravation from your mum and the same from the boys in the shop – he was in the middle of 'em all.'

After the Clerkenwell raid, Dad called Gerald and told him to get down to the shop straight away. 'We've got a problem,' he said. When Gerald arrived, he was astonished to see this giant ovoid wonder sitting unguarded on the desk in Paul's office. 'Leo and his lot couldn't make it work,' he wheezed, shaking his head at the memory. 'It was like telling jewellers to make a car. They might have been able to get the tyres on but they hadn't got a chance with the engine. Leo tried to be clever. He tried to do everything himself.'

The next morning, Paul smuggled the egg into Sanitt and Stein's Soho workshop, once again wrapped in dark green Harrods plastic bags, sweating as he lugged it up the narrow stairs. 'The rest of the blokes were in shock,' Gerald told me. 'It was so bloody massive. We had to work out how the bleedin' thing had been put together. We took it apart screw by screw, scratching our heads to work out how to fix the mechanism.'

Drumming his fingers against the egg's shell, Gerald considered his next move. Part of him wanted to teach Paul a lesson for cutting them out at the start, but their businesses were too closely linked. If the House of Kutchinsky went under, so did Sanitt and Stein. Also, the sheer absurdity of the situation amused him. Only Paul would end up in a pickle like this.

Retreating to his office at the back of the workshop, he was lost in thought when the phone rang. He knew it was 'God' the minute he put his ear to the receiver because the line was so crackly. Paul's love of gadgets meant he'd recently bought a brick-sized car phone, partly so he could make secret calls to Anna undetected, but also so he could stay abreast of all Project Egg developments.

'I can't bloody hear you,' Gerald bellowed, slamming down the receiver and leaving it off the hook. He needed time to think. Flicking through his Rolodex, he found the contact he was looking for. There was only one person in the trade who might have the answer to the egg problem: Chris Walton, director of design and technology at Goldsmiths' Hall. If he couldn't work out how to fix the mechanism, the only option was to melt the entire structure down and start again. Gerald grimaced at the idea of breaking the news to Paul that it was game over. When Chris answered the phone, Gerald outlined his problem and asked if Chris knew where to buy a small but extremely powerful motor for a giant gold egg.

Several hours later, Gerald was hurtling in his red Jaguar saloon down the motorway towards Heathrow Airport. The address he'd scribbled down during his call with Chris fluttered precariously on the dashboard – it had nearly blown out of the window earlier. Chris had warned him there was no guarantee of success, but it was Gerald's only hope. A dark blue road sign flashed up as he careered off the motorway – RAF Northolt. He was headed for a military base.

As he pulled up outside the gates of the sprawling airfield, he noticed a pack of fierce Alsatians patrolling the gates. The dogs bared their fangs and growled in his direction. Shouting the name of Chris's contact at the security guard, he breathed a sigh of relief as the barrier lifted to let him through.

A short runway cut through the middle of the site, ringed by trees that were just regaining their spring lustre. As Gerald drove around the edge, he passed an aircraft hangar where private jets and military helicopters were stationed. The only other vehicles on the road were army trucks. His directions led him to a big factory with a rounded, corrugated iron roof where engines and other parts were repaired. Confronted by a man in overalls with goggles pushed up on his head, he repeated the request he'd made on the phone, aware of how strange it sounded.

'See, I've got a problem with this giant gold egg ...'

As he was ushered into a small office, with piles of official-looking documents on the desk, he was perturbed to see another Alsatian tethered to the desk. Scenting fear, the dog got up and started sniffing in the direction of his crotch, straining against the lead.

Just then, a smartly dressed man strode into the room and shook his hand. Caught off guard, Gerald stammered his request. As they sat down, he pulled out some pictures of the egg and the motors he'd unscrewed from its base and placed them on the desk, launching into a technical explanation of the problem. The man frowned, scrutinised the motors and turned them over in his hand. Then he excused himself to consult with a colleague.

Alone again, Gerald puffed out his cheeks and shuffled further away from the Alsatian. When the man returned, he was holding an official document. 'We can help you,' he said, his voice imbued with seriousness, 'but before we go any further, I'm going to have to ask you to sign the Official Secrets Act.'

He dropped a piece of headed paper onto the desk in front of an open-mouthed Gerald and presented him with a pen. 'I'm not signing the bleedin' Secrets Act,' he sputtered. What happened if Paul, who could be reckless, contravened it? It would be Gerald who got banged up in prison.

'Look, mate, it's my boss you want,' he said, pleading. But there was no other option. The man shook his head and informed him that they were willing to manufacture two motors at a cost of £7,000 each, but given the top-secret nature of their work, signing the act was non-negotiable. Bewildered, Gerald scratched his head. He had no idea what their normal line of work was or why it would be shrouded in such secrecy, but time was running out.

Muttering a Jewish blessing under his breath, he scrawled his signature and grimaced. What had he done? He wrote down the shop's address and telephone number and told them to send the bill to Paul. He would be fuming – the total cost was more than double the budget he'd given Gerald – but there was no other choice.

The man smiled and extended his hand, reassuring him that the motors would be ready in just a few days.

When Gerald got back to the workshop, a quick follow-up call to Chris Walton confirmed his suspicion. The company he had just done business with was a Ministry of Defence provider. The motors he had bought were originally made to power missiles.

'Your dad was desperate, sweetheart, we all were,' Gerald said. 'The motors that went into these missiles were made with total precision; they weren't meant to fail. That's how we got the egg to work.'

Gerald took a sip of Scotch and licked his lips. Over the course of our conversation, he had grown animated, buzzing from the whisky and the memory of his past triumph.

* * *

Finally, Kutchinsky's egg was finished. There was one last moment of panic, when Dad realised the photo frames in the portrait gallery were still empty. The original plan had been to engage an art firm that specialised in hand-painted miniatures.

KUTCHINSKY'S EGG

But the expense of the new motors forced him to abandon this final grand gesture. Instead, he and David O'Connor, Kutchinsky's archivist, cut out pictures of wig-wearing historical figures from my school textbooks and other images from glossy magazines like *Tatler* to fill the gaps.

Neither of my parents were home much during the egg's creation. If they weren't out at charity functions, they were having dinner with clients or Dad was playing tennis, often his alibi for seeing Anna. It felt like we had babysitters almost every school night. I'd started acting up in class, to the point that my parents were called in to speak with my head teacher after I'd caused a disruption with a few friends.

'Has anything changed at home recently?' the head teacher asked in the meeting. I stared at the floor. Mum gazed angrily at Dad. He stayed resolutely silent. Nobody mentioned the egg.

On the drive home, I sat in the back of the car and tried to block out their bickering, but fragments filtered through. Dad was repeating his promises to buy Mum a new car, take us all on a big family holiday, add a swimming pool to the house. Our lives could finally start again. After the egg.

* * *

The first stop on the egg's world tour was the Basel Fair in Switzerland, but it nearly didn't make it. A last-minute panic threatened to derail its debut, when customs demanded the House of Kutchinsky supply an invoice stating the egg's value, origin and purpose, which would allow Swiss officials to work out how much import duty and tax was owed on it. Aware that a no-show at the fair would fuel gossip and tarnish the egg's reputation, Paul was forced to swallow his dislike of Leo de Vroomen – which was mutual after Paul's raid on the Clerkenwell workshop – and ask him to resupply the final invoice, having ripped the original up in a fit of pique. Later, Paul's solicitor would claim that this was in no way an admission that he owed the Dutch jeweller the inflated sum, despite that having been de Vroomen's impression at the time.

Founded in 1917, the Basel Fair attracted the great and good of the jewellery trade for a week-long industry carnival of meetings, long lunches and extravagant dinners. From the minute the doors of the conference hall opened, the egg caused pandemonium. The organisers displayed it in a custom-built glass and marble case that was so heavy it took six men to lift it. Rumours about it spread like wildfire through the 90,000 delegates, until every jeweller, diamond dealer, goldsmith and journalist in attendance was desperate to see it. Like a flock of hungry pigeons, they converged on the Kutchinsky stand, to coo in wonder at the jewelled treasure. Paul received the adulation of his peers with a mixture of joy and disbelief. When he caught his father's eye, Jo nodded in approval and curled his lips into a tight smile. Paul beamed back. But beneath his smile, his anxiety was surging. Several times a day, he'd excuse himself and head to the toilet. He kept a bottle of Benylin tucked in his suit pocket to swig in secret when he felt his nerves jangling.

The truth was, the electronics were still temperamental. The souped-up motors worked better but the doors still regularly jammed. Paul was left with no choice but to display it with the shell fixed open and pretend it was intentional. 'I was amazed we got away with it,' Mum recalled. 'Everyone was dazzled by the sheer scale of the egg. I had to fight my way through crowds of people to get to the stand.'

While Paul stayed with the egg, soaking up the praise, Brenda toured the maze of cavernous halls with Jo, who was treated like jewellery royalty wherever he went. 'The crowds parted before him like the Red Sea before Moses,' Mum recalled, with a wry smile.

It wasn't just the egg that Paul was launching at the fair. His dream to create a watch worn by the world's top tennis players came to fruition at the same time. Modern and sleek, with a chain link strap, it was almost diametrically opposed to the bejewelled wristwatches his father had designed and for which the House of Kutchinsky was known. It was a risk, Brenda told him wearily, with the business already creaking under the financial strain of the egg. But Paul wouldn't listen. His plan was to build on the buzz created by the egg, solidifying the House of Kutchinsky's status as a global luxury brand. The marketing materials for the fair showed the egg in all its golden glory, nestled next to the watch with the slogan: 'Having crafted the ultimate egg, we now bring you the ultimate sports watch – the Premier.'

The watch was also a way of indulging his passion for tennis. By sponsoring players to wear it, including the British number one at the time, Chris Bailey, he was guaranteed tickets and VIP treatment at tournaments including Wimbledon, with which he had a lifelong love affair. The Wimbledon final was an almost religious event in our house. Dad would draw the living room curtains, turn the TV volume up to full blast and regale us, yet again, with how he had snuck into the historic final between Björn Borg and John McEnroe in 1980, shimmying up a pillar to peer through a gap into the famous Centre Court, before hustling his way in. Never miss a chance to break the rules, he'd say, a mischievous glint in his eye.

At the end of a triumphant week in Basel, hopes of a sale were running high. Paul had just returned to London when he received a call from an excited David O'Connor. A German count had invited the egg to go on show at a private chateau just outside Hamburg, should he accept? Ever since the press launch in the shop at the start of April, Paul had found himself ping-ponging from one surreal situation to another. At this point, not much surprised him, but first he needed to make sure this wasn't a scam.

The story of the egg's brush with the German aristocracy was another part of its legend that as a child I just accepted. Now, tasked with tracing its journey and tracking down the count himself, I realised I had no idea where to start. Mum's and David O'Connor's memories were hazy and I was reduced to randomly googling German chateaus, until scouring Dad's papers for clues, I spotted the grand-sounding name of Count Johann Villavicencio and references to a manor house in northern Germany. Typing his name into Google, I sent a message to a sparse LinkedIn profile that matched his name not feeling hopeful of a response. So I was taken aback when a short, enigmatic reply appeared almost instantly, asking to hear more about my quest and including his phone number. Feeling trepidatious, I dialled it. His voice was warm and he spoke English fluently with aristocratic inflections. When I explained that Dad had passed away, he expressed great sadness and described Paul as a 'most humorous and generous gentleman', who had helped him out in his time of need.

KUTCHINSKY'S EGG

Like Dad, Count Johann Graf Villavicencio, who was then the flamboyant, well-dressed director of a prestigious Hamburg-based jeweller, had attended the sell-out Fabergé exhibition in Munich in 1986 and fallen under the Russian master's spell. Through contacts at the top auction houses, Johann, who was in his early thirties, set about wooing Malcolm Forbes, the American media tycoon with one of the world's most significant collections of Fabergé eggs. A plan was hatched to exhibit these treasures for one night only at a glittering party at a private chateau outside Hamburg.

Johann sent out 600 invitations to the cream of German high society, including descendants of the Romanovs and members of the House of Wickenburg, one of northern Germany's most aristocratic families. There was huge excitement about the return of Fabergé's treasures to Germany and Johann, who was still in the early stages of his career, was amazed he'd pulled off such a coup.

Then with just weeks to go before the exhibition, disaster struck. Malcolm Forbes died suddenly of a heart attack in late February 1990, aged seventy. Lawyers for his estate refused to allow his Fabergé eggs to leave the US, on the grounds that their ownership was unclear at that moment. Johann was faced with a dilemma: cancel the event and lose credibility or find something equally spectacular to form the centrepiece.

Searching for inspiration, Johann travelled to the Basel Fair, where he noticed a huge crowd gathered around one particular tent. 'I asked my assistant what was happening,' Johann recounted to me. 'He said that this crazy guy from England had made the world's biggest Fabergé-style egg and it could be my lifeline.'

Exhausted, Dad had flown home a day early to spend time with us kids, leaving David O'Connor and his identical twin brother, Dennis, who also worked for the House of Kutchinsky in sales and marketing, to pack up. When Johann, wearing a panama hat and an expensive suit with a silk handkerchief poking out of the pocket, approached the stand, the brothers charmed him with their Irish twin act. 'They were smoking about a hundred and fifty cigarettes a day,' Johann said, chuckling at the memory, and 'drinking Bloody Marys in the morning.'

The timing was tight – the egg was due to go on show at the Victoria and Albert Museum in just a few days, but this was a chance to attract a buyer from European royalty. Paul was buzzing – the deal of a lifetime was within touching distance.

'We'll make it happen,' he promised Johann, on a phone call during which the two men shared their mutual love of Fabergé's treasures.

After a raucous final night in Switzerland, the egg's burly security team, which included ex-SAS operatives, roused the bleary-eyed O'Connors from their beds at dawn. 'We had a party the night before we took the egg to Germany,' David recalled. 'We got absolutely pissed and then these ex-SAS boys woke us up at about 5 a.m.' Ignoring the twins' grumbles, the bodyguards bundled them onto a plane next to the egg, which was transported in a coffin-shaped wooden box. As it was far too precious to go in the hold, Dad's creation had its own seat in first class, which was booked under the name of Mr Egg. The O'Connors were strapped in on either side of Mr Egg, and the bodyguards sat behind them.

Paul's flight got in later that afternoon at Hamburg Airport and a helicopter was dispatched to fly them directly to the chateau in time for the reception at six o'clock. There wasn't enough room on the helicopter, so Paul and Dennis went on ahead while David stayed behind in Hamburg and arranged to meet them later for dinner at a different manor house.

The epitome of understated European wealth, the chateau's imposing main building was painted a mix of lemon and cream, with a sloping roof of red tiles and two adjacent annexes. It was surrounded by neatly manicured grounds where deer grazed. Paul and Dennis exchanged excited glances as they disembarked the helicopter. Would it be here, amid the ancient artefacts, marble columns and fine furnishings of this spectacular manor house, that the egg would find a buyer?

In the spirit of Fabergé, Count Johann decided to use the egg's late arrival to add a theatrical element to proceedings. The party was already under way when the noise of the helicopter brought the guests rushing to the windows, speculating about who or what might be arriving. Prolonging the suspense, Johann bundled the egg's entourage in through a set of French doors into a small library where Dad assembled the egg. As Johann threw the doors open to reveal the star attraction, a hush fell, broken only by exclamations of wonder from the crowd.

That night, high on champagne and flattery, Dad reeled off his spiel about the egg to multiple party attendees. Since the press launch in the Knightsbridge shop earlier that month, his life had become a whirlwind of parties and press interviews. This type of attention was new to him. Typically, the jewellery trade was built on discretion, and his high-end clients usually wanted their treasures to remain secret. But the egg commanded centre stage. Sometimes, he joked that he was simply the egg's plus one, tagging along in its golden shadow. It irked him when the popular breakfast TV news show, *TV-am*, featured the egg alone, without its creator.

As he toured the room, shaking hands and making the same joke about how he'd only take £6.999 million for what felt like the hundredth time, he felt his chest constrict. The failure of the Sultan of Brunei's agents to express interest during Basel had unsettled him. Normally they snapped up his *objets d'art*, almost as fast as he could make them. Had they somehow got wind that it didn't work properly?

The air was heavy with the smell of perfume and cigarettes. Pushing through the crowd, he followed the trail of smokers out into the vast grounds and gulped down the spring air. The stars shone in the inky black sky as he loosened his tie and picked the ever-growing scab on his finger. The quiet was broken only by the distant chatter of the guests and the voice that whispered in Paul's head. A buyer wouldn't be found tonight. He could sense the resistance in the room. It was too extravagant. Too expensive. Too big. It belonged in a museum, he'd heard someone mutter. He dealt with his disappointment by getting uproariously drunk.

After the exhibition, the egg was packed up and the group flew to Wulfshagen, a smaller manor house which was surrounded by a lake and ancient oak trees, to dine and continue the party. Copious amounts of champagne were imbibed and by the end of the evening, Dad and the O'Connors were on top of the wooden dining table with their arms around each other singing Irish and Jewish folk songs. Finally, Dad crashed out in the 'Blue Room' on the top floor, which had housed the famous American conductor and composer Leonard Bernstein a few years previously when he conducted a concert held in the grounds. 'We had so much fun,' said Johann, for whom the whole venture was quite simply a great success. 'It really was a crazy, funny evening.'

The next morning it was time to fly back to London. With the star-studded launch at the V&A just hours away, it was essential that everything went smoothly. Timing was already tight. The egg needed to be installed and the security detail put in place well before the guests arrived. But on the way back, the trouble began.

A German customs official demanded to open the egg's coffin-shaped travel box, explaining that until he was confident it didn't contain a corpse, guns or drugs, he couldn't let them fly. Shielding the egg's box with his body, Paul refused, worried that if the rest of the passengers knew he had a £7 million egg, his life could be in danger. He grew irate, shouting, swearing and spraying saliva into the face of the official. Armed police with sniffer dogs appeared and escorted him and the egg into a side room, while David and Dennis waited in the airport bar.

Eventually, Paul gave in after police threatened him with a night in the cells. By now, they'd missed their flight back and were perilously behind schedule. Luckily, they managed to grab business-class seats on a plane that was leaving for London in a few hours. I picture him grimacing, as he handed over his company credit card, the bill totalling thousands of pounds. How was he going to explain this to Roger?

Once on board, with the egg safely installed, Paul perked up, ordering champagne while recounting the custom officers' shocked expressions at seeing the egg. Laughing like a seal, he swigged the fizzy gold liquid and smacked his lips as cold bubbles trickled down his throat, soothing his hangover. David O'Connor nodded silently; there was something about his boss's feverish behaviour that unsettled him. Strapped into his seat in front of the egg, David exchanged a nervous glance with his brother. Would they make it in time?

When they finally landed at Heathrow Airport, about a half-hour drive from our West London home, Paul rushed to a payphone. The clock was ticking; they had just four hours to get their precious cargo to the museum. First, he called Brenda. 'She was going ballistic,' recalls David O'Connor. 'She was thinking "Where the fuck are they?"' The twins heard him barking orders, telling her to lay out a clean suit for him and make sure the girls were dressed and ready to go. Then he called Roger, who was waiting at the shop, to reassure him that they hadn't been kidnapped, and the egg would be there soon.

Just as the taxi was pulling up to take them to Knightsbridge, the O'Connors realised they'd lost Paul. He'd headed off to buy a coffee and never returned. Rushing back into the terminal, David spotted him hunched over a different payphone, talking in a low voice with a faraway expression on his face. As David approached, he hurriedly hung up, mumbling something about calling his parents. As they rushed to the taxi, David was fairly sure his friend was lying, but he didn't yet know there was another woman in Paul's life.

12

The Grand Tour

The exhibition launch at the V&A was the first time I saw Kutchinsky's egg. I was so excited to finally be in the same room as Dad's creation and had scarcely believed it when Mum granted my plea to attend the party. Skipping up the museum's stone steps in my favourite pink denim skirt and sequin jumper, I noticed fleets of chauffeur-driven cars clogging up the entrance and a jostling crowd of photographers waiting outside, ready to snap the arrival of Marina Ogilvy, a minor royal who had sparked a scandal by falling pregnant to her photographer boyfriend before they were married.

We arrived just as the egg was being transferred into its display case in the centre of the grand room with its red-tiled floor and walls lined with gilt-framed pictures. Gerald was there polishing the shell and testing the electronics. The doors of the case weren't yet locked, and with my parents engrossed in conversation with a museum official, I seized my moment. Creeping up behind Gerald, I stood on tiptoe and reached out my hand, caressing the egg's cool, hard surface.

My sister, Katrina, crossed the room and was about to copy me when one of the security guards stepped in. I grabbed her hand and rushed out of the room, pushing through the crowd that was gathering in the foyer. Together, we ran through the corridors of the museum with Mum careering after us, her stiletto heels click-clacking on the floor. I could hear Dad cursing in the distance. My grip on Katrina's hand tightened, and she cried out in pain. Sliding to a halt, I pulled her down behind the life-size statue of a semi-naked man. We crouched, our hearts racing. I knew I was in trouble, but I didn't care. Finally, I had touched the egg.

* * *

After the exhibition, like a pop star enjoying a meteoric rise, the egg embarked on a world tour. The first stop was Tokyo, where the pink diamond market was booming. The city's most prestigious department store, Mitsukoshi, where Kutchinsky had a small boutique, would showcase the egg, putting it on the radar of Japan's newly minted billionaire class.

Mum didn't join Dad in Tokyo. Far away from home, he could lose himself in the city's pulsing neon lights, towering skyscrapers and backstreet drinking dens, thousands of miles from his splintering marriage and financial woes. But during that trip, another relationship started to fracture. There was a growing perception on the Argyle side that the House of Kutchinsky was hogging the limelight. David Fardon, who headed up Argyle's corporate affairs team and was in Tokyo, was unimpressed when he discovered the egg's name had been translated into Japanese simply as The Library Egg. He wrote to Mitsukoshi's general manager on 9 May 1990, insisting its full title be used. He also wrote to Paul, asking him to make the point clear.

An imposing pair of black lion statues, modelled on those in Trafalgar Square, guarded the entrance to Mitsukoshi's flagship store, which sat on a busy crossroads in an upmarket district. The night before the egg went on public display, Dad and the Argyle representatives attended a grand dinner there – a feast of the finest Japanese cuisine with ingredients partly sourced from the store's lavish food halls. He thought of Anna as the translators passed greetings to his hosts, while he swirled a large blossom of wasabi paste into his soya sauce bowl and dunked a quivering slab of sushi into the earthy liquid. His eyes watered as the horseradish spread fire through his sinuses. He was courting disaster with his affair at a time when the stakes had never been higher.

As talk turned to potential buyers, he picked the scab on his thumb, crusty shards of skin falling onto the table. Looking up, he caught a look of horror on his Japanese host's face. His interpreter gently nudged him; 'Bad manners,' he whispered. Paul brushed the table clean and squirmed in his chair. Suddenly, he just wanted the night to be over.

Tokyo went the same way as the egg's previous outings. Rapturous headlines, a stream of superlatives from onlookers, but no hint of a sale. The next stop was New York City, where the egg would make its US debut at Christie's prestigious auction house. This time Brenda joined Paul, as – to her excitement – did their friends, Philippa and Nick. Paul had been distant lately but she put it down to stress and a lack of family time together. 'He was obviously having his affair then,' Mum recalled. 'I could feel he was disengaged but I just tried to brush it off.'

They flew on the Concorde, sharing the supersonic flight

with the former Prince Andrew and his then wife, Sarah Ferguson. As the jet steadied itself after take-off, they toasted Paul's success. Lurking behind them, strapped in alongside its bodyguards, the egg served as a constant reminder this wasn't a holiday.

For four jam-packed days, they trailed the egg around the city, doing interviews with everyone from *The New Yorker* to *Brides* magazine and *The Today Show* on NBC. The climax of the trip was the 'Ultimate Event' – a glittering cocktail reception at Christie's affording the great and good of New York society a glimpse of the 'Ultimate Masterpiece'. 'We did everything we could to find a buyer,' Mum said. 'Short of hawking it in the street and walking up and down Broadway with a sign saying "Egg for sale"'.

On the final day, the foursome carved out time to sneak off for lunch at Windows on the World, the celebrity hotspot which sat atop the World Trade Center's North Tower. The waiting list was months long but Dad pulled strings to get a table for lunch. Dubbed the 'most spectacular restaurant in the world' by *New York Magazine* when it opened in 1975, its allure hadn't worn off. Even the lift was an experience: a famous a cappella group serenaded them with Broadway classics as they sped up to the 107th floor. It was so surreal, Brenda and Philippa kept snorting with laughter. When the doors opened and they stepped out into the blue-carpeted restaurant, its floor-to-ceiling windows separated by pillars, all four of them fell silent, awestruck by the majestic view of Manhattan. Squeezing into one of the sophisticated beige banquettes, where the likes of Robert De Niro and Warren Beatty had previously warmed their bottoms, it occurred to

Brenda that the egg's success had literally taken them to the top of the world. Turning to smile at her husband, she was struck by how dark the shadows under his eyes were, like purple tattoos imprinted on his flesh. She reached for his hand under the table, his fingers briefly brushing hers before he pulled away.

After lunch they hailed a cab to JFK Airport. By this stage, it was clear that, despite his love of gold bling, Manhattan local Donald Trump wasn't going to buy the egg. Malcolm Forbes, the famous Fabergé collector, had also been on Dad's hit list until his sudden death earlier that year. The mood on the three-and-a half-hour Concorde flight back from New York was subdued. Both couples were exhausted and slept most of the way, Brenda resting her head on Paul's shoulder, wishing he would stroke her hair like he used to.

* * *

It had been a hectic few months, but Paul had no time to breathe just yet. Repairs were urgently needed to the 'Big E'. The electronics were more erratic than ever, and he feared Argyle would soon realise the extent of the problem. The egg went straight back to Gerald in the workshop, after which it was due to return to Hamburg and go on display in Count Johann's jewellery shop for two weeks. As for his personal life, the first thing he did upon his return from America was arrange to see Anna. He'd thought about her constantly while he was away, guilt and lust driving him crazy in equal measure. Retreating into his romantic fantasy cocooned him from the growing tensions at work and the reality that time was running out to make a sale. Jo tried to hide his concern but Roger didn't hold back. 'You are going to destroy our business,' he hissed. Paul just shrugged and walked away. He'd gambled everything on selling the egg. But the lack of interest from the Brunei royal family, to whom he had been so confident he could 'knock it off', was a serious concern. Had his luck finally run out?

On the surface, he stayed calm. 'All good things come to those who wait,' he'd say breezily, when asked about the egg's prospects. The launch of his new line of watches was a welcome distraction. But there were problems with the Premier watch too. Jo had made no secret of his dislike of the timepiece's minimalist look. 'Give 'em a show, make it bigger,' he'd said in disgust, when his son first showed him the prototype. It had also received a mixed reception in Basel, with a rival jeweller accusing Kutchinsky of copying their design. So, it was a relief when orders started rolling in.

The watches were a big hit in the Middle East. In late spring, Paul and David O'Connor toured Oman and Bahrain, showing the sample collection to its top jewellers, who snapped them up.

'We were so excited,' David recalled. 'We sold a load.'

The trip was a much-needed success and Paul was in good spirits on the flight back, sipping a vodka orange and shovelling in his favourite pistachio nuts, dropping the shells in the ashtray of his armrest. David, who had hurt his back lugging their heavy bags, was laid out awkwardly across three seats. From his prone position, he eyed his boss, who kept mercilessly mocking his plight. Having seen Paul in full flow over the past few days, he was convinced that if anyone could sell the egg, it was him. Meanwhile, the orders they had secured for the Premier had bought him, and the House of Kutchinsky, more time. Feeling reassured, David closed his eyes and tried to sleep.

*   *   *

The summer of 1990 stands out in my memory as the point at which the threads binding our family started to unravel. We spent the start of the school holidays at Jo and Lily's flat in Marbella, southern Spain, while Dad stayed in London. I could sense Mum felt aggrieved, left alone to look after three young children. 'Bloody egg,' she would mutter under her breath when she thought we weren't listening. The flat was close to the beach and had a small garden. I spent hours reading books, listening to my portable CD Discman and collecting shells with my sisters. At night, we feasted on pizza and ice cream and tried to gloss over Dad's absence. Unlike other summer holidays when he would join us at regular intervals, this time he wasn't coming at all, Mum informed us, looking pained.

That was the year Saddam Hussein ruined my birthday. After I pleaded with Dad to fly out and celebrate me turning eleven, he eventually succumbed. He arrived the day before, on the morning of 2 August, and we drove to a nearby water park. Typically, he and I would team up to conquer the most stomach-churning slides. But this time, as I climbed the stairs to the fearsome Kamikaze, I found myself alone. I'd thought Dad was right behind me, but looking over at the sun loungers where the rest of my family were sitting, I saw no sign of him. Packed into the balconied stairwell, I carried on upwards, thinking that at any moment I'd hear him call my name. But soon it was my turn and there were too many people jostling behind me to turn back. Careering down the slippery blue slab, twisting and sliding like a fish caught in a current, I felt a sense of foreboding that didn't go away even after I eventually found him, clutching a day-old newspaper with a worried expression on his face. He spent the rest of our time at the park buried in its pages, muttering to himself.

On the drive back to the flat, Dad was even more distracted and irritable. When we got inside, he turned the TV on and called the shop. News was breaking that Iraq's president, Saddam Hussein, had sent his forces to invade neighbouring Kuwait. The United Nations immediately condemned the invasion, and an Allied Coalition was formed to drive Saddam out of Kuwait. Prime Minister Margaret Thatcher was clear on her position: Saddam, whom in private she called a 'selfish, despotic dictator' and likened to Hitler, must be prevented from gaining control over a large swathe of the region's oil fields.

Dad spent most of my birthday glowering on the sofa, muttering profanities. The implications for the House of Kutchinsky were clear: if war broke out, the Middle East's heads of state would be too busy protecting their oil fields to splurge on supersized jewelled objects. The geopolitical strife also imperilled the sale of other luxury items like watches. That night, we drove to Puerto Banús, a fashionable marina built to resemble an old Spanish fishing village. Superyachts and sailing boats bobbed about on the water, while the shell-like silhouette of La Concha mountain glowed in the evening sun.

Over dinner at an Italian restaurant, Dad perked up and

started waxing lyrical about how making his egg was like making a pizza, with all the different ingredients fusing together to make a work of art. Maybe he should make the world's largest jewelled pizza next, Mum said tartly, raising an eyebrow. Dad's smile tightened. Once we got home, the simmering tension between my parents erupted. The spare bedroom, where Katrina and I slept, shared a thin wall with the living room, making it impossible to escape the shouting. Lying in the dark, crickets chirping in the distance, I pulled on my headphones and tried to block it out with the latest Kylie Minogue album.

Dad took me to play tennis the next evening. After he'd put me through my paces, we sat on the terrace of a nearby cafe and shared some chips. He always treated me more like an adult than an eleven-year-old child and didn't hold back from telling me when things were going 'tits up'. He had to return to London, he explained and didn't know when he would be back. A war was brewing which could stop him selling the egg.

'I'm worried it might end up being my *Mona Lisa*, Cece,' he said, looking pensive.

I stared at him blankly. 'Whaddya mean, Dad?' I asked, slurping my Diet Coke.

He sighed. 'Well, there's a famous painting in the Louvre Museum in Paris . . .'

'I know what the *Mona Lisa* is, Dad,' I interrupted.

The *Mona Lisa*, he explained, had a price tag of about $1 billion, which was so high that no one person could ever own it. The work was now so fragile, and the cost of insuring it so stratospheric, that it was unable to leave the Louvre and could only be seen through a glass case. Lapsing into silence, he took a swig of his beer. 'I'd like the egg to be in a museum one day,' he said, sounding more philosophical. 'But right now, I just need someone to buy it.'

He looked so downcast that I moved round to his side of the table and hugged him. 'Don't worry, Dad. Even if nobody wants it, I still love you.'

He smiled and reached out to ruffle my hair. 'Thanks, Cece Bear,' he said quietly, turning his head away and rubbing his eyes.

The next morning when I awoke, he was gone.

* * *

As the situation in the Gulf escalated, all the watch orders Paul had taken on his triumphal tour of the Middle East were cancelled. Amid fears that a lengthy war could disrupt the global oil market, the region's royal families reined in their spending. It was a catastrophe for the jewellery trade and terrible timing for Paul, who watched as his dream turned into a nightmare. Hundreds of hand-crafted timepieces, made at great expense, were left to gather dust in the workshop. The egg was also grounded, with no money left to fix it.

Meanwhile, Paul's attention was consumed by the turmoil in his personal life. Aside from his worries over the business, the egg and his marriage, his mother, who'd been his champion all her life, was slowly dying of cancer. Lily's diagnosis the previous year had been a terrible shock. Even during her gruelling treatment, she'd retained her elegance and glamour, even insisting on wearing a satin kimono in hospital rather than the standard gown. She'd recovered well, so the news that the cancer had returned and spread from her bowel to her lungs was shattering. Dad's attempts to block it out only threw him further emotionally off-kilter.

By this stage, he was struggling to keep his affair a secret. Not long after our return from Spain in late August, Mum dropped into the shop to see Dad and run through their upcoming charity commitments, including the Queen Charlotte's Ball with which she was now heavily involved. According to an article in the *Jewish Chronicle* about the changing role of 'ladies who lunch', Brenda was now part of a 'high-powered band of women' who used their power and influence to raise money for worthy causes. She had successfully infiltrated English high society, following Jo and Lily's carefully laid plan for their family.

But when she arrived at the shop that day, there was no trace of her husband. He wasn't in his office and he wasn't answering his car phone. The refrain of: 'Where the fuck is Paul?' echoed around the shop. As she lit a cigarette and took a soothing puff, Brenda spotted a few staff members exchanging guilty, almost pitying, glances.

'Do you think he's having an affair?' she asked David O'Connor, putting him on the spot.

'He wouldn't dare, darling,' he said, giving her arm a reassuring pat. 'He'd be crazy to risk pissing you off,' he added, and they both laughed uneasily. To pass the time, they staved off the horror of betrayal by making a list of possible suspects. Brenda's top guess was his Australian secretary. Anna's name wasn't even on the list.

Shortly after, Paul went away for the weekend to Amsterdam, ostensibly to scope out a buyer for the egg, but

David O'Connor later told Mum he took Anna with him. When he returned on Sunday night, Brenda knew something was terribly wrong. While he was away, she'd crashed her car and, although unscathed, was still a bit shaken. Instead of comforting her, he was stiff and cold, recoiling when she kissed him. Bewildered, she went to sleep in the spare room, only to be awoken by Paul bursting in and announcing that he didn't love her anymore. There wasn't anyone else, he assured her, but surely she must accept they hadn't been getting on for a while, probably since before Hollie was born, if they were being honest. She just stared back at him open-mouthed, her brain not making sense of his words. Their children. Their house. Their life. Why was he blowing it all up?

'I was just shocked,' said Mum. 'I didn't realise what was going on.'

After a sleepless night, she called Philippa. Distraught, she begged her friend for help. Philippa was close to Paul – maybe she could talk sense into him. It was not knowing what was behind it, Brenda sobbed, that was unbearable. She still refused to believe he could have betrayed her. Philippa promised to help and soothed her friend's fears. Paul loved her and the girls, she reassured Brenda. He would never leave.

Towards the end of that week, Philippa dropped into the shop on the pretext of collecting a piece of jewellery. It was late in the afternoon. Paul ushered her into his office and closed the door. There was a restless energy to him that she didn't recognise. When she confronted him about the state of his marriage, she was shocked by his confession. He'd fallen in love, he admitted, an agonised smile pasted across his face. He hadn't gone looking for someone else, it had just happened. Philippa nodded, white-faced. Long-lasting relationships could be difficult, but when children were involved, she reminded him, it couldn't just be about your own selfish desires.

'Those three girls are my best creations,' he said, wringing his hands, his lisp becoming more pronounced, as it always did in times of stress.

'Then you know what you need to do,' Philippa advised, trying to sound sympathetic but stern. 'End the affair. Cut off all contact. If you're not prepared to do that, then you have to tell Brenda the marriage is over. You can't go on torturing her.'

He knew Philippa was right. But he was conflicted. He felt a passion for Anna that was unlike anything he'd felt before. At first the attraction was physical, but her vivacity and sharp mind also beguiled him. Was it love or just lust? He wasn't sure but when he was with her, he felt free – it was a part of his life that nobody owned, not his father, not Brenda, not the kids.

He was probably having a mid-life crisis, he joked poignantly to Philippa, who nodded tersely. Think very carefully before destroying your family, she said, getting up to leave. You'll live to regret it.

The next day, Philippa drove to Hollybush House. She wasn't going to break the news of the affair, that was up to Paul, but she needed to warn her friend that the situation was far more serious than she ever imagined. When Philippa told her it looked hopeless, Mum broke down.

'Why?' she kept asking over and over, tormented.

'You need to talk to Paul,' Philippa said, hugging her tightly.

That weekend they were due to attend the wedding of an

old neighbour's daughter who now lived in Belgium. Brenda had been looking forward to it as a chance to have some time away together. But her hopes were dashed when Paul, still too cowardly to confess, told her that if she went alone, they would talk and sort everything out upon her return. He could also enjoy some quality time with 'his girls', having missed us terribly while travelling with the egg. Desperate to save her marriage, Mum agreed.

In reality, we barely saw him all weekend. Once, I heard his voice and raced into the kitchen, hoping he might want to play tennis or take us out for pizza, only to catch a glimpse of him crunching across the gravel and driving out of the gates. He had come back to change his clothes and left again without so much as saying hello. The next day, he was due to collect Mum from the airport but when his car pulled up in the driveway around mid-afternoon, there was no sign of her. Grim-faced, he got out and slammed the door.

His friend, Gordon, had arrived to play tennis and they disappeared into the garden and started thwacking balls across the net. About an hour later, the buzzer of our electric gates started ringing incessantly. Standing at the big window in my bedroom, I saw Mum staggering through the gates, her body shaking with sobs, mascara-streaked tears pooling behind her sunglasses, as she dragged her weekend bag behind her.

After he picked her up, Dad had driven them to a restaurant in town. His frosty demeanour made it clear this wasn't going to be a romantic reunion and Mum, who had barely slept all weekend, was in a state of panic.

Once he started talking, the words came tumbling out. He had been cheating on Brenda for months with a mystery woman who was terribly ill. He didn't want to leave his family but if he ended the affair, the stress of it could pose a risk to this woman's life. This last bit was fiction. Although Anna had a minor health condition when she was younger, by the time she met Dad, it had resolved itself.

Mum sat opposite him, numbed by shock. 'I was just thinking "who the fuck is it?" she recalled, wincing at the memory. Their food arrived, but neither touched it. Mum pushed her spaghetti vongole around her plate, tears running down her cheeks. For a moment, she was paralysed between hurt and anger, like a broken compass whose needle is spinning erratically between north and nowhere. They sat staring at each other, until Mum crumpled, her shoulders shaking. 'The sex better be worth it,' she choked, wiping snot and tears from her face.

Arsehole. Bastard. Cheat.

She needed to get out of there. Away from him. Grabbing her bag, she ran out of the restaurant. Wandering in a daze, she stared at the immaculate white townhouses, leafy squares and clusters of well-dressed people sitting at cafes, enjoying their weekend. How could their lives just carry on, she wondered, when her world was falling apart. Lighting a cigarette, she took a drag and then stamped it out, the rush of the nicotine making her head spin. As she ground the glowing stump into the pavement, she imagined it was her own heart beneath Paul's heel, being crushed to nothing.

Eventually, she found a phone box and dialled her mother's number. Her sister, Anne, answered and, in between sobs, Brenda filled her in on the nightmare that was unfurling. Promising not to worry their parents, Anne booked herself on the first flight down to London from Scotland. After she hung up, Brenda threw herself into the path of an oncoming black cab. As it screeched to a halt, she wrestled open the door and collapsed into the back. Why was this happening? It didn't make any sense. The person in the restaurant had looked and sounded like her husband but she didn't recognise him. He'd seemed possessed, just like he had when he'd first conceived the idea for the egg. When she got home, he was playing tennis and drinking with Gordon, as if nothing had happened. Exhausted from all the emotion, she put us to bed and waited for her sister's arrival, trying to sleep.

The next morning, I was surprised to find Aunty Anne in the kitchen. 'I'll be taking you to school today,' she announced, trying to sound cheerful. Dad had left for work, she explained. Confused, I looked around for Mum, who was standing in the doorway, still in her dressing gown, clutching a mug of black coffee. Her hair was wild and her eyes were red and ringed by dark patches. She'd barely slept, racking her brain for clues as to when the affair had started, torturing herself by picturing Paul having sex with someone else. As soon as we'd filed out the door, she ran to the toilet and retched.

Later, with Anne's help, Mum got washed and dressed and drove up to Knightsbridge for crisis talks. As she walked into the shop, the doormen greeted her cheerfully and she briefly wondered if this was a bad dream she was about to wake up from. Hiding her swollen eyes behind large sunglasses, she walked into Paul's office and closed the door, her heart racing. Caught between anger and despair, she begged him to reveal his mistress's name and commit to giving her up. But Paul refused. He just needed time to think, he kept repeating, like a record stuck in a groove.

When he got home that evening, Mum was at breaking point. All summer she'd suppressed her suspicions, hoping he would snap back to his normal, affectionate self. After their crisis talks at the shop had ended in tears, she had called his parents and told them everything, begging them to reason with him. I remember getting home from school to find my grandparents there, pale under their ever-present tans; from the looks on the adults' faces, I sensed something was terribly wrong.

With everyone locked away in my parents' bedroom, I was ushered upstairs to the playroom by my aunt, who made soothing noises and promised me chips for dinner if I did my homework. It was only when my grandparents left, having failed to steer Dad away from his latest obsession, that the screaming started. Katrina's bedroom was next door and she came creeping in, looking scared. Our Scottish nanny, Pauline, appeared cradling a crying Hollie, who was almost four, in her arms, and turned up the volume on the TV as the row escalated. They'd been arguing a lot recently but this sounded worse. The shouting was louder, the sobs more jagged, the insults more bitter.

Later that night, as Mum was putting Hollie to bed, Dad appeared, hovering by the door. 'You wouldn't cope if I wasn't here,' he taunted.

'Of course I would cope,' she replied, determined to stay calm.

Turning his back, he stomped downstairs and she heard him pick up the phone. He wouldn't be so blatant as to call his mistress from their house, would he? Kissing Hollie goodnight, she closed the bedroom door behind her and sprinted down the stairs.

'Who are you calling?' she demanded, her legs shaking.

'Nobody.'

'Liar!' Mum screeched, wrestling the receiver out of his hand and waving it in his face.

'I was calling Philippa, if you must know,' he retorted. 'I thought she might be able to calm you down.'

'Liar! Your mother will be disgusted,' Mum spat back, slamming the phone down and holding it out of his reach. Dad, furious, snatched it from her and slapped her across the face, a violence he would later try to explain away as an act of desperation.

Upstairs, we pretended not to hear the commotion. If we just pretended it wasn't happening, then maybe it would all go away. The shouting and sobbing got louder and louder, then there was a thud. Mum was screaming at Dad and he was holding her by the wrists and shouting in her face, clumps of spittle spraying from his lips.

Hollie woke up and started wailing. While Pauline rushed to soothe her, Katrina and I sheltered in the playroom watching our favourite movie, *Grease*. It was getting late, and with no sign of the shouting stopping, I dragged over our giant Mickey Mouse teddy, a present from Disney World, and we both hid our faces in its black furry bulk. Curled up together on the pink sofa under a blanket we were just drifting off when the noise of an engine revving roused us. I ran to the window and threw it open, craning my neck to watch as Dad sped away into the night. Foxes howled in the darkness, while Mum staggered back inside, laid her head on the kitchen table and wept. For the first time, she realised their marriage could really be over.

When I spoke to Philippa years later about that night, she said: 'Serena, the story was written. Nothing anyone could have done could have made any difference, of that I am sure.'

* * *

Slut. That's how Anna was always known in our house. A word that Mum would spit out in hurt and anger. 'Trading up' for a younger model was common behaviour among powerful men, and several other women in my parents' circles had suffered similar fates. Early on, Mum rightly staked her claim to the moral high ground and clung to it as her life collapsed. Refusing to use Anna's name was part of how she survived but it meant I grew up with a deeply conflicted image of the woman who stole my dad's heart. Throughout their relationship, she remained a mystery to me and when he died, I imagined our paths would never cross again.

But when I started searching for Kutchinsky's egg, I knew the time would come when there were questions only Anna could answer. Tracking her down proved tricky; she wasn't on social media, I didn't have a phone number and all I could find online was a single picture of her at a charity ball. Until one day, on maternity leave during the pandemic, I was scrolling Instagram absentmindedly, looking for clues, when I saw a face that looked remarkably like the Anna I remembered. I knew immediately it was her daughter.

I typed out a message, asking if her mother once knew a man called Paul Kutchinsky and quickly pressed send, feeling like I was betraying Mum. I forgot about it until one day a message arrived confirming my hunch. Her mother was away on business, Anna's daughter wrote and was unsure when she would get back to me. Assuming that was a polite excuse for not wanting to be in touch, I breathed a sigh of relief. She obviously never really cared about Dad if she had refused my heartfelt request to share her memories. She was still 'Slut'.

Until about a month later, my phone rang in the middle of the day, displaying an unknown number. The baby was napping and, curious, I answered. The voice on the line sounded uncertain, faltering, yet strangely familiar.

'This is quite surreal,' Anna said, with a mix of trepidation and warmth. She'd thought long and hard before responding to me but in the end, she explained, she hoped it might help me find closure. A chance encounter with an old business contact in the Middle East, whom she hadn't seen since my father took her there in a last-ditch attempt to sell the egg thirty years ago, had convinced her it was time for us to talk.

My heart raced. Would I have chosen to do this, to make contact all these years later, if it weren't for the egg? But Anna was a part of the egg's story, my father's story. This was my opportunity to fill in some of the blanks that had haunted me over the years.

'I don't know what to say. I don't know what you think of me but a long time has passed. I'm sure everything that happened had a life-changing effect on you and I'm happy to tell you anything I know.'

* * *

The morning after Dad's confession, Anna arrived at work in Hatton Garden, oblivious to the emotional tornado that was about to hit. She'd been dealing with her own romantic dramas, navigating the fallout from her recent split with Jimbo. 'Painful but inevitable' is how she described it to me, years later, as we sat, sipping wine, in her stylish Notting Hill mews flat. For five years, she and Jimbo had 'worked, lived and breathed' together but her job at the jewellery shop took her into a different realm. Even before she met Paul, she was growing weary of the nocturnal nightclub world, Jimbo's mercurial character and spendthrift nature. For her, the fling with Paul was the final proof she'd outgrown that relationship. After delivering the news to Jimbo, she packed up her stuff and moved back to her mother's house in a leafy South London neighbourhood.

Single for the first time in five years, she felt a rush of freedom. Until the realisation dawned that Paul was labouring under the illusion she had left for him. It was true their relationship had intensified over the summer but she'd never imagined he might actually leave Brenda. Now, suddenly, he was making promises and plans for the future, and Anna was starting to panic. As much as she was charmed by him, and he made her feel like she was starring in her own *Pretty Woman* fantasy, she didn't want the rupture of his family on her conscience. But the more she withdrew, the more demanding Paul became.

'You have a wife and three children,' she'd said, almost pleading with him at their last meeting. 'This is not okay. I don't feel good about it. You've got to figure your shit out.'

'Why are you doing this?' he demanded, crossing his arms across his chest and sulking dramatically. The rest of his life was crumbling around him, and he was determined not to let this precious gem out of his grasp. But Anna was adamant; she'd left Jimbo for her own reasons, she told him, and wanted a new start. As long as he was married, they were done.

She had walked away, feeling lighter. The guilt had been

eating her up. So, it was a shock when just three days later, he called the Hatton Garden shop, sounding fraught.

'There's bad news, I'm afraid,' he said, solemnly. 'Brenda knows.' There was a pause, as Anna, who found herself strangely calm, weighed up her response.

'What happened?' she asked.

Unable to explain the elaborate story he'd spun to Brenda about Anna's health, he opted for the most obvious of excuses. 'Your name just popped out,' he fibbed.

'What do you mean? How?'

Paul mumbled a web of excuses, effectively insinuating that he'd blurted out her name while in bed with Brenda. Stunned, Anna hung up the phone, trying not to panic. Instead, she went straight to speak to her boss at the jewellery shop, Viktor. He just laughed at first, assuming she was joking. When he realised she was serious, he turned pale and swore under his breath.

The phone started ringing again in the shop, and Anna answered it, out of habit. It was Brenda. 'She was, understandably, very unhappy with me,' Anna recalled, wincing at the memory. I can only imagine the rage and hurt that poured out of Mum, as she confronted the woman who had stolen her husband's heart.

'I'm sorry,' Anna repeated, aware of how hollow it sounded, knowing it didn't make any difference. The damage was done. After that, Viktor bundled her upstairs to see the Vainers and warn them about the personal and professional storm that was brewing. The phone rang again. It was Paul. He was coming over for crisis talks, he announced. Anna nodded silently, feeling nauseous. She sat down in a corner of the Vainers' boardroom, which occupied the top floor of their Tardis-like building, and tried to make herself invisible.

For a while, nobody said anything. Anna, Viktor and the Vainers sat in silence, while the phone rang incessantly. Eventually, Milos ordered his secretary to block Brenda's calls. The tension was broken about thirty minutes later by the screech of tyres and slam of a car door, announcing Paul's arrival.

Anna stiffened as she heard the sound of his loafers slapping against the stairs. When he entered the room, he looked grey under his olive skin. As he glanced at her, his eyes burning with unabashed adoration, she felt her chest constrict. If only she could rewind to that first night in the car and make this horrible mess go away.

Realising there was far more at stake than just their affair, Anna offered to hand in her notice and escaped downstairs to collect her belongings. Seizing his chance, Paul followed her with a hangdog expression and offered her a lift home to her mother's house in South London, where she'd been living since breaking up with Jimbo. After carrying her box of stuff to the Aston Martin, he helped her into the passenger seat, put his foot down and sped towards the River Thames.

'I'm going to leave for good,' he said solemnly, filling her in on the row he'd had with Brenda at the shop that afternoon.

'Don't do it for me,' she told him again. 'Go home, see if you can work things out.'

Paul sighed. He promised to call her later. He would try, for the sake of his children if nothing else, but he couldn't stop thinking about what life with Anna might be like.

That evening, after Anna had explained the situation to her mother, the phone rang. It was Milos Vainer, telling her she was expected at the shop tomorrow. In his eyes, her private life had no bearing on her ability to do her job. It's possible that Milos, a known philanderer, thought it would have been a double standard to have fired someone over having an affair. And I also imagine he saw the value in having a beautiful woman behind the shop counter.

Weak with relief, Anna thanked him and hung up before he could change his mind.

Then, at around 10 p.m., the doorbell rang. Anna and her mother exchanged glances. They weren't expecting anyone, especially at this time of night. When she opened the door, Paul was standing there, his glasses crooked, his suit crumpled and his grin anxious.

'I've left,' he said. 'Brenda's furious with me. I've got nowhere to go.'

Shocked, Anna struggled to speak.

'Can I come in?' he said, shuffling his feet.

She acquiesced. 'I wouldn't say I did it out of pity,' she told me. 'I just thought okay, fuck it. So, I said to stay and we slept on a mattress on the floor in my mum's house for three months. Your dad properly forced my hand. I'm not painting myself as naive and stupid but I got caught up in something and . . . everything just snowballed.'

Once Dad's departure seemed like it might be permanent, Mum descended into a pit of despair. She stopped eating, hardly slept and struggled to get out of bed. She wept constantly. I can still remember the sound – like a newborn baby that's been wrenched from its mother. There's a Scottish word 'greeting' which describes a loud cry that expresses deep emotion, and Mum was greeting her eyes out.

'He said if I did certain things, like go to marriage counselling, he would come back,' Mum recalled wearily. 'He kept me dangling until I nearly had a breakdown. It got to the point where I said: "Either you come back today or not at all." I gambled and lost.'

A letter Paul sent her a month after he left gives a glimpse into his conflicting emotions. He sounds deluded, asking Mum to accept they need marriage counselling while simultaneously making excuses as to why he couldn't move back. 'We would be at each other's throats within a short time ... You must see the sense of my not coming home before we have had counselling,' he wrote, adding that if he did, 'things would not work out between us.'

'Both you and your solicitor have put all the blame on me,' he wrote, his tone growing defensive. 'Whilst I formed my friendship with Anna, this was the culmination of several years of a deteriorating relationship between us and indeed unhappiness at home ... I never intended to form a relationship with anyone else. It was just one of those things that happened and perhaps part of life. As you know, I am prepared to make a real effort to see if we can get back together again.'

He also expressed his desire to spend more time with his daughters. 'It is vital that the children have an ongoing relationship with me,' he wrote. 'Otherwise they will think I can't be bothered with them. You know how much I love the children and I miss their company dreadfully.

'As you know the company is going through a critical period, particularly because of the egg and the problems in the Gulf. I have more than enough to worry about in relation to the future of the company, on which I have to try to concentrate without constantly thinking about being deprived of the pleasure of seeing our children.'

Writing this is hard. Back then, aged eleven, I didn't understand the nuances of adult emotions. Now, my own ragged memories mingle with those of the different women involved. The Mistress and The Wife. And it's possible there were other parties involved. Mum has always maintained that the Vainers used Anna to ensnare Dad because his name was Kutchinsky and carried weight in the jewellery world. Although obviously untrue, this wasn't solely the product of Mum's heartbroken imagination. It all stemmed from Lily who, furious at Paul for prioritising sex over his family, hired a private detective to dig up dirt on her son's mistress, hoping to persuade him to return home. When Lily discovered Anna's links to Jimbo, and his involvement in the world of nightclubs and glamour photography, it seemed to give substance to the idea that Dad was the victim of a honeytrap. Mum remembers poring over photos of Anna from her nightclub days, which she eventually ripped up and burned in the fire. *Trash.*

Outraged, Lily decided to take action. By this time, Anna and Paul had moved into a flat in north-west London owned by Leon Gold, Paul's childhood friend. When Anna, who was home alone, picked up the phone, Lily unleashed a tirade of abuse, calling her a prostitute and a gold-digger, and warning her off her son. Anna, shuddering at the memory, told me she felt as if she had become the 'punchbag' for the Kutchinsky family's problems.

Trying to discern the 'truth' in a situation of such emotional carnage is futile. Dad always swore that he never meant to leave us but the fact remains that after the initial shock of his infidelity wore off, Mum would have done anything to have him back. Whatever the truth, the outcome remains the same: their split was the catastrophe that marked the end of my childhood. When you've seen your parents shouting and screaming, knocking each other's glasses off and pushing each other into holly bushes, it's hard to see them as heroic figures any longer.

Amid all the screaming, shouting and shagging that the grown-ups were doing during this painful time, I just missed my dad. The first time I saw him after he left is carved in my memory as the start of a new and difficult chapter. To avoid further upsetting Mum, her sister drove us to meet him at the nearby parade of shops. I remember seeing his Aston Martin, parked forlornly outside the local Indian restaurant. As soon as the car stopped, I rushed out and threw myself into his arms, breathing in his familiar scent of aftershave, coffee and cough syrup. Dad was here; he still loved me. My body felt weak with relief. Katrina's reaction was different. Instead of hugging him, she pounded him with her nine-year-old fists. How dare he upset Mummy like that, she shouted before getting back in the car and refusing to come out.

The visit, which was meant to have included dinner, had to be aborted. As we drove away, Dad stood on the pavement, looking crushed. Hating to see how sad he looked, I rolled down my window and blew kisses until we were out of sight.

13

The Sale

As 1990 drew to a close, the House of Kutchinsky teetered on the brink. A buyer for the egg still hadn't materialised, a global recession was starting to bite and the bank was threatening not to extend its credit. Personally, Dad was still in limbo; torn between the agony of hurting Brenda and not seeing us girls, and the ecstasy of being with Anna. He missed his home comforts and was bitter that he was now living 'like a student' while Brenda stayed in Hollybush House. Both my parents had consulted solicitors but so far, they were locked in a stalemate.

The final stop on the egg's publicity tour was Australia. Argyle had arranged for it to be a star attraction of the 1990 Melbourne Cup, of which it was a sponsor, but had hoped it would be sold before the horse racing carnival rolled around in November. This '$16 million thoroughbred' (as one newspaper advert described it) would be revealed to an audience of almost 300,000 racegoers. A press conference was planned to show it off to selected media and launch it in the southern hemisphere.

Paul agreed to the plan but he was worried the egg's notoriety was becoming problematic. The longer it went unsold, the more speculation mounted as to what the reasons for that might be, leaving him to face the stark reality that nobody loved it as much as he did. He'd had some troubling feedback recently from a US-based diamond dealer who pitched it to a wealthy Wall Street banker, only for the banker to respond, 'That old egg from Oz? Don't waste my time on that lemon.'

From conversations with Dad's old Argyle buddies, Ray Sparvel and Ron Currie, who have long since left the mining company, and David Fardon, whose memory is sharper than most, I have some idea how things played out during Dad's second Melbourne Cup trip. When he flew out to Australia, he left Anna in London, not wanting to broadcast the news of his infidelity and shatter his business partners' image of him as a family man.

Upon landing in Western Australia, he was whisked to a swish hotel, the Rockman's Regency. Exhausted, he ordered room service and a bottle of red wine and flopped on the bed. Unused to being alone, he filled the silence by flicking through the latest TV news bulletins about the situation in the Middle East, grimly sipping his wine. The United Nations had just passed a US-led resolution authorising the use of force to compel Iraq to withdraw from Kuwait. War looked unavoidable. He was fucked. Turning the TV off, he heaved a stack of legal papers out of his briefcase and tried to decipher the unfamiliar language of divorce. One thing was clear – the costs of his own marital war were also eye-watering.

Falling into a jet-lagged slumber, he was awoken the next morning by the room phone's shrill ring. Argyle's Ron Currie was calling in a panic. There was a problem: the egg's doors wouldn't open. Trying to sound surprised, Paul dressed and rushed upstairs to the suite where the showcase was due to take place. When he arrived, Ron had his suit jacket off and was wrestling with this giant golden egg, desperately trying to prise open its shell, while David Fardon and a few other Argyle executives looked on, grim-faced.

It was amazing that he'd been able to hide the fact that it didn't work properly for so long. The same problem had occurred numerous times before, including during its press debut in the Knightsbridge shop and on the *Today* programme set in New York. But this was the first time his Australian partners had witnessed its failings up close.

Ignoring the fact it was almost midnight in England, Paul called Gerald. Once the workshop manager had stopped cursing about his sleep being ruined, Paul explained the problem. If the slightest misalignment occurred when the egg was slotted into its marble display cabinet, the mechanism that powered the doors would fail. It required exact precision and for various wires to be taped together to hold it in place for it to work.

'If you get desperate, just tip it upside down and rattle it around,' Gerald wheezed, as he hung up. At that moment, there was a knock at the door. Paul's shoulders slumped. It was too late. Their only hope was to say the egg had been damaged in transit from London and hope the journalists believed it. 'A publicist's nightmare' was the verdict in the free weekly news magazine *TNT*, which described how:

> The waiting media watched eagerly as Argyle Diamond executives tried to prise open the $16 million Argyle Library Egg ... With the doors stuck fast, the precious

contents – more than 20,000 rare pink diamonds crafted into a glittering miniature library and enamelled portrait gallery – remained out of view.

Always a good talker, Paul survived the press conference, moving through his repertoire of egg puns and joking about suing British Airways £7 million for repairs. 'That wasn't too bad,' he whispered to Ron as the press pack started filing out. His friend winced. No amount of witty banter could hide that this was a total humiliation.

'Let's just focus on fixing it,' Ron said bluntly. Wrapping his arms around the egg's golden girth, Ron tried one last time to manoeuvre it into place, while Paul stabbed the power button and held his breath. As if by magic, the doors jerked apart. Breathing a sigh of relief, Paul slapped Ron on the back and instructed the egg's handlers to keep the shell open at all times. Looking around the room, suppressing his desire to order a Bloody Mary, he wondered why the faces of the Argyle staff were still so grave.

As if this weren't enough, rumours were flying that a criminal gang was plotting to pose as police officers and seize the egg from its display inside the stadium during the Melbourne Cup. The story leaked into the local newspaper, *The Age*, under the headline: 'Diamonds may be target for bogus police' after a spate of thefts from police stations of uniforms and radios. Security was being increased at the racecourse but everyone was on edge, and it highlighted the uncomfortable truth: the egg was becoming a liability. In a bid to lighten the mood, Paul suggested generating some positive press by organising a photo shoot with the newly crowned

THE SALE

Miss Melbourne Cup. 'There's not many problems a beautiful woman can't fix,' he joked.

The next day, Natalie O'Donnell, an elegant blonde in a sequin dress, was escorted over to the Argyle enclosure and photographed draped across the Argyle Library Egg. The photograph was picked up by the media, including TNT, who added a final paragraph to their report detailing how the egg was 'quickly fixed' for the races.

But one successful stunt wasn't enough to repair Paul's reputation with Argyle. Whereas the previous year everyone had been clamouring to shake his hand, this time he heard whispers behind his back and noticed scathing glances. The drunker he got, the more paranoid he became. He responded as he used to when being bullied at boarding school – by inhabiting a bigger, brasher version of himself. Swaggering over to Ray and Ron, he started slurring that it wasn't his fault the egg wasn't selling. When he launched into a bitter diatribe about the stress he was under with the looming Gulf War and recession, his friends exchanged glances. Maybe it would be better if Paul headed back to his hotel and got some rest, they gently suggested. Thinking that perhaps he could secretly call Anna, who would be waking up soon, Paul nodded.

Surveying the marquee, he noticed that the path to the closest exit was blocked by a cluster of Argyle executives. To avoid being seen, he dropped on all fours and crawled towards what looked like a side door. The Argyle bosses watched open-mouthed as the famous jeweller from London they'd all heard so much about, slithered into a storage cupboard and slammed the door shut behind him. The realisation quickly dawned, even in Paul's befuddled state, that this was not the way out. 'Whoops, another boo-boo,' he muttered.

The next morning, Paul awoke fully clothed, face down in his hotel room, his throat parched and a metallic taste in his mouth. Groping for the painkillers he kept in his briefcase, he staggered into the shower and turned the tap on full blast, cringing as memories of the previous day flooded back. The cupboard incident would be funny eventually, he told himself. His flight left in a few hours and while the thought of seeing Anna raised his spirits, it was dampened by guilt. He also needed to speak to Brenda. It pained him to admit it, but he'd missed her on this trip.

He flew back to London without the egg. Argyle had arranged for it to go on display at a local museum. Although he was happy to have a break from handling its logistics, it was the first time he had been separated from his golden ego. Leaving it behind, he felt a conflicting rush of freedom, rather like blowing up his marriage. As the flight attendant poured him a vodka orange, he flicked through the in-flight entertainment and saw the film of the egg's creation was featured on the programme list – the result of a sponsorship deal with British Airways. Plugging in his headphones, he covered himself with the thin blanket as the familiar Bach cello music soothed his throbbing headache. 'A grand tradition has been revived,' the disembodied voice said, 'with the design of a magnificent work of craftsmanship.'

He sighed bitterly. He'd risked so much to make Kutchinsky's egg, and now at the point where he should be reaping the benefits, he was heading home with nothing to show for his obsession, save for a skull-crushing hangover.

THE SALE

* * *

The festive bonus was a House of Kutchinsky tradition. For the best performing salesmen, it could total around £25,000 (about £65,000 today). It boosted morale and kept people loyal – a vital attribute in the cut-throat world of sales. When Jo found out that this year the staff might not get a bonus due to the company's precarious finances, he was furious. Do whatever it takes, he advised his sons, but make it happen.

Paul's lifeline came in the unlikely form of a pocket watch. For several months, a wealthy Japanese doctor had been making regular trips to London to purchase pieces for a mysterious 'client' (rumoured, though never confirmed, to be a member of the yakuza, a powerful Japanese criminal network) with a passion for pocket watches. Nasser Ghahramani, a Kutchinsky salesman and personal friend of Paul's, was sourcing and selling scores of watches to the doctor for 'crazy money'. Desperate for anything that might boost the business, Paul gave Nasser bundles of cash and sent him off to tour antique markets in search of vintage timepieces. He also instructed him to hit up their wealthiest customers to see if they had any to sell. Even Solly was persuaded to hand over his favourite Cartier pocket watch which he loved and had pledged never to part with. But those sales weren't enough to keep the House of Kutchinsky afloat.

Then, just as Paul was about to give up, a contact in the Middle East sent word of a truly exceptional timepiece, which the owner wanted to sell discreetly. It was one of several jewelled pocket watches believed to have been commissioned by the Sultan of Oman as gifts for the rulers of different Middle Eastern nations. Each one had a country map on the front, picked out in diamonds, with its capital city marked by a large ruby.

Paul flew to the Middle East and brought it back to London. Nasser, who knew nothing about its origins, was then charged with flying to Tokyo to present it to the doctor. At first, everything went to plan. The doctor's client was wowed by the watch and the deal was done within hours. But then Nasser panicked. The doctor had delivered millions of yen in cash to his hotel room. Under no circumstances was Nasser going to carry that sort of money back into Britain. He loved Paul. He loved his job. But he wasn't prepared to take that risk. 'I've done my bit. This is your responsibility,' he told his boss over the phone, imagining his wife's reaction if he ended up in a Japanese jail.

Paul booked the next flight to Tokyo, scrambling to re-arrange meetings and pack at short notice. When he arrived, he and Nasser met for dinner at Inakaya, in the vibrant Roppongi district, a meal Paul would later describe as one of the most memorable of his life. The whole experience was so distinct to Tokyo – theatrical yet understated. Diners sat at a long U-shaped wooden counter with a charcoal grill sizzling in the middle. Chefs, kneeling on cushions, wielded long metal skewers garlanded with a cornucopia of delights, as orders were shouted out. The bill was eye-wateringly expensive, but Paul charged it to the company. Afterwards, they went for a drink at Trader Vic's, a fashionable tiki bar, before heading back to Nasser's hotel room, where Paul packed the cash into shoeboxes and hailed a cab.

Travelling back through Narita Airport, Nasser was stopped at customs. Paul, who had the money stashed in his hand

THE SALE

luggage, sailed through, while a stern-faced official ripped open all the beautifully wrapped gifts Nasser had bought for his family. After paying a few hundred pounds in excess charges, he was allowed through.

Now they just had to get through the security scanners. Paul, calm and practised, coolly sat his shoulder bag on the conveyor belt and watched it trundle through, followed by his briefcase. As he collected it, he heard the sound of an alarm. His heart sank. A few years earlier, a salesman he'd dispatched to Saudi Arabia had been caught at customs with £250,000 worth of jewellery. The stock had been impounded, and the salesman briefly jailed. Trying to act cool, Paul glanced back to see what had triggered the alert – and then remembered. Tucked into a pocket in his briefcase was a Swiss Army knife, a birthday present from Brenda that he always carried and had completely forgotten about. The guard dropped it into a plastic bag and labelled it. It would be returned to him after the flight, the official explained. Paul exhaled. He, and the Christmas bonus, were on their way home.

Once they were safely back in London, the shop's security men were sent out across town to bank the money in small amounts to avoid detection. Dad also requested they pick him up some of his favourite cough syrup, as his local pharmacy was refusing to sell it to him. None of the staff asked why their bonuses were being handed out in envelopes stuffed with cash. The implication was clear: the House of Kutchinsky was in trouble. When the last person had collected their envelope, Paul closed the door and slumped against it. He'd bought himself more time but was it enough? His desk phone started ringing. It was probably his mother calling to give him an earful, he thought, gingerly picking it up and holding it at a distance. Instead, it was Nasser. There was good news from Japan. During the previous visit, he had discussed the egg with the doctor, aware that the pink diamond market in Japan was just taking off. Now, his mysterious client wanted to see Paul's creation. There was just one catch: he wasn't interested in it as an artwork but instead wanted to melt it down and flood the jewellery market with its rare stones. Six months earlier, Dad would have rejected his offer, but now he was desperate.

The doctor arranged for a viewing to take place at the top of Tokyo's World Trade Center. This time, the egg, which had returned to the Sanitt and Stein workshop for further repairs, and its marble case were packed into crates and flown out by a private security company to reduce insurance costs. Flying alone, Nasser tried to ignore the dark thoughts fizzing in his brain. Were the yakuza planning to steal the egg? Was he walking into a trap? What happened if the sale fell through? He could see the stress was affecting Paul. He'd been shocked at the change in his boss at their last meeting. His normal good humour had deserted him, his clothes were crumpled and dark shadows sagged under his eyes. He'd heard all the lurid details of Paul's infidelity from his wife and had even come home one night to find Brenda chain-smoking and sobbing in his wife Ferry's arms.

In his view, Paul running off with that 'Beeatch', as Ferry called her, was a terrible mistake but it wasn't his place to say so. Instead, he was determined to do everything in his power to repay the kindness his friend had shown him when he first moved to London. After meeting and marrying Ferry in Iran, Nasser came to the UK in 1979, fleeing the Iranian revolution.

THE SALE

He had lost everything and although Ferry was a qualified doctor, she was pregnant and soon would be unable to work. In a twist of fate, Ferry ended up working at the same hospital where Brenda was a social worker and the two couples became close. One Sunday afternoon, over lunch at their old house, Paul detected a note of despair in Nasser's voice. He had applied for what seemed like thousands of jobs and been rejected. Despite Nasser having no experience in jewellery or sales, Paul offered him a job on the spot.

It was late afternoon, Tokyo time, when Nasser arrived at his hotel and phoned the doctor to let him know that the egg and its entourage were on their way to the World Trade Center to prepare for the presentation. Enigmatic and polite as ever, the doctor arranged to meet him in the lobby of the skyscraper in just over an hour. Adrenaline fluttered in Nasser's stomach as he shook the wrinkles out of his suit and pulled on a fresh shirt. Did the egg's bodyguards carry weapons, he wondered, before dismissing the thought. He trusted the doctor, despite knowing little about him or his client.

It was mid-December, a damp chill hung in the air and the days were short, with darkness gobbling up the sun just after four o'clock. Speeding through Tokyo in a cab, Nasser marvelled at the festive illuminations that lit up its buildings and public squares. Thousands of brightly coloured lights shimmered in the darkness, as if a trove of precious gems had been sprinkled across the city. In his job, he was surrounded by beauty, but there was something about this sparkling spectacle that moved him. The taxi pulled up outside the towering forty-storey building which lay close to the watery expanse of Tokyo Bay.

The doctor came out to meet him, leaning on a mahogany cane. He was in his eighties, smartly dressed in a suit and overcoat. His eyes darted around as Nasser explained that the bottle of Scotch whisky he'd brought with him as a gift had been confiscated at customs. Smiling, the old man reached into his coat pocket, produced a steel hip flask and thrust it towards Nasser. The peaty sting of Japanese whisky flooded his veins as a group of several men, dressed in mink coats, black leather hats and sunglasses, entered the lobby. They walked straight towards the lift, motioning for Nasser and the doctor to follow. He squeezed in, avoiding eye contact, his senses on high alert. An aroma of expensive aftershave mixed with tobacco smoke filled the small space. As the lift shuddered upwards, he noticed the intricate tattoos adorning his fellow passengers' bodies – colourful dragons peeking out of their sleeves, lotus flowers grazing their collarbones. He wondered idly which other parts of their anatomy might be similarly adorned. Trying not to stare, he shifted his gaze to his feet and silently rehearsed his sales pitch.

The oppressive silence of the lift was broken only by the ping of the doors sliding open. A vast boardroom lay ahead with stunning panoramic views of the city. At the end of a long mahogany table, the egg stood surrounded by its bodyguards. The men quickly pulled down the blinds, threw off their heavy furs and extracted an array of special lights and magnifying glasses from their briefcases. They peered at the pink diamonds, asking questions which the doctor translated about the clarity and cut of the stones. Nasser was transfixed by the jewellery they were wearing: diamond rings, bejewelled watches and extravagant pendants. After they'd finished interrogating him, he was escorted back to the lift and asked to await a decision at his hotel.

The next morning, the phone in his hotel room rang. It was the doctor. He had received his client's decision and wished to speak in person. There was an ominous note in his voice that made Nasser's stomach clench. When the old man arrived thirty minutes later, parking his souped-up Mercedes on the busy road outside the hotel, the look of sorrow on his face confirmed Nasser's worst fears.

The answer was no.

'I'm so sorry,' the old man repeated. 'They didn't like the diamonds. They are not used to that type of pink. They think they are cheap. I tried to explain . . .' he said, his words trailing off. Nasser was amazed to see tears form in the old man's eyes. 'It's so beautiful, such a wonderful piece of art. I have let you down terribly. You have come so far.' He was crying now. Nasser put his arms around the old man and comforted him, the irony of the situation not lost on him.

The phone call to London was short and painful. He'd expected Paul to urge him to persuade the Japanese that the diamonds were worth another inspection with the puppyish determination that usually characterised his boss's approach to sales, but this time his voice was thin and flat. Their conversation lasted barely a few minutes; the egg would fly back that evening and Nasser would follow the next morning. Paul had run out of money and time.

* * *

In early 1991, the House of Kutchinsky owed the bank more than a million pounds.

Without an injection of capital, there would be no way of paying salaries, let alone dealing with their ever-growing pile of creditors. Their bank manager made it clear he wasn't prepared to wait any longer for Paul to sell the egg.

After all the years of bad decisions, murky dealings and mud-slinging, the end when it came was sudden and brutal. Almost a hundred years of history – wiped out. I've always wondered why the business couldn't be saved. Were the debts really so catastrophic and the family rifts so deep that nobody could work together to find a solution? Or did Dad secretly see the bonfire of the business's fortunes as his release from the pressures of a life he was already untethering from? Was he led by the same self-destructive impulse I sometimes feel simmering below the surface, polluting my happiness and whispering in my ear: 'This life is good, but could something else be better?'

In his darkest hour, Brenda rallied to support Paul. Putting on a brave face, she styled her hair, perfected her make-up and slipped into one of the new figure-skimming dresses she'd bought to lift her spirits. She'd barely eaten for weeks after Dad left and had slimmed down to a slender size eight. Swallowing her pride, she visited their wealthy friends, begging the likes of gambling impresario Jimmy Thomas for investment. The business had been a huge part of her life for two decades; she'd taken on a formal role helping Paul with publicity and was paid a salary. It was her and the children's livelihood on the line too, she pointed out. But nobody was willing to take a risk on a business that was crippled with debt and overwhelmed with stock it couldn't sell. The rejection from these people, who'd flocked to her side when invites to glitzy parties were forthcoming, stung Brenda, adding to the hurt and humiliation she already felt at being abandoned for a younger woman.

It didn't help the House of Kutchinsky's case that during the violent eruption of their marriage, the majority of their friends had taken Mum's side. I suspect the wives, horrified by Dad's actions, made it clear to their husbands that their sympathies lay firmly with Brenda, and under no circumstances were they to socialise with Paul and his new girlfriend. Eventually, Dad gave up trying to contact his old friends and moved on. But there were friendships, like that with Nick Cooper, that he mourned the rest of his life.

Around this time, he started smoking weed every night. He'd always loved a spliff but had kept his habit under control when my sisters and I were small. Now, with his life spiralling out of control, he sought comfort in its soothing numbness. According to Anna, who declined to ever smoke with him, he was living in 'survival mode', careering from one crisis to the next. It's as if he thought, 'Fuck it, everything's going tits up. I'll just change my entire life,' she told me. I imagine Dad was also reluctant to admit the degree to which money and status were ebbing away from him. The more he lost, the more his reliance on Anna, as a means of bolstering his self-esteem, tightened.

As rumours about the firm's future reached fever pitch among staff, Jo stepped in to help secure a sale. If he was going to witness the destruction of his life's work then he was determined to get the best deal possible, otherwise there was nothing to stop a rival jeweller 'stringing his sons up like a kipper'. There was emotional urgency too. Lily's cancer treatment was expensive and he couldn't risk not being able to provide the 24-hour care she needed. The only thing he loved more than his business was his wife, so if he had to sacrifice one to save the other then so be it.

A sales memorandum was compiled, outlining the company's illustrious history and giving a detailed breakdown of its bank balance, assets and debts. Dad's passion, and self-delusion, permeates the pages of this document. It paints such a positive picture of the business it's hard to believe it was in its death throes. The House of Kutchinsky, it stated, was suffering from a lack of capital at a time when interest rates were 'at their highest levels ever' and when lending by banks was 'severely curtailed'. The Argyle Library Egg is described as a 'heroic project' and 'one of the most precious treasures of the late 20th century', with its failure to sell couched in careful language. 'No decision has yet been made as to the permanent home of the masterpiece. It remains available as a publicity vehicle for its proud parents, Kutchinsky and Argyle.' If it was sold for a modest £2.5 million, the House of Kutchinsky could still hope to receive a cash injection of £600,000, the memo stated.

It makes painful reading in places, describing Paul as 'one of the bright young men of the jewellery world' and laying out plans for a future that never materialised. Later, it explains how the promotion of the Premier watch had to be significantly scaled back after sales from the Middle East were scuppered by 'factors beyond the control of a mere jewellery company'.

At the back was a list of every precious stone the company possessed, including its weight and its estimated price. This was the stuff that would arouse interest in potential buyers – a chance to snap up several hundred precious stones, worth more than half a million pounds. There were several *objet d'arts* left unsold too, including a spectacular gold and red enamel drum that featured in the film of the egg's creation, which was priced at a whopping £243,000. The most expensive item was a barometer with a clock carved from rock crystal, valued at £350,000, which Dad had commissioned on a whim in spring 1990, before Saddam's invasion caused chaos in the Middle East.

The memo ends on a rousing note. 'The company is seeking far-sighted investors,' it reads, 'who can see past the present depression, the Gulf crisis and the property slump, towards the day when Kutchinsky clients, past, present and future, feel confident enough to invest once again in the jewelled masterpieces for which Kutchinsky has earned a well-deserved place in the history of the art of jewellery.'

Reading beneath the formalities of the sales memo, it's clear Dad still harboured a secret hope that the egg would save him. That a future buyer might see the value in keeping him in place as the creative brain behind the brand, giving him more time to sell his precious creation. He was a drowning man clutching a giant gold buoy. What if Argyle could be persuaded into buying the business? They were due to fly over for a meeting to discuss the future and it seemed the perfect opportunity to make a pitch. But his hopes were dashed when it transpired the real reason behind their visit was to take possession of the egg. From this point forwards, the egg was solely the property of Argyle, who had covered most of the manufacturing costs and provided several million dollars' worth of precious stones, on the basis that a sale would more than cover their initial investment. At the time, Dad was in too vulnerable a position to argue.

As the threat of bankruptcy loomed, the race to find a buyer intensified. The mood in the shop was grim. Dad and Roger spoke even less than usual, and his relationship with Lily was strained. She had sided firmly with Mum, stubbornly refusing to meet Anna, and the loss of his mother's adoration added to Paul's sense that his old life was being ripped from him.

He continued to approach other big players, including the great Italian jewellery house Bulgari, Mitsukoshi, as sales of Kutchinsky jewellery were flourishing in Japan and Chopard, who didn't have a London shop of their own. But each time the answer was a resounding no. In the end the only serious offers came from the House of Kutchinsky's fiercest rivals, which was a galling experience, especially for Jo. But he put on his best suit, took a sip of whisky and sat down to negotiate with Laurence Graff, the young pretender who'd stolen his crown as the leading light of British jewellery. Born in Stepney in 1938, Graff had been determined to escape the East End, like Jo. The son of a Jewish tailor, he left school at fourteen and started out scrubbing toilets as a jeweller's apprentice. But he rose fast. By the time he was in his early twenties, he had two shops in Hatton Garden, where he set about wooing the Middle East's wealthiest people. A ferrety figure, small in stature with a shock of blond hair and exceptionally well-tailored suits, Graff had already stepped on Kutchinsky territory, opening a branch just a few doors down on Brompton Road and hiring Lily's disgruntled nephew, Stanley Dessau, who was pushed out when Paul and Roger took over. Graff would go on to become a billionaire with a global network of shops and an honour from the crown.

THE SALE

'The first hint we got that the firm was up for sale was when Graff came in,' Peter Stein told me. 'It was obvious then the sale was going to go ahead.' For almost half a century, the workshop his father co-founded with Len had only made jewellery for Kutchinsky. If the shop went, the workshop was also doomed.

* * *

The deadline set by the bank for a sale to go through was early March 1991. As it approached, negotiations with Graff stalled. Jo felt his offer was too low and baulked at accepting it. By all accounts, Graff had big plans for the business but wouldn't agree to retain the Kutchinsky name and provide jobs for Paul and Roger, which was a deal-breaker for Jo. A last-ditch meeting was arranged and when Graff arrived, the two legendary jewellers retreated into Paul's office.

Time wore on. Then, so the story goes, at around five o'clock the door opened and Jo appeared, smiling and holding a crystal tumbler of whisky. Everyone in the shop stopped what they were doing and turned in his direction. The deal was agreed. Jo had given Graff his word. The House of Kutchinsky would be sold.

Just as Jo took his first sip, the shop door swung open. Like a shark smelling the blood of her prey, Alisa Moussaieff, the most feared woman in British jewellery, appeared with her arms folded and her lips pursed. She was there to buy the business, she announced, eliciting gasps from the staff who were transfixed by the drama playing out in front of them. Sensing an opportunity, Jo licked his lips and swooped down to greet her.

Known as Mrs M in the trade, she cut an intimidating figure, dressed for business in her trademark trouser suit, with her greying light brown hair styled into a soft bob and glasses resting on the bridge of her nose. Alisa had been born in Austria, then married into an Israeli jewellery dynasty, which traced their roots back to the twelfth century and claimed to count the Mongolian warrior Genghis Khan among their earliest clients. She and her husband had moved to London in 1963 and opened a boutique in the Hilton Hotel on Park Lane, then a hotspot for international jet-setters. From there, she built a network of discerning collectors, including celebrities such as Frank Sinatra and Elizabeth Taylor, and amassed a collection of jaw-dropping jewels.

Speaking with a quiet authority, Alisa conveyed her message: whatever offer was on the table, she would exceed it. I can only imagine what was going through Laurence Graff's mind at that moment. He'd spent hours negotiating and was moments away from inking the deal. He wasn't prepared to go higher – he'd made that clear. And now Alisa Moussaieff, who he respected as a shrewd operator, had him on the ropes. He was, I'm told, furious but powerless to stop it. Escorting Mrs M into Dad's office, Jo made it clear to his sons that he would handle the negotiations. Staff were summoned to extract trays of stock from the safe and parade them in front of Mrs Moussaieff.

'She had all the stock out, weighing it, looking at it, trying to value it. She was going through it like it was a jumble sale!' a staff member said, harrumphing at the memory.

Discussions continued late into the night. Copious cups of coffee were drunk and Jo's chauffeur was dispatched to collect

THE SALE

takeaway food and pick up beer and wine. Mrs M was joined by her husband, Shlomo, who typically focused on the designs while she handled the financial side, and Paul and Roger were brought into discussions. Eventually, sometime around midnight, terms were agreed.

For Jo, money was important but legacy mattered more. There was a rumour he made it clear he would only open negotiations with Mrs M if she agreed to keep the Kutchinsky name above the door, retain several key staff members and work with his sons. Ultimately, that was what made the difference between her and Graff. Recollections of the final price vary but I'm told it was about £2.6 million (about £7.12 million in 2024). Mrs M also promised to give Roger and Paul payouts of £150,000 each if she ever got rid of them.

After the deal was done, the two families, rivals for decades, marked the moment. I suspect Roger sidled off home, and perhaps Mrs M did too, while Jo, Paul and possibly Shlomo stayed drinking until dawn, bidding the House of Kutchinsky a final farewell.

The next morning, when the staff arrived to open up, they got a shock. Whisky and wine bottles littered every surface of the normally pristine showroom and there were red wine stains on the carpet. Ashtrays were filled with cigarette butts and an odour of nicotine and vomit hung in the air.

The following Monday, Paul arrived at work, determined to make the best of his new reality. His Aston Martin had been sold earlier in the year. That loss hurt him almost more than anything else; he loved the way driving that car made him feel. He'd begged Brenda to ask their friends to loan him the £17,000 he needed to buy it outright, but nobody would.

He'd hidden the impending loss from Anna as long as possible, perhaps anxious he might be less desirable to his young girlfriend without a sports car. Meanwhile, Brenda still expected him to provide for her and the children. The realisation had started to dawn that supporting his family and his new life with Anna was going to cost him dear.

The way Dad told it, Mrs M had assured Jo his sons would be looked after, and their roles retained in some form. Perhaps he thought Mrs M might effectively be a silent partner, allowing him to carry on almost unchecked. Either way, what happened next surprised him. Arriving at the shop that Monday morning, he was surprised to find Mrs M seated behind his desk, waiting patiently for his arrival like a spider spinning her web. A signed cheque for £150,000 sat on the notepad in front of her. As Paul sat down, she pushed it towards him.

'We will never work together,' she said. Dad's legs shook. He hadn't expected this final humiliation. He struggled to speak but the words wouldn't form. Why hadn't she just told Jo she was planning this and paid him off when the sale was agreed?

'Take this and go,' she added, easing out of his chair. It occurred to Paul that he could ring his father and ask him to beg on his behalf, but he sensed her mind was made up. She would keep Roger on to run the accountants, she explained, but there wasn't room for Paul.

In a daze, he decided to visit the workshop to say goodbye to Peter and Gerald, and check if there was any lingering stock that had escaped Moussaieff's clutches. Winding his way to the workshop through the backstreets to Soho, the route so

THE SALE

familiar, he remembered his early days at the bench when he was so hungry and hopeful for the future. How had it all gone so wrong? In that moment he feared that, like the egg, he was now damaged goods.

'He was a bit shell-shocked,' Peter Stein recalled. 'He and Mrs M were oil and water; it would never have worked. But it was the way she did it, letting him think he was going to keep his position and then throwing him out. There is no nice way to tell somebody "I don't want you here" but you can give a man his dignity.'

As he left the workshop, Dad took a detour through Hyde Park. It was early spring, the air was cool but the sun was shining. Trees were starting to bud back into life and clusters of daffodils and snowdrops coloured the lawns. Feeling his spirits lift, he started to whistle, the sting of rejection fading. It was almost a year since the launch of Kutchinsky's egg, and his life looked dramatically different. Finally, he was free.

14

'THE GARDEN'

Who was Paul Kutchinsky after the egg? When I search through the shadows of my father's past, conflicting images emerge. 'He lost his moral compass,' Mum always said, and I would nod, acquiescing to her narrative. It was easier that way. But like all of us, he inhabited different personas. *Warm. Generous. Sociable.* Alongside less flattering versions. *Selfish. Spoiled. Stubborn.* And towards the end, like his egg: *broken.*

For the first time, Dad had gambled and lost. Perhaps he consoled himself that he wasn't entirely empty-handed; he still had Anna and the faded glory of his family name. Desperate not to seem diminished in her eyes, he showered his young girlfriend with gifts of designer clothes and jewellery, and encouraged her to slim down, just as he had done with Brenda. At first, Anna was flattered. A snippet in a national newspaper, from September 1991, shows them looking loved up at a gallery opening, under the headline 'Sparkling form'. Sensing a scoop, the gossip columnist honed in on the photogenic pair, and was surprised to find Paul 'bubbling with delight' despite having lost his business, failing to sell his 'astounding £7 million Fabergé egg' and facing a messy divorce. Was the source of his happiness an engagement to his 'new love'?, who was was sporting a 'colossal' diamond ring on her fourth finger, the reporter enquired.

'It's more a statement of intent,' Anna said coyly, describing their situation as 'very complicated'.

'There was I,' the journalist wrote, 'thinking it was one of the simplest and oldest situations known to man – which, of course is exactly what it is, with Anna emerging as the bejewelled victor.'

While Anna smiled and showed off the ring, Dad was relegated to a supporting role with half his body cropped out of the picture; a satellite orbiting around his statuesque, Scandinavian beauty. In his mind, as long as he had Anna on his arm he was still Paul Kutchinsky, bright young thing of the jewellery world. It wasn't the first time whispers of an engagement had swirled around them. A few months previously, just after the dramatic sale of the business, Dad had taken Anna to the Caribbean island of Antigua, where he had sponsored the annual tennis week at a luxury resort called Curtain Bluff. In exchange for a free holiday, he had donated watches as prizes for the annual tournament.

While they were away, Lily received a surprise phone call.

'Mazel tov,' croaked Ethel Bloom, an old friend of hers from Jewish circles. 'I hear your son just got engaged!'

Ethel just so happened to be staying at Curtain Bluff and had overheard Paul announcing his 'engagement' to Anna in the hotel bar in front of a crowd of guests.

Did Ethel see Anna wearing the dazzling 'ring of intent' on her index finger and jump to the wrong conclusion? Or perhaps she overheard Paul making a poorly judged joke?

Anna denies there was ever a proposal but admits that Dad was determined to marry her as soon as he was free. 'His impression was that we would get married. He talked about it all the time,' she said, not mentioning if she shared his desire.

Either way, Lily was furious. I imagine her sitting bolt upright in bed, the shock cutting through the fog of cancer and morphine. After informing Ethel she was mistaken and that he wasn't yet divorced, she got straight on the phone to Brenda. Lily was adamant: 'Paul's Prostitute' would not be joining the Kutchinsky family. After all the other blows they'd suffered due to her son's follies, the stigma of divorce was to be avoided at all costs. Lily had spent her life building her family's reputation and she was determined to preserve what was left of it.

While Lily was alive, Mum still had an ally. Lily was furious with Paul for destroying the business and disgracing his family by having an affair. Their relationship, always so symbiotic, broke irrevocably. Paul barely visited her in her final few months, sulking that he didn't want another telling-off. 'I hope you never know what it feels like to have a child turn on you like this,' Lily whispered to Brenda in her last days, clutching her hand.

I was on a school trip to France when my grandmother died. The decision was made not to tell me, so I unwittingly missed the funeral. I knew she was ill but the word cancer was never used around us, and I don't think I knew what it meant. The first sign that something was wrong was when I got off the plane and found both my parents there to meet me at the airport. Not only that, they were being civil to each other. They took me home, ushered me into the living room and told me the news, staring at me as if expecting tears to appear on cue. I refused to give them the satisfaction, irritated by their sudden ability to act like grown-ups in front of each other, rather than petulant toddlers, as if the past two years had never happened.

After that brief truce, relations between Mum and Dad worsened as their divorce negotiations rumbled on. At first, Mum refused to agree to the divorce, blocking him from marrying Anna, which enraged him. It was all a terrible mess, with my sisters and I caught in the crossfire. We stopped celebrating Jewish holidays. Mum was no longer welcome on these family occasions and so by default neither were we. In Mum's eyes, aside from Lily, the family never really accepted the working-class shiksa from Scotland. Now was their chance to get rid of her, she would tell friends after we'd gone to bed, her words floating up the stairs.

The final blow came when Mum discovered that Jo had welcomed Anna into his home. During an awkward weekend visit to see Grandpa Jo, our paths accidentally crossed with Dad and his girlfriend. As Mum tells it, after being alerted to their presence by the housekeeper, Katrina discovered them 'hidden out in the conservatory at the back' and 'she went through and chased her [Anna] right out of the bloody house ... we were *persona non grata* after that.'

After that, our trips to see Grandpa Jo dwindled, and my Jewishness became just another part of my childhood that vanished after the egg.

* * *

Lily's death was a release for Dad. Finally, he could escape from the pressure and expectation that came with her all-consuming love. If the bitterness of their final fall-out haunted him, he pretended not to show it, remarking flippantly to Mum that he was glad his mother was no longer alive to scold him.

As he settled into his new life, Dad exuded a Teflon optimism. 'I'm down but not out,' he'd exclaim, banging his fist on the kitchen table and making Anna jump. Moments like that, when she didn't know if he was joking or not, reminded her how little they knew about each other. Determined to show he was still a force to be reckoned with, Dad set up a new business in the basement of the Vainers' building in Hatton Garden. Unable to trade under his family name (part of the agreement with Mrs M), he called it PK Limited and made Anna an equal partner, which infuriated Mum. 'He's dick struck,' she would wail down the phone to her friends. He also changed his will, leaving everything to Anna. A decision he would later try to reverse.

A member of the Kutchinsky family, with their hundred-year-old heritage, moving into London's jewellery quarter was big news. At first, the trade was cautious that Paul might have West End airs and graces but he soon won them over. He stopped wearing suits, opting instead for jeans and flamboyant jumpers. He still wore a blazer, filling the inside pocket with cash, diamonds and a sliver of hash. 'Paul was so charismatic, everybody fell in love with him, you'd do anything for him,' recalled Brian Jocelyn, a diamond mounter who worked with Paul in 'The Garden', as locals called it. 'He had a huge reputation coming from the shop, but he'd messed it up a bit with the egg.'

It wouldn't be long, Paul promised Anna, before he was

'THE GARDEN'

back at the top of his game. He was now in his early forties and refused to accept that his career may have peaked. As much as the egg had brought him international renown, he was painfully aware that it risked becoming his nemesis. There were no photos of it on the wall of his new office and when it inevitably cropped up in conversation, he would quickly shut it down, affirming sharply that the terrible timing of the Gulf War made it so ruinous; that was certainly the story I knew. Only when he was drunk did his residual pride in his creation come pouring out, although he would still lament how petty jealousies had tarnished it.

Until the egg, every gamble Paul had taken had paid off. His belief in himself as a creative genius had been fostered by those around him, from the workers in the workshop to his parents. 'I've got the Midas touch, Cece,' he would joke, explaining the story of the ill-fated, avaricious Greek king who asked the gods to turn everything he touched to gold and then regretted it when he could no longer eat, drink or embrace his loved ones. Realising the error of his ways, Midas begged the gods to reverse his wish. The story goes that Dionysus, the god of wine and festivity, granted his request and let him wash away the enchantment in the Pactolus River (near Sardis in modern Turkey), leading to it becoming rich in gold deposits.

Unlike Midas, the one thing Dad could never admit was his mistake. That if he had taken the egg straight to the Sultan of Brunei, it would have kept its mystique and sold. It was his desire to parade it in front of the media, and be hailed as the next Carl Fabergé, that ruined its chances. In the sultan's eyes, the egg was worthless once the world knew about it. Whenever Dad had sold him golden treasures in the past, the sales were always conducted with the utmost discretion. It added to the item's allure and was safer that way. But beguiled by the celebrity status the egg bestowed on him, Dad got swept up and took a different path.

If he had kept it out of the public eye, then it would likely have sold for several million pounds as planned and the House of Kutchinsky would still exist today. Had the other pillars of his life remained intact, Dad might have been less inclined to abscond with Anna, and he could even still be alive today to hold his grandchildren and read these words.

The failure of the egg shook Paul's confidence and his ability to persuade others to believe in him. In my mind he was like a TV superhero who had been stripped of his powers but was stuck recreating his past heroics in a low-budget, spin-off series. While he looked and sounded like Dad, with the same bad jokes and penchant for silly hats, the light in his eyes had dimmed.

Searching for a scheme that would outshine the egg, and restore his reputation, he had hit on the idea of designing a range of jewellery that would rival Chopard's bestselling Happy Diamonds. He had started working on it in secret before the House of Kutchinsky was sold and his concept hinged on the fact that although the gems inside Chopard's necklaces, rings and watches moved freely, their metal setting dulled their sparkle. What if there was a way to free the stones so they could reflect light from every angle? His design featured gems suspended between sheets of glass, shimmering like frozen meteorites. He christened it Solid Rock, and after setting up his new company, obtained a patent at significant expense.

His next step was to find a permanent home for PK

'THE GARDEN'

Limited. After about a year of renting space in other workshops, he took out a lease on a space at the top of number eight Hatton Garden, a tall off-white Victorian building with a smog-stained facade. There was no lift, and the stairs were steep and narrow. Every morning, Anna would clatter up them in high heels, sprinting ahead of Paul, her long blonde hair bouncing off her neck, where sometimes her pet parrot nestled, giving her the air of a power-dressed pirate. A small sign on the fifth floor proclaimed their presence: PK Limited. Inside the hulking metal door there was an office and workshop with just five benches, a far cry from the forty workers the House of Kutchinsky had in its heyday.

PK Limited got off to a good start, boosting Paul's hopes of a comeback. Business in the Middle East was picking up, he made a clock for Argyle with some of the leftover stones from the egg, and Mrs Moussaieff agreed to sell some Solid Rock pieces in the Kutchinsky shop. PK's bestseller was a romantic pendant with initials picked out in rubies. Orders poured in, especially around Valentine's Day, but production came to a screeching halt when several necklaces exploded due to a manufacturing fault. The heat of the display lights in the shop window melted the glue that held the stones in place, shattering the glass and sending the gems flying into orbit. Undeterred, Paul poured money into finding a solution. He tried transparent silicone moulds provided by a medical company and then rubber versions, which were more precise but still not cost-effective for mass manufacture. Solid Rock was rapidly becoming a black hole but he refused to give up, painfully aware that another failure would ruin him.

In 1992, he swallowed his pride and returned to the Basel

Fair, booking a small stand and flying over with Anna. 'We were lucky to be there,' she said frankly. 'We tried to pad the collection out to make it look as rich as possible but it was pitiful.' How did he feel, wandering through the familiar halls eyeing the large stands occupied by the big houses such as Cartier and Bulgari, and his former rivals Graff and Moussaieff. Where once he had mocked Leo de Vroomen for being small fry, now he barely even qualified as that. In just two years he had gone from the star attraction to a sideshow.

But with bills to pay, his bitter divorce from Brenda spiralling and Anna to impress, he had no choice but to go out and hustle. Luckily, despite his egotism and eccentricities, people were fond of Paul and liked his designs. Basel was a relative success, and he returned to London feeling optimistic about the future.

However, he'd failed to realise the limitations of a small workshop, which was already close to capacity. 'It was one job after the other, and they were big jobs,' recalled Darren Weeks, a gruff diamond setter from South London who worked in the Hatton Garden workshop. Anna had suggested I speak to him and when I reached out, he responded warmly, inviting me to visit him at work. Creeping up the stairs of a tall, narrow building, typical of those in 'The Garden', I found him, dressed in the goldsmith's attire of polo shirt and jeans, sketching designs on a pad, surrounded by piles of wooden-handled jewellery tools and wearing what looked like a head torch with a pair of mini binoculars attached to allow him to set gems with absolute precision. His memory was sharp and he spoke about his time working alongside Dad with genuine affection. 'When

Paul came along, I started earning a lot more money ... He could go anywhere and get an order.' But there were limits. 'It was too much – there weren't enough hours in the day.'

The final straw came when Paul demanded a jewelled bangle be made for a friend's fiftieth birthday to an absurdly tight deadline. The craftsmen refused point blank, and realising he had a mutiny on his hands, Paul resorted to melodrama.

'I might as well jump out of the window if this order falls through,' he exclaimed, looking forlorn. Silently, all five craftsmen stood up, pulled a chair up to the window for him and walked out of the workshop.

From time to time, Jo would visit Hatton Garden, staggering up the steep stairs to breathe in the familiar workshop smell of chemicals and molten metal, sweat and cigarettes. Without the pressure of a shared business and no longer competing for Lily's love, Dad found a new closeness with his father, although Jo would later exact a bitter revenge on his son for his reckless ways.

Unlike Paul, who the craftsmen affectionately mocked as an artistic dreamer, nicknaming him 'Thumbs' due to his tendency to break things, his father commanded respect. 'Jo was a jeweller's jeweller,' Darren said. 'Paul had no idea how to manufacture things. Once a group of us were standing in the workshop, trying to figure out why a job wouldn't work. You could see Paul, taking a half-step backwards and then another half-step, until he'd created enough space so he could turn around and walk out. But your grandfather stayed and worked out the problem with us. That was the difference between them.'

KUTCHINSKY'S EGG

* * *

In my memories after the egg, Dad plays a caricature of the father I knew from childhood. Louder, brasher. He became more of a grown-up friend, telling eye-opening stories about how he used to secretly grow weed in the bathroom when I was a baby. I liked this version of Dad. He was exciting to be around and no longer nagged me about my homework. In the early days, I would wait awkwardly at the gates of Hollybush House for him to collect me for our fortnightly tennis and pizza outing. Although my mum and sisters called me disloyal for seeing him, I didn't care, secretly revelling in having him all to myself.

Whenever I asked Dad where his egg was now, he'd just shrug. 'Dunno, Cece. Could be anywhere. Could be on the bloody moon for all I know,' he'd say, honking with hollow laughter. I was perplexed. How could he go from being so consumed by something to acting like he didn't care about it? At the same time, everything else about Dad's life was different now, so maybe it made sense that there was no space for Kutchinsky's egg. But under his clownish defence, he mourned the image of himself as the talented trailblazer at the head of an historic family firm. A bright young thing destined for greatness.

In the past, Dad rarely gave interviews, due to his parents' worries it would make him a target for kidnappers. But, in 1984, many years before the egg, during a business trip to Singapore and far away from Jo's control, he spoke to *The Straits Times*, the country's biggest selling daily newspaper. The piece shows a picture of Dad, his face framed by oversized, round spectacles, under the headline: 'Kutchinsky has a gem of a family'. It depicts him as the humble heir to a glittering dynasty, who keeps a low profile and eschews the trappings of wealth. 'The few luxuries he allows himself are family skiing holidays and a second-hand 1977 Aston Martin that he bought from the Duke of Westminster,' the writer gushes. At the weekend, 'easy-going' Paul likes nothing better than taking his young daughters to the park. 'Once off the job, he tries to concentrate on his family.'

After the egg, that part of his identity was also lost. Until, that is, he launched a reckless bid to reclaim it. I was twelve when the secret trips started. He picked me up one Sunday, having promised me a trip to my favourite theme park, Chessington World of Adventures. But when I got in the car, chattering excitedly about which ride we would go on first, he fell silent. Then he started asking if I understood how sometimes adults fall in love. I squirmed, sensing what might be coming. As he talked, I noticed we weren't going the normal route.

'We missed the turning, Daddy,' I interrupted.

Gripping the steering wheel, he stared silently ahead. Would I like to meet Anna? he asked, glancing anxiously in my direction.

'I really wanted to go on the pirate ship,' I sulked.

'I know, Cece, but Chessington will always be there. Anna would love to meet you,' he pleaded, in a voice I found hard to resist. I'd heard so many horrible things about Dad's girlfriend, but at the same time I was curious to meet the woman who'd stolen him away, and short of jumping out of the car, it seemed I didn't have much choice in the matter. I nodded, feeling a mix of fear and excitement as Dad accelerated up the motorway.

Our destination was a house in a seaside town on the Sussex coast belonging to friends of Anna's. As we pulled up, a young woman, dressed in jeans and one of Dad's jumpers, came bouncing out and greeted me warmly. Her friendliness surprised me. Was this the villainous, gold-digging woman that I'd heard so much bile about? Breathing a sigh of relief, I followed her inside where lunch lay in wait.

At first, I enjoyed being treated like an adult. But as the meal wore on, and they started making private jokes about how they got drunk the night before, my mood slumped. I missed my sisters. Eagle-eyed, Anna jumped up and suggested we walk along the beach where there was a small funfair. Among the small collection of rides were fast-spinning waltzers, which I loved but Dad loathed. After the ride, we had ice cream and walked along the pebbly beach, making the most of the warm weather. Driving back to London that night, Dad blasted Pink Floyd from the stereo. When it came to his favourite track, 'Another Brick in the Wall', with its anthemic refrain of 'We don't need no education', we all sang along, Anna and I thrashing our hair around.

Dad deposited Anna in a nearby pub before dropping me off. Both of us were silent as we approached the house, nervous about what lay ahead. 'Don't tell Mummy,' he warned, as I jumped out. 'It's better for everybody that way.' And then he was gone, speeding back down the dark, narrow road to his new life.

As the summer wore on, I saw more of Anna and her family, including her younger sister, Flora, who was around

'THE GARDEN'

my age. Together, we tasted our first glass of champagne and amused the adults by play-acting drunk. Dad also took me to watch the tennis at Wimbledon, once with Anna and another time with her teenage brother, Hugo. I was enjoying spending time with him, and the truth was that Anna's presence made hanging out with Dad, who was often at a loss as to how to entertain his pre-teen daughter, less awkward. He seemed happy, and that was enough for me. But at the same time I was finding it hard to keep up a front at home and had started having trouble sleeping. The more evasive and defensive I became, the more Mum's suspicions were aroused.

Eventually, after a day out with Dad and Anna's younger siblings, who were also on their summer holidays, I cracked. He'd taken us to Rock Circus, a new Madame Tussauds exhibition focusing on rock stars. As well as the normal wax figures, the finale was a 'live' show featuring an array of all-singing, all-dancing robotic pop stars including Michael Jackson, The Beatles and Elvis. It was late by the time Dad dropped me back and he must have had a few drinks. When Mum came out of the house to meet me and ask him for money to help her buy petrol and food, a row broke out. Demanding to see Katrina, who was sleeping, Dad grabbed Mum's house keys and refused to give them back.

'He really resented the fact I was still living at Hollybush,' Mum said, long-buried emotions stirring in her voice. 'He would get almost violent. I think the guilt made him completely flip out.'

Upset by all the animosity, I ran into my room and slammed the door, sobbing. The next morning, when Mum started grilling me about where I'd been, I broke down and confessed. Shocked and furious, she got straight on the phone to her divorce lawyer, who insisted she take a statement from me detailing Dad's sneaky behaviour.

'I noticed that Serena often had sleepless nights and was weepy and appeared to be under a lot of pressure,' Mum wrote. 'She has now said she doesn't want to see her daddy unless he changes. She felt knotted up inside and could not keep all this inside her any longer.'

Reading it now brings back a wave of conflicting emotions. While it was horrible being forced to lie to Mum, I had enjoyed having Dad back in my life and was desperate not to lose him again. When it all came pouring out, scared of upsetting Mum, I said what I thought she wanted to hear, twisting the narrative to such an extent that an afternoon at a country estate watching Dad play cricket was somehow transformed into a story about a decaying squat where people were openly smoking marijuana.

After my confession, I didn't see Dad for a while. The secret visits achieved the reverse of what he wanted, fracturing our relationship. He became a disembodied figure, an absent presence. A distracted voice on the phone. A name in the divorce papers. An awkward figure in the courtroom, telling us he loved us and missed us. *Lies*, Mum said tearfully. *He left you, too.* While it was true that his attention was focused on Anna, as if she were the centre of his universe, I knew that underneath it, he was deeply lonely. His obsession had robbed him of his friends, his children and his status. All he had left was Anna, and no matter how much affection she gave him, it would never be enough to fill the egg-shaped hole in his ego.

'THE GARDEN'

'The sale of Kutchinsky to Mrs Moussaieff badly affected your dad,' the goldsmith Tony Bellingham told me. 'If you're the family member who inherited a position as the head of an old company and then lost it . . . that's a very harsh thing to happen.'

Although he tried to hide it beneath the artifice of wealth, Dad was fatally wounded. Like a hunted stag that's taken a bullet but keeps running with his head high, his legs trembling and blood trailing behind him. It was only a matter of time before he stumbled and fell.

* * *

By the mid-nineties, it was clear that PK Limited was never going to rival the big brands like Chopard. As he approached fifty, Dad still loved the artistry of jewellery but his burning ambition had dimmed. 'Work hard and make enough money, so you don't have to work,' he'd say, in the jokey, conspiratorial way that signalled he was imparting wisdom. I was confused. Being a jeweller was a huge part of his identity. What else would he do?

It was around this time that Dad sensed Anna pulling away. She was less indulgent of his foibles, laughed less at his bad jokes and smirked at her friend's impression of his lisped endearments. The more distant she grew, the more needy he became. He started smoking weed during the day, scoring off a supplier in Hatton Garden, and grew paranoid and possessive. Darren remembers him muttering about how other jewellers were out to get him, and complaining about diamonds going missing from the safe. If someone walked past his desk he would contort his body, shielding the precious stones from view. Simultaneously, he tightened his grip on his most precious jewel: Anna. Her refusal to marry him gnawed away at what was left of his self-esteem.

Why didn't she want to be the next Mrs Paul Kutchinsky?

Meanwhile, Anna was establishing her own identity, away from Paul. Approaching thirty, she was about to embark on a new business venture: a gift shop with her close friends, Lorna and Angela, which would be based in the Vainers' building. The Chancery Trading Company opened in September 1994. In the past, her dealings had been mainly with Milos Vainer, but now she found herself drawn to his son Richard who, with his wealth, arrogance and good looks, was one of London's most eligible bachelors. Rumours of an affair swirled around Hatton Garden. If they were seeing each other, then it was all conducted in great secrecy as, I'm told, Richard had an upper-class girlfriend his mother was desperate for him to marry. According to Anna, while there was 'harmless flirting' between her and Richard, she was never unfaithful. But is flirting ever without danger?

At home, Anna started to feel like a prisoner. Paul was policing her movements and checking their shared mobile phone. If she broke away from him at a party, he would swoop in and shut down her conversation or pick a fight, demanding to know why she didn't want to be seen with him. If she went for a drink with a girlfriend, he spent hours sulking. A dinner with a business contact, while he was away in the Middle East, led to a three-day tirade during a holiday in Spain. When Anna, in despair, went to sleep in a different room, he followed her, prodding her awake. Once that subsided, he circled back to talking about marriage again, as he and Brenda were now officially divorced. They already had a mortgage, a business

'THE GARDEN'

and a life together – wasn't that enough? Anna pleaded. His passionate nature, once part of his charm, now repelled her.

It was early 1995 when Anna ended it. When she first broke the news, in the living room of their waterfront flat, the lights of the River Thames reflected in the murky waters below, Paul refused to accept it, drowning out her words with his own verbal missiles.

Wracked with grief, he begged her not to leave. *Darling. Baby. My world.* When he realised her mind was made up, he begged her not to tell anyone. It would be bad for business, he said, pulling at the leash that bound their lives together. Every indignity had been bearable while he still had Anna. Everything Brenda had predicted would happen when he first set out on his ill-fated mission to become the modern-day Carl Fabergé had come true.

Anna agreed to keep her departure quiet. For three months, they kept up the charade at work. When Jo came over for fortnightly dinners, Anna returned from her mum's house to cook, as all Dad was capable of whipping up was egg and chips smothered in chilli sauce, followed by a dessert of frozen grapes. 'I felt bad for Paul,' Anna said. 'I know he loved me very much, but I'm not sure how normal that love was.'

A few months after she moved out, friends of Brenda's spotted Anna at Annabel's with Richard Vainer. Relieved that the charade of her and Paul still being together was shattered, she broke the news to Paul the next morning at work. She wanted him to hear it from her first. He didn't take it well, flying into a furious rage. If the workshop hadn't known about their break-up before, there was no hiding it now. The thought of her with anybody else, let alone Richard, who was younger and wealthier, must have been soul-destroying. In that moment, all his suppressed grief over losing his family, his business, his mother and his egg, came roaring out. He stormed out of the office.

*   *   *

The collapse of his relationship with Anna made Dad feel like a loser. When he wasn't working or playing tennis, he threw himself into flings with a string of unsuitable women, even joining a Jewish dating society, which surprised me given he'd spent his entire adult life dating outside his religion. There were also rumours he started taking cocaine.

Sporadically he would try to get his life back on track. But just when things were starting to look a bit better, his luck took a turn for the worse when he was arrested on a business trip to Bahrain. He had hidden a few extra pieces of jewellery in his luggage to sell without paying import tax. 'One for customs, one for me,' he would always say, with a roguish grin. As his bag went through the scanner, officials confronted him about the concealed items. Before he knew what was happening, armed border guards were shepherding him into a side room while waving the disclaimer he'd signed earlier in his face. Panicking, his fingers went automatically to the stash pocket in his blazer where he kept his hash. As his fingers curled around a soft, sticky lump, he caught his breath. Shit. He'd been smoking so much post break-up, he'd forgotten it was there. Bahrain, like many Gulf countries, operated a zero-tolerance approach to drugs and carrying even a small amount of hash risked a severe penalty.

The idea of trying to make a run for it flashed through

'THE GARDEN'

Dad's mind, but he was outnumbered. Instead, squeezing the hash between his fingers, he tried to drop it behind his back. But it was too late. The guards caught him in the act, picked it off the floor and dragged him away, shouting and swearing. After attempting, and failing, to bribe his way out of trouble, the gravity of his situation started to sink in, as he was transferred to the nearest prison, steel handcuffs cutting into his wrists. He was most likely held in Muharraq Police Station, a whitewashed building close to the airport, which had a reputation for interrogating political prisoners. Trying to exude an indignation he didn't feel, he demanded a phone call. His agent in the region, Zayd*, who acted as a broker between manufacturing firms like PK Limited and high-end retailers, also had a range of private clients including the Bahraini royal family. Paul's hope was that Zayd could use his contacts to negotiate his release. The alternative didn't bear thinking about.

'Why didn't you tell me you wanted hash?' Zayd said, sounding incredulous, as Paul explained his predicament. 'We could easily have got you some.' For the first time since his arrest, Paul managed a weak smile.

Don't worry, his agent reassured him, he would make some calls. He was confident he could get Paul out.

Back in his cell, which he shared with about seven other prisoners, Paul slumped on a hard wooden bench and tried to sleep. How the mighty had fallen. The next day, he telephoned the PK Limited office, praying Anna would answer. When she picked up, he felt weak with relief. Although they were

---

* Name has been changed

no longer together, she was still the closest person to him at that moment.

'Don't panic, but I'm in prison,' he said, his nervous laugh echoing down the line.

'What the fuck?' she replied, stunned. 'Whatever for?'

When he told her, he could feel the disbelief radiating through the receiver. 'What were you thinking?' she demanded.

'I forgot it was there,' he blustered, reliving the horror he'd felt during that moment of discovery at the airport. But the sound of her voice soothed him; surely he'd be home soon.

Almost a week later, the news finally came. Zayd had worked his magic and secured Paul's release. He had to pay a hefty fine, would be immediately deported and could never return to Bahrain. While it was a blow to his business, it felt a small price to pay in exchange for his freedom.

Later, Paul would turn the story of being 'banged up in Bahrain' into a comic misadventure, but there was no denying the experience shook him to his core. How many close scrapes could he survive? Unable to afford the mortgage on his flat, he moved in with his father to save money – a development I found troubling. I was living in my own student house by this point, while Dad, it seemed, was regressing.

But in the back of his mind, a plan was brewing. Buying his freedom in Bahrain had cost him dear and the business needed a serious cash injection. The thought of asking Argyle to give him one last chance to sell his lost masterpiece buzzed at the back of his mind like a wasp trapped in a glass jar. He'd always believed that someone, somewhere, would fall in love with his egg. Was now, almost a decade after Kutchinsky's egg first made its debut, finally the right time?

'THE GARDEN'

* * *

As Dad prepared to turn fifty, his life seemed stuck in a downward spiral and his longing to start anew intensified. Tennis became his obsession. He immersed himself in the sport and social scene, and I think he felt he'd found his tribe. He also started secretly designing a new range of gold and diamond cufflinks adorned with miniature enamel eggs and sold them to a friend in the West End who ran a high-end men's fashion outlet. His life was nothing like it was before the egg, but he clung to fragments of his old image.

In the intervening years, Mum had reluctantly sold Hollybush House and returned to Scotland. There were too many memories in London; it was time for her to go home. The village pub in Pennan came up for sale in 1999. She'd clung onto our holiday cottage there, using the money from the sale of her parents' house after their deaths. Now, in search of a new challenge, she decided to base herself in the village full time and bought the pub. I had already left home to go to university and Katrina was planning to take a gap year and study abroad, so it was just Hollie who moved with Mum to live permanently in Aberdeenshire.

In the summer of 1999, I spent a month working behind the bar to raise money for a backpacking trip to China, a country whose history fascinated me. In buying the pub, Mum had fulfilled a dream she and Dad had shared when they were still married, and fuelled by a mixture of envy and curiosity, he offered to pick me up and drive me back to London to catch my flight to Beijing. When I reminded him it was a twelve-hour drive to Scotland, he just laughed. He knew that drive so well, it was nothing to him. To my surprise, he stayed all weekend. I remember leaving him and Mum sitting in the restaurant talking late into the night; it was the closest I'd seen them since the split. I even overheard them discussing visiting Katrina, who would be living in Paris after the summer.

But not everyone from his old life was ready to forgive him.

Philippa, Mum's closest friend, was also there helping to redecorate. It was the first time she'd seen Paul since he'd confessed his liaison with Anna to her almost a decade ago, and she was determined to stop him worming his way back into Brenda's affections. 'I was like a wild animal,' she recalled. 'I shouted and swore and he just took it. He was a broken man.'

Dad was put to work fixing a bathroom in one of the rooms above the pub. The surrealness of seeing Paul on his knees scrubbing the toilet sent the two women into hysterics. 'We were like witches,' Philippa recalled, laughing bitterly. 'It was his punishment.' When it was time to leave, my parents shared a friendly hug. Driving away from the village with Dad, I felt lighter. My parents were no longer at war, and my sisters had also shown signs of thawing towards him too, that weekend.

Was it possible our family might be reunited? So much had happened since the divorce, I was sceptical that my parents' romantic partnership could be repaired. But, years later, one of Dad's female companions told me he had expressed surprise at how much his departure had devastated Brenda. He had mistaken her frustrations over the egg for something greater and thought she'd stopped loving him. Had he known the truth, he would never have left – or so he said. As he told her this, his friend listened, feeling a mix of pity and irritation.

'THE GARDEN'

Paul was clearly full of regret, but still failing to recognise the part he'd played in his own downfall.

A few months later, Anna told Dad that she was pregnant with Richard's baby. They should probably think about wrapping up the business, she said gently over lunch at the Bleeding Heart. Dad nodded; he'd suspected something like this was coming. Amid the sadness, he felt a sliver of relief. Seeing Anna at work every day was stopping him from moving on.

As they left the wine bar, he wished her good luck, feeling only the faintest pang. He returned to the office and started making plans for his future. He already had his new cufflink range, which he was hoping to expand, and had set up a property company with his cousin, Melvyn – the son of Lily's sister, Millie. Paul Kutchinsky would always be a jeweller, it was in his blood, but increasingly he wanted a different life, where he worked less, played more tennis and made up for the time he'd lost with his children.

If he could just pull off this last big sale – the notorious egg – his reputation would be restored and he would be able to pick and choose the jobs he took on, rather than scrabbling around for work. He dusted off the brochure from almost a decade ago and resolved to take it with him on his next trip to Dubai, now a booming market for international jewellers, and show it to a few agents he worked with there. His relationship with Argyle had cooled, but he was certain he would have heard if they had sold the egg. If the price was right, he felt confident he could persuade them to give him one last shot. He whispered his hopes down the phone to me at night, telling me it was our secret.

As the new millennium dawned, he started planning a big

party for his fiftieth birthday. The very last time I saw him, he was so excited about it. I'd called him in a panic as I'd spent all my student loan and was too ashamed to tell Mum, who had already helped me out more than she could afford. Happy to be my hero, he sped down the motorway to Oxford to see me the next day. When I'd won a place at the famous university the previous year, Dad had been embarrassingly proud, spouting off about it to all his girlfriends. Later he even sent them copies of my articles in the student newspaper. As the familiar burgundy BMW drew up outside the back gates of Balliol College, I clambered in and hugged him. He handed me £200 in cash, telling me to hide it under my bed. He couldn't stop because he was going to play tennis with a lady friend, he said, before reminding me about his party.

'It's on Saturday 4 March at my new tennis club, the Cumberland, in North London. We've got the whole bar booked out,' he said, grinning. 'It's going to be great, Cece, people are even coming from America for it. You have to come.'

'I'll be there, Dad,' I promised, kissing his cheek as I slid out of the car.

15

THE CALL

The accident made the papers. 'Jeweller killed in Spanish road crash,' declared the *Jewish Chronicle* in its report, which made no mention of Kutchinsky's egg. Instead, it described Dad as a manufacturing jeweller from Hatton Garden; 'the third generation of the family which successfully built up the prestigious shop in Knightsbridge'. Even in death, his father's achievements still overshadowed his.

It was a rainy Monday morning when I got the call. I was ensconced on the sofa in the living room of my student house with a friend, drinking tea and swapping gossip from the weekend. The shrill ring of the house phone drowned our laughter. I had decided not to go to Dad's party at the last minute. I was worried that I wouldn't know anyone, except the unsuitable girlfriends, whose names I struggled to remember. My sisters weren't going and, although things were better between my parents, I felt uneasy – as if showing up to party with him and his friends from his new life would be betraying them. So I stayed in Oxford, celebrating the birthday of a close friend at a student house party, where we stayed till dawn.

I'm told Dad had a great time at his party. Almost a hundred people crowded into the wood-panelled private room at the Cumberland Tennis Club, which had become the epicentre of Dad's social life, to celebrate his half-century. Jo was there, sipping whisky and holding court, as were Dad's cousins, and even Roger showed up, flanked by Yvette.

I did feel a stab of guilt that night. Usually, I was prepared to be the odd one out when it came to Dad, but I had nowhere to stay in London and reasoned that he had always put his own pleasure first. So, I left a message on his voicemail, apologising and promising to explain over supper in London next week. Maybe that's him, I thought, wobbling over to pick up the receiver.

It wasn't Dad. But it was about him.

'Bad news,' Mum said, choking out the words, sounding as if she were drowning. 'There's been a car crash. In Spain. Your father . . .' Her voice trailed off into jagged sobs.

'Is he okay? What happened?' I said, panic rising in my chest. I'd never heard her sound like this, not even during the darkest moments of their divorce. Time stood still.

'He's dead, Serena.'

I screamed and dropped the phone. My knees buckled beneath me. Mum's voice was still sputtering from the receiver but I couldn't bear to listen. Dad would never call me back.

'I don't understand,' I repeated over and over. 'Why was he in Spain?'

'There were two American women with him,' Mum said. 'He wasn't driving.'

For years, that was all I knew. That at least his death wasn't his fault. Back then, lost in the darkness, I wondered if that was a fabrication, intended to lessen the pain. The truth was,

THE CALL

Dad was notorious for drink-driving and I found it hard to believe he wasn't behind the wheel. It hurt to think about it, so I pushed it away. Nobody ever told me the names of the women involved, and I never asked, assuming they were part of Dad's doomed dating life.

Amid the shock and sorrow, there was a niggling thought that the crash was the inevitable outcome of the direction Dad's life had spiralled in, ever since Kutchinsky's egg. Mum was the first to say that if only he hadn't risked everything to make it, he'd still be alive. His reckless ambition had ruined him.

*   *   *

When Paul discovered that his close friend Terry Walker, an American he knew through the tennis scene, had booked a last-minute trip to surprise him on his birthday, he couldn't stop smiling. Determined to show her something beyond the tennis club where the party was, he asked Jo if he could take Terry and her childhood friend, Bunny Ginsburg, who was accompanying her, to continue the celebrations at his flat in Spain.

There was a special bond between Dad and Terry. They were the same age, both came from Jewish backgrounds (but had married outside their religion) and they both loved to socialise. They had met nearly ten years ago on the paradise island of Antigua at the Curtain Bluff tennis tournament. A great listener, Terry had provided a sympathetic ear after the split with Anna. They had a close, almost sibling-like relationship, and Terry left her husband Ross at home in Texas with their two children and flew to the UK for Dad's party.

She was excited about the trip; her daughter had left home to go to university and her son was in his final year at high school. Finally, she could start having adventures of her own. When she heard Paul had booked flights to Marbella, she was thrilled. Their plan was to soak up the glamour of the Costa del Sol in the evenings and spend the days playing tennis and making the most of the warmer weather.

Dad had made numerous trips to Spain over the years, often driving the whole way. It took him about a day and he loved the adventure. I joined him once when I was about fourteen, bringing my friend Edwina along. Anna turned up a few days into the trip, walking into the flat resplendent in a white bikini and stilettos. Her presence made me fade into the background, but I didn't mind. Every night, Dad would buy us sangria at dinner and then send us off shopping with some pocket money while they sloped off to various bars. Intoxicated by this sudden freedom, I quickly worked out which bars served people underage and got drunk for the first time in my life.

But this time, they only had a few days so Dad decided it was better to fly and hire a car, likely a jeep, at the airport. They arrived on Sunday late morning, bleary-eyed from the night before. While the Americans, who were still jet-lagged, got some rest, Dad drove off to meet a friend for lunch. That evening, the trio made the short journey into Puerto Banús for dinner, where we had celebrated my eleventh birthday all those years ago.

When they left the restaurant later that night, a thick sea mist had descended, cloaking the harbour. I imagine Terry, who hadn't been drinking, insisted that Paul was in no fit state to drive. Or perhaps he had a sneaky spliff after dinner and,

THE CALL

after three days of partying, it knocked him out. However it happened, Dad was in the back and Terry, who didn't know the roads, was in the driver's seat.

The route back to the flat was a ten-minute drive along a treacherous stretch of coastal highway where accidents were a common occurrence. I remember seeing the aftermath of a motorbike collision there, with broken glass, severed limbs and bike parts strewn across multiple lanes. The image haunted me and I used to worry about Dad driving the route, especially at night, but he brushed it off. 'You don't need to worry about me, Cece,' he would say, smiling.

There are so many 'what ifs' with accidents, it's hard to accept that split-second decisions can cause lifelong heartache. Running low on fuel, they stopped at one of the late-night petrol stations dotted along the roadside. After filling up, Terry got back in the car and twisted around to check on Paul before fastening her seat belt. As she pulled out, her sight of the road ahead reduced by the fog, she made a fatal error. Mistaking the entrance for the exit, she steered the car straight into the path of oncoming traffic.

Did she scream in terror when she realised her mistake?
Did they see the Porsche speeding towards them?
Did the commotion wake Dad from his hazy slumber?

Or was it deathly silent until the screech of brakes and the sickening crunch of metal colliding, as vehicles folded into each other, steel bending like rubber, glass popping and shattering in a glittering, blood-smeared spray.

At the moment of impact, as car alarms wailed and the acrid smell of burned rubber and leaking petrol filled the air, their bodies would have jerked forward, hitting the roof or

KUTCHINSKY'S EGG

dashboard. I was told that Dad, who I doubt was wearing a seat belt, died quickly. That it was too fast for him to know what was happening or feel any pain.

I always assumed both women died too. But while Terry perished with Paul, as did the Belgian driver of the other car, her friend Bunny survived. She is still alive today but has no memory of the accident or the days leading up to it. She'd never met Dad before, so he too is wiped from her mind, her husband told me when I reached out to them. The impression I got from him, and Terry's family, was that the trauma of the accident wasn't something Bunny wanted to revisit. I understood; for years I blocked it out.

Dad was dead; it didn't matter how it happened. But now it does matter, because how could I ever truly understand my father without knowing the circumstances that led to me losing him again, this time for good? Above all, I'm glad he wasn't alone.

Today, thousands of miles away in a home in California that I have never visited, there is a picture of Terry and Dad on her daughter Sara's bedside table. It sits in a small frame, with a cherub on top, its gilded edges faded.

The photo was taken at Dad's party. In the photo, his arm is around Terry and their heads are touching. He looks startled, almost as if surprised by the photographer's presence but she is beaming, her big smile lighting up her face.

It was the last photo ever taken of them alive.

*   *   *

The crash happened in the early hours of Monday 6 March 2000 but the news didn't trickle back to London until later

THE CALL

that morning. Dad's cousin, Melvyn, was the first to hear. Melvyn, a retired hairdresser, was never fond of his aunt Lily, finding her haughty and cold, and the feeling was mutual. But after Lily died, and Jo sunk into alcoholism and loneliness, Melvyn grew close to his uncle, paying him almost daily visits. Relegated to a bit part in my memories, it didn't occur to me to track Melvyn down until I discovered Dad had gone into business with him just before he died. And I had no idea, until we first spoke in early 2025, that it was him who told Jo his youngest son was dead.

Melvyn was in the office of his stepson's property company, early on Monday morning, when the phone rang. The call was from someone claiming to be Corrarado, the chauffeur Jo used when he was in Marbella. 'Come on, Paul,' Melvyn said, knowing his cousin's love of pranks. 'I'm busy, I'm at work . . .' Once it sunk in that it was serious, he called Roger, who was working in the West End at the time. 'I'm coming straight over,' Mervyn told him. 'We'll have to break the news to your father.'

Jo was in bed, sleeping off the previous night's whisky, when there was a knock at the door. It was 11 a.m., little more than twenty-four hours since he had kissed his youngest son on both cheeks and bid him farewell. What on earth were Melvyn and Roger doing here? he wondered as the housekeeper announced their arrival. By the time he eased himself into his armchair, still in his silk pyjamas and dressing gown, he knew something was badly wrong. His older son and nephew stood in silence in the living room, barely able to meet his gaze.

'What's happened?' he slurred, still not fully sober.

Melvyn spoke first. 'Paul's been in an accident, Uncle.'

'He's dead, isn't he,' Jo said numbly, his voice flat. Roger and Melvyn nodded. There was a brief, pained silence before Jo started barking orders at them.

'You'd better get over to Spain and sort everything out. Book a flight. Leave now and you'll be there by the afternoon.'

After some frantic phone calls, both men were on their way. Before they left, Roger called Brenda to break the news. How did he feel as he dialled Mum's number? Relations were strained but they all knew how much she still cared for Dad. After the horror of relaying the stark facts, there wasn't much more to say. Desperate to hang up before she broke down, Mum promised to tell me and my sisters and make arrangements to travel to London.

When Roger and Melvyn arrived in Marbella, the haunting scene of a holiday cut short greeted them. The women's suitcases were still mainly unpacked, with a few possessions strewn about, their tennis racquet bags stood expectantly in the hall and Dad's bed had not been slept in. On the answerphone, Melvyn heard a message which he assumed was from Terry's husband, Ross Walker. 'I haven't been able to get hold of you,' he said cheerily. 'But I hope you're having a fabulous time playing tennis with Paul.'

The mortuary was on the outskirts of Marbella just across the road from one of Jo's favourite restaurants. On the way back from identifying the body, Roger turned to Melvyn and lisped: 'I guess everybody in London wishes it was me that had been killed.' Even in death, he was unable to shake the lifetime habit of comparing himself to his brother.

'Don't be silly, Roger,' Melvyn said.

THE CALL

Over dinner that night, he surveyed his cousin. 'It's like you've won the pools and the lottery in one day, isn't it?' Melvyn said, between mouthfuls. Later, as they walked back to the car past a row of designer shops, he pointed out a handbag his wife would like. In a flash of generosity, Roger insisted on paying for it, settling into his role as the sole heir to Jo Kutchinsky's legendary fortune.

Officially, Dad died with nothing. Just a litany of debts. But 'A Kutchinsky does not die penniless,' Melvyn, who spent a lot of time at Jo's house when Dad was living there, told me. 'I was with Paul a lot. He always had little plastic bags of gems in his pockets. He always had nice watches. The only watch that was ever found was the one that was on him in the accident. I bought it home from Spain in a plastic bag.'

I was too grief-stricken at the time to care. But the murkiness around his finances, and the fact he died without finalising his new will, which would have reinstated his three daughters as his sole beneficiaries, would come back to haunt me during my search for Kutchinsky's egg.

* * *

When it came to Dad's funeral, the combination of bad blood, religious differences and the horror of sudden death turned it into a family battlefield. Shocked into a robotic state, existing but feeling nothing, I sparked into life when in the run-up Uncle Roger tried to stop me from saying a few words and giving a reading. It wasn't tradition, he sneered. Panicked at the idea that Dad might be laid to rest without people hearing how much he was loved, I accosted the rabbi during a visit to Grandpa's house. A warm and sympathetic man, whose own father had married my parents twenty-five years earlier, he agreed to grant my wish.

Now all I had to do was write something coherent and find the right piece of prose to read. This was easier said than done, I discovered, when your emotions are pinballing around at high speed. Mum had rented a flat in London, through friends, so we could all be together but I kept returning to my student house in Oxford, seeking escape. Unable to sleep one night, squeezing the fluffy Eeyore my friends had bought me for comfort, a passage popped into my head that meant something to Dad. Jumping up, I wrestled a small, hardback tome, that he had given me as a child, off the shelf, where it was squeezed between my history textbooks, and flicked through it impatiently until I found the words I was searching for.

The day of the funeral dawned drizzly and cold. In the run-up, my sisters and I also had to fight to have Mum sit with us in the chapel, as it was common practice at Jewish funerals that the front row was reserved for the immediate family, and as the ex-wife, my grandfather's view was that Mum didn't qualify. At eighteen and twenty, Katrina and I were older, but Hollie was only thirteen and it seemed cruel to make her face such trauma without Mum by her side. In the end, Grandpa Jo gave in and the four of us stood grasping each other's hands, our knuckles whitening, as Dad's simple coffin was wheeled in on an iron cart. 'They brought him in on a wheelbarrow,' Katrina recalled. 'It was more like an old-fashioned trailer that horses would pull,' corrected Hollie. 'Plain black. Very bare.'

I don't remember the trailer. But I do remember the dizzying panic that hit me when I realised Dad was in that box. He was there, but he was gone. As the sing-song intonation of the rabbi's voice rose above the wails of the crowd of more than a hundred mourners, I felt an out-of-body sensation akin to extreme drunkenness. Maybe it was all a terrible mistake. Maybe he was still in Spain. Maybe we would soon see him sauntering down the aisle, pulling on his blue kippah, grinning at having pulled off such a successful prank.

At the back of the packed chapel, another drama was playing out. Anna had arrived. Dressed in black, visibly pregnant with Richard's child, she looked haunted. She had come to say goodbye. But her attempt to slip in unnoticed failed, and during the service, Jimmy Thomas and his family, who were standing behind the rows of chairs, shuffled backwards, creating a wave that edged Anna out into the foyer.

Mum had made it clear beforehand that she didn't want her there. 'She destroyed your father. If it hadn't been for her and that bloody egg, he'd still be here.' But at that moment, standing in front of the packed chapel, desperate to avert my eyes from Dad's coffin, I found myself searching for Anna's face. After Kutchinsky's egg was gone, her love had become the life raft keeping Dad afloat, until she pulled it away and left him to drown. And yet, despite everything, I felt he would have wanted her there. I must have seen her when I stood up to do my speech, because I can picture her now, her pregnant belly swelling beneath her black dress.

I used to say that delivering my speech that day was the hardest thing I'd ever done. And it was, until I decided to find Kutchinsky's egg. Reading the eulogy now, it's not much of a tribute. None of his triumphs were mentioned, no funny stories recounted to lighten the mood. Desperate not to further upset Mum, I avoided making any reference to his great golden egg, his world record fame or his ambition to be the modern Carl Fabergé. Instead, it was steeped in the outrage of unexpected loss. I struggled to finish, my words strangled by sobs. Mum leapt up and rushed to my side. Desperate not to let Dad down, I read the passage that had drifted through my mind during that sleepless, grief-stricken night. 'It's about a dreamer,' I said 'and it's called *Jonathan Livingston Seagull* by Richard Bach.'

The original cover of this celebrated fable is deceptively simple, like the book itself. It features a stylised photograph of a seagull, its chalky, white silhouette framed against an inky blue background. When I read it again before Dad's funeral, I saw in it a coded message about his motivation for making Kutchinsky's egg. The hero of Bach's story is Jonathan, a seagull who develops a passion for flying, while the rest of his flock peck and squawk around for food. Exiled for being different, he soars ever higher, finding fulfilment and purpose in the purity of flight. It's a tale aimed at those, like Dad, who follow their hearts and make their own rules, whatever the consequences.

> 'You will begin to touch heaven, Jonathan, in the moment that you touch perfect speed. And that isn't flying a thousand miles an hour, or a million, or flying at the speed of light. Because any number is a limit, and perfection doesn't have limits. Perfect speed, my son, is being there.'

I didn't go to the grave that day. Mum spared my sisters and me that horror, despite it being tradition. Looking back, perhaps she needed space to give in to grief, unfettered by parental concern. I later found out from her friend Philippa, that as they walked behind the coffin, Mum broke down and started desperately calling Dad's name. 'I've never seen anything like that love,' Philippa said, still moved by the memory. 'She was holding my arm so tight, it was completely bruised. It was an unbelievable love.'

Later that day at the shiva (the Jewish wake), as sorrow turned to alcohol-fuelled nostalgia, stories were shared and tales told, but nobody spoke a word about Kutchinsky's egg. It was as if Dad's greatest creation was buried with him.

*   *   *

Eight months later, we attended another funeral. Jo Kutchinsky's official cause of death was pancreatic cancer, but we all knew that the pain of outliving his son was too much to bear. Grief had wrapped itself around my grandfather like a parasitic weed, squeezing out any lingering goodness. Losing the business and Lily in rapid succession had hit him hard but he'd carried on living, clinging to the vestiges of his humanity. His grand, gloomy house had become a shrine to his dead wife. Long after she was gone, her clothes still filled the wardrobes, her scent hung in the musty air and her jewellery sat unloved in drawers. Jo never moved on, but he survived – until his son's death shattered him, slipping a noose around his neck. I can still picture him, slumped in a brown leather armchair, his hand curled around a crystal whisky tumbler, drinking himself to death. Ever since Lily died, he'd been averaging about a litre of whisky a day and Paul's death tipped him into oblivion. 'He was crying like a baby at your dad's funeral,' David O'Connor recalled, his voice trembling. 'It was terrible to see a grown man so broken.'

KUTCHINSKY'S EGG

Jo's death was marked by notices in the *Jewish Chronicle*, as was customary. The main tribute was written by Roger:

Kutchinsky, Joseph passed away peacefully on Thursday, October 26, aged 85 after tragedy and illness so bravely borne. He is now at rest reunited with his beloved 'Choochie' and son Paul. His strength of character and warmth will be dearly missed by his loving son, Roger, daughter-in-law Yvette, granddaughters Tanya and Natasha and all those who had the privilege of knowing him.

There was no reference to us in the cluster of notices that followed from various family members, who all sent their condolences to our cousins. It was as if we were being erased.

Grandpa's funeral was an austere affair and one which hammered home our outsider status. The Orthodox service was conducted primarily in Hebrew, a language we didn't speak, and men and women were segregated, which I found jarring. The hostilities evoked by Dad's funeral lingered between us and the rest of the Kutchinskys. Feeling the sting of his absence, we didn't linger at the shiva, which this time was held at Uncle Roger's house. The only person who remembers that day clearly is Hollie. Uncle Roger tried to talk to her but she rebuffed him. That was the last time any of us spoke to him.

While Jo's death wasn't a shock, what happened after was. From beyond the grave, my grandfather had laid out one last manoeuvre. Three weeks after Dad's death, he had changed his will, valued at £1.5 million (about £3 million today), making Roger the sole beneficiary and leaving nothing to us, not even a keepsake. All we merited was this sharp-edged sentence: 'I have decided for personal reasons not to leave any part of my estate to the children of my late son, Paul Samuel Kutchinsky.'

Why did Jo Kutchinsky, whose creed was always family first, so brutally disinherit his grandchildren?

Before Dad died, Jo, who had become crabby and curmudgeonly, would often bemoan his children's shortcomings. 'I have two sons,' he would sigh dramatically. 'Paul's a *ganef* (a thief) and the other, Roger, is a numbskull.'

He loved his children, they were his blood, but he knew their natures; after all, he and Lily created them. Jo had no moral code; it's what made him such a wiley businessman. He was a liar, a swindler and a smuggler. After he died, people shared stories about his more nefarious activities including his involvement in a diamond cartel. Batches of the world's finest gems would regularly be shipped from Siberia, where they were mined, to London's Docklands. While most of the stones passed legitimately through customs, several thousands of carats were lobbed over the side of the boat and caught by divers sent out by an East End gem dealer who sold them on to Jo. In later years, it's rumoured that Jo befriended the head of security at a major UK airport who regularly helped him smuggle jewellery into the country.

If Dad was a thief, he took after his father. Jo taught him everything he'd learned in the East End, and turned a blind eye to most of his son's misdemeanours, but the crime he could never forgive him for was bringing down the House of Kutchinsky with what he saw as a vanity project. Jo blunted his anger with booze, leaving it to curdle below the surface. 'I never wanted it,' he snarled, whenever Paul mentioned the egg. 'If you weren't my son, I'd have put you in prison.'

But Paul was his son, and so he forgave him. Later, their mutual loneliness brought them back under the same roof. When he was stuck for cash, Paul would sell off some of his late mother's jewellery, keeping it off the books to avoid inheritance tax, giving Jo a cut and ploughing the rest back into PK Limited. During this time, a cousin who was visiting from America, Judy Wolkovitch, asked Jo for help selling a stash of diamonds she'd been left by her father-in-law. He delegated the task to Paul, who successfully sold the stones for £140,000, ensuring discretion by using a diamond dealer outside Hatton Garden. Before Paul died, he handed over about £100,000 to Jo, meaning there was still £40,000 unaccounted for. Since there was no record of the sale, and nobody knew the name of the mysterious gem dealer, there was no way of tracing the money.

After Paul's death, Jo was incandescent with rage. 'Somebody must know something,' he seethed. He was adamant that he'd given Paul other 'bits and pieces' to sell, including some more diamonds and twelve bars of platinum (worth about £300,000 today). Did he believe the *ganef* had struck again? He wouldn't have put anything past his son; after all, Paul had stolen from him before. But when they checked the office safe and the safe deposit box he still shared with Anna, which was stashed in a Hatton Garden bank, they were empty save for a large set of silver cutlery which Anna, who knew nothing about the extra diamonds and platinum bars, returned to Jo. Paul hadn't planned to die, so it didn't make sense – why would he have cleaned everything out?

Determined to get some answers, Jo hired a private detective. One theory was that Dad had opened a new safe deposit box under a fake name but there was no record of it anywhere.

THE CALL

When his bedroom was searched, a bag of white powder and a collection of porn movies were found hidden in his wardrobe. Jo handed the detective photographs of women whom Dad had been close to and told him to make enquiries. Among the rumours circulating was the notion that Dad had been selling cocaine to his rich tennis club friends.

In the end, it was Roger who found the £40,000, stuffed in the back of Dad's dresser. When it was counted, thousands of pounds were missing. I assume he spent some of it celebrating his birthday and used the rest to maintain his wealthy lifestyle. Now, it makes sense why he told me to hide the cash he gave me that day in Oxford, under my bed. It was stolen money.

Did Jo decide that his son's final act of theft was too much and that Paul's children should pay the price? Personally, I suspect my grandfather's obsession with the missing money was a diversion from the brutality of his son's sudden death. He was also drinking so much by this point that perhaps his memory was blurred and some of it was a hallucination. There was also the 'Brenda issue', as Jo called it. Oblivious, Mum paid the old man a final visit after Dad's funeral. Despite all the bad blood, she was conscious Jo had lost his son and wanted to check on him before flying back to Scotland. Just after she arrived, the phone rang. Speaking in Yiddish, Jo said he needed a visit from Brenda like a '*lokh in kop*' (a hole in the head). Mum had studied German at school and understood the meaning. 'I went mad,' she said, her voice rising at the memory. 'How dare he speak about me like that? After what I'd been put through by his son and his family! I was furious.'

Jo tried to bluster his way out of it. But the damage was done. Sitting there, in that living room where so many scenes from her life had played out, Mum had snapped. She stormed out of the house and never saw him again, although she encouraged Katrina to visit him in hospital when he was dying. In her eyes, there was no distinction between her as the ex-wife and us as the grandchildren; we were intermingled and inseparable, and so any slight to her was a slight to us.

'We were cast into the wasteland,' Mum said bitterly. 'We weren't Jewish. We weren't anything to him.'

It was the final severance between us and the rest of the House of Kutchinsky, but the break had been a long time coming. Dad's death was a release in a weird sort of way. I had started to sense that beneath the bad jokes and bravado he had given up, and at least I was no longer the outsider with Mum and my sisters. At the time, I rolled my eyes whenever he mentioned finally selling his egg, dismissing it as a sign of his ongoing mid-life crisis. Now, at almost that same age, I understand the panic he felt. Time was running out; if he left it any longer, he would have to accept that far from being the next Carl Fabergé, he was a fifty-year-old failure.

16

THE FINDING

Being a writer was always my goal, but it took time for me to realise it was Dad's story I needed to tell. Looking back, it's as if an invisible thread was pulling me back into my family's past, back beyond the people I had known and to my earlier ancestors nearly a 150 years ago. In the mid-noughties, I unknowingly moved to the part of London where my great-grandfather Moshe first established the House of Kutchinsky, where the story began. I had thought, perhaps, that this was all ancient history, best left in the past, best forgotten. It took the jolt of nearly losing someone else I loved, fifteen years after Dad, for me to realise that there were ghosts from my past that I needed to confront, before it was too late.

Alex Allen was kind and handsome but without the ego that often makes pretty men poisonous. We'd circled blindly around each other for two decades, sharing the same friends, attending the same weddings and parties but only meeting at the perfect moment when both of us were single and ready for a relationship. Our first proper date was at Notting Hill Carnival in 2015. He turned up to meet me with a box of fresh strawberries and a bottle of bubbles. As we danced through the crowded, colourful streets he kissed me and told me I was beautiful, and I felt giddy and light. Then, after three blissful weeks, I nearly lost him.

That September morning, he left my flat shouting, 'Goodbye, beautiful Serena,' as he skipped down the stairs. Still in bed, I pulled the duvet over me, savouring his warmth. The accident happened about seven hours later, as he was driving back from a work meeting in Brighton. It was raining apocalyptically when his car broke down on a busy bend. A relatively new driver, surrounded by cars travelling at high speed, Alex was paralysed by fear. Before he had time to get out and call for help, a large lorry, transporting broken down cars, slammed into the back of his small, stationary Fiat Punto.

When I first got the call from his flatmate, I assumed the worst. I knew how this story ended. Desperate for news, I rushed round to their shared flat in North London, despite having never met them before. That was the first night I spent in his bed, curled up in one of his t-shirts, breathing in his smell.

I awoke the next morning, determined to visit him in hospital in Brighton. He had broken his neck in three places and suffered a severe brain injury. The editor of the current affairs magazine I was working on was confused when I called to explain my absence. 'What boyfriend?' she replied, clearly thinking I was making it up. However crazy it was, I was already in love and acting on instinct. The surrealness of it all intensified when in the intensive care unit, the doctor went round his family, asking who we all were. When he got to me, I paused. 'Girlfriend, I think?'

When Alex awoke, he disagreed. Memories of our short

time together had vanished from his bruised brain and nobody knew if they would come back. As the weeks passed, he grew stronger but still showed no signs of recognising me – until I found myself unexpectedly alone with him on a Friday night, sitting next to his hospital bed. At a loss for what to say, I started telling him the story of Kutchinsky's egg. Suddenly, out of nowhere, he reached for my hand. 'Where's your dad's egg now?' he asked, staring at me, his big brown eyes sparkling. I just shrugged and shook my head, feeling bad for disappointing him.

Later, he walked me to the door of the ward and kissed me goodbye. 'Your dad was amazing, just like his daughter,' he said, making me blush in front of the hospital staff. 'If anyone can find his egg, it's you.' I walked home to my flat, smiling; it had felt almost like our first kiss but had meant so much more. Lying in bed that night, my sleep-hazy mind intertwined romantic scenes with Alex with memories of the Scotsman I had met at Glastonbury, all those years ago. I awoke with a start, remembering the early morning pledge I'd made to keep telling Dad's story. It was time.

After three long months, Alex was released back into the real world. As he recovered and came back to me, I couldn't shake the feeling it was a sign that anything was possible. Our relationship moved fast. Two years after the accident, our first child, Caspian Paul Allen-Kutchinsky, was born. We bought a house. Then in August 2018, we got married on Alex's mother's alpaca farm in Devon, three years to the day that we met.

Kutchinsky's egg was still lost but I no longer was and, for a while, that was enough. I avoided talking about the egg and if anyone brought it up, I would stutter out a hail of excuses as to why I'd abandoned my search. After our second child was born – beautiful, dark-haired Finlo who looked as eerily similar to me as I did to Dad – we moved house again, in the midst of the global Covid pandemic, and I put the photo of Kutchinsky's egg that I'd always kept on the mantelpiece away in a drawer and tried to focus on family life, and forget.

Then, in June 2022, I was made redundant from my job at a youth-orientated digital publisher, a depressingly common occurrence in journalism these days. It was an anxious time but gave me the space to confront my great unfinished task, the photo in the drawer, the father I had faded out. Kutchinsky's egg. I avoided telling Mum about my decision to reopen my investigation, fearful of the family strife it would spark. The previous year, when I had plucked up the courage to tell Katrina I'd made contact with Anna, she'd gone ballistic, framing it as the ultimate betrayal. She had called me selfish, and in a sense, she was right. But I was determined to reclaim the egg, transforming it from a source of shame into a symbol of pride – not just for me but for my whole family.

Eventually, I was connected with David Fardon, now the CEO of a jewellery company in Western Australia, who became the egg's babysitter after it left our workshop. Talking to him was like unlocking a human archive. Ruddy-cheeked, bespectacled and precise, Fardon regaled me with his memories of the egg and its adventures over a series of video calls.

After the House of Kutchinsky was sold, the egg had continued its globetrotting. During an exhibition hosted by Argyle in New York, it had broken again and Gerald had been summoned across the ocean to fix it. For its swansong, it travelled to Seville for Expo '92, a sprawling universal exhibition which welcomed 41 million visitors over six months. The egg was the single most expensive item on show and the star attraction of the Australia pavilion.

While the Expo put the southern Spanish city on the map as a tourist destination, for Kutchinsky's egg it was almost the end of the road. It had become overexposed; a glittering albatross, hanging around the neck of its owner and racking up unsustainable costs. Sometime in the mid-Nineties, Argyle decided the best option was for the egg to go dark. For about a decade, Kutchinsky's egg was secreted away in a bonded warehouse, a facility that helps those importing high-value items to avoid paying customs duties. It was rarely visited and faded from view.

Behind the scenes, Argyle still harboured hopes of a sale but as the years passed, and even enquiries from con artists dried up, they started to accept defeat. Then, two years after Dad died, the call came. There was interest, and this time it was serious.

Whispers of a giant jewelled egg, made in the Fabergé tradition and encrusted with cherry blossom diamonds, had reached the ear of a secretive billionaire, known for his extravagant tastes. A mood of cautious excitement pervaded Argyle's Perth headquarters. Once they established the enquiry wasn't a hoax, and the agent making the call was acting on behalf of one of Japan's richest men, they sprung into action. At some point in 2002, Kutchinsky's unsellable egg was sold. By a margin of just two years, my dad wasn't here to see it happen.

But the information Fardon declined to offer up was the thing I most desired: the identity of the egg's purchaser. Client confidentiality was everything in the jewellery trade, he reiterated. Until finally, he realised I wasn't giving up and admitted there was somebody who might be able to help. An old contact who had been involved in the sale and might be able to get a letter to the mysterious owner. Promising to speak to him and report back soon, Fardon ended our video call.

But the answer, when it came, was bad news. The billionaire owner, whose name he still declined to share with me, had died some time ago and nobody knew what fate had befallen the egg. Fardon's tone as he relayed this information was solemn, his manner suggesting it was time for me to admit defeat and move on. 'I've drawn a bit of a blank,' he said, adding that neither he nor his contact had links to any of the family members. The trail had gone cold.

I was devastated. What if Kutchinsky's egg had been melted down? In 2020, the Argyle mine ceased production, sending the value of its pink diamonds stratospheric. Its rare gems were now more in demand than ever, and it was very possible that the owner's offspring had seen dollar signs and decided to sell off its stones. Alternatively, it could have been sold discreetly into another private collection and vanished into the ether.

Trying not to feel downhearted, I turned to an art detective. These Indiana Jones-like figures investigate high-profile art crimes, often working alongside the police to help return lost or stolen artworks. They understand the criminal networks that allow hugely valuable pieces to be transferred between countries without leaving a trace. While I had no reason to suspect the egg had fallen into malevolent hands, I was looking for advice on how to locate it.

Chris Marinello answered my call. An American based in London, he was an amateur artist and former lawyer with salt and pepper hair and a piercing blue-eyed stare who, in the course of his career, recouped hundreds of millions of pounds' worth of stolen luxury goods including Rolexes and Ferraris, a Matisse looted by the Nazis and ancient illuminated manuscripts. 'Everything is possible – it depends what level you want to go to,' he said. His work typically consisted of wrangling with governments, galleries and private individuals who were in possession of stolen artworks. Since the egg had been legitimately sold, my case fell outside Chris's remit. My best bet, he explained, would be a global firm of investigators called Kroll, who specialised in this type of conundrum, but they would charge me tens of thousands of pounds, which I didn't have.

I was determined to find another way but weeks turned into months and my quest seemed to have stalled once more. In the end, it was a call to Barry Turner, the former policeman who had helped Dad hijack the egg from de Vroomen, which determined my course of action. He was eighty now and in a wheelchair, but his mind was still sharp. 'Kroll will find it for you,' he said, unprompted. It seemed I had no choice but to follow my grandparents' example and engage private investigators.

In November 2022, I contacted the Kroll UK office. Conscious that they normally work with government agencies, law firms and high net-worth individuals, my plan was to pretend I could afford their services, in the hope that by the time they realised I couldn't, the eccentric nature of my request might have engaged their interest. I sent a message through the contact form on their website. A few days later, a response arrived, asking me to outline my enquiry. Once they had got to grips with my case, Jonathan, one of their UK directors, would consult with their Tokyo office and draw up a rough quote. Reasoning that it was worth a shot, I sent it over and waited.

Then a Christmas miracle happened. The night before we were due to leave to spend the festive period in Devon with Alex's family, an email arrived from one of Kroll's UK directors, Jonathan Harman. I was frantically packing and almost missed it. Racing upstairs to the loft, I opened my laptop. I still remember how I felt when I read it – the chill of disbelief that spread through my nervous system; the shiver down my spine that electrified the hairs on my neck. Kroll's scoping research had revealed a golden nugget of information. The Argyle Library Egg was no longer privately owned. It had been sold to an art museum in Japan and was rumoured to be going on show to the public in 2025. But, cautioned Jonathan, that didn't mean it would be easy to find. It was common practice, he explained, among Japanese art museums to keep the purchase of high-value items secret until they exhibited them.

As I ran downstairs to share the news with Alex, I tried to ignore the eye-watering quote of £16,500 that accompanied this bombshell. If I wanted to find the egg's exact location and trace its previous owner, it would cost me dear. This was the closest I'd ever come but there were still obstacles in my path. There were about 600 art museums in Japan. Even if I did find the right one, there was no guarantee they would let me see it while it was locked in a vault. The thought of waiting another three years for it to be on public display made me want to weep from frustration.

For the next seven months, I exhausted every option to

avoid pouring thousands of pounds into what could easily be another dead end. A Japanese researcher – recommended by a journalist friend of Chris Marinello – helped me begin the painstaking task of contacting every art museum where it might have landed. But each came back with a similar response: they had never heard of the Argyle Library Egg by Kutchinsky. My frustration was intense.

Eventually, I gave in and contacted Kroll again. They arranged a meeting for me with the man who had given me that glimmer of hope, Tadashi Kageyama, managing director in their Central Asia office, based in Singapore. As I sat fidgeting in front of my laptop, a smartly dressed man in a navy suit and tie appeared on the screen, blinking behind his gold-rimmed glasses. Warm and friendly, he put me immediately at ease. He had stumbled across this information on the egg by pure chance, Tadashi (who goes by Tad) explained in his mellifluous transatlantic accent. When he first heard about my search, Tad reached out to a friend in the art world and asked whether he'd ever heard of a giant jewelled egg. By some extraordinary stroke of luck, he struck gold – the friend not only recognised the object but knew the very person who had brokered its sale to the museum. Tad had kept that first conversation with his contact brief. But, he asked gently, with what I would later come to recognise as his signature discretion, would it be alright to share my family story, and my name, in the hope of finding out more specific details?

Suddenly I found myself weeping. I had told myself repeatedly it didn't matter if the egg stayed lost. That Dad would be proud of me for even getting this far. But I knew I was lying.

'It's wonderful after so long, after so many dead ends,' I

sniffed, my voice trembling. 'Tell your friend that I lost my father over twenty years ago and never got to say goodbye. The egg is the only piece of him I have left. It would be like seeing him again, in a way. I don't want to buy it or anything. I just want to see it.'

Wiping my eyes, I took a breath. Over the past year, I'd become well versed in the language of the super-rich. 'I could sign an NDA or whatever was required . . . It's just about that emotional moment.'

Tad nodded. Normally, he explained, Kroll's information would be obtained via open-source intelligence work, interviews with art collectors and galleries in Japan, and even some 'underground elements' who broker illegal sales of such artefacts. That was the work Kroll's original quote was based on. But in this case, luck had intervened early on. 'These things don't happen every day,' Tad said. 'We were very, very fortunate.' For the first time, instead of another closed door, someone was saying yes. They weren't going to help me for free, but we agreed on an hourly rate that I could just about afford.

After that, there was silence. For two months, I heard almost nothing. My emails went unanswered. I went about the motions of daily life, working – I had started a new job at Sky News – and parenting. Finally, in early September, Tad replied. He'd been on holiday and then fallen ill with Covid-19. He apologised and then dropped another bombshell. His contact had discovered that the egg was due to go on display for a short period at the end of the coming month rather than in 2025, but due to security concerns, its location was still unknown. Shocked, I read his email over and over,

THE FINDING

then began frantically searching the internet for news of this forthcoming exhibition. I also checked in with the Japanese researcher. Surely, the re-emergence of this priceless treasure would have attracted the attention of the media in Japan? But there was nothing. I had no choice but to trust Tad and hope his information was correct.

Life seemed to speed up. Within two weeks, Tad had an answer. The egg wasn't in an art museum. Instead, it had been donated to the National Museum of Nature and Science in Tokyo, which at first glance seemed a strange home for a giant jewelled artwork. And there was more good news. The egg's new guardian, the museum's head of geological research, Mr Ritsuro Miyawaki, had offered to give me a private viewing, on a day when the museum was shut to the public. It would only be on show for a short period (23 October to 5 November 2023), after which it would be locked away again, while they raised the funds to cover the cost of having it on permanent display – the conservation, security and sheer logistics of exhibiting such a treasure – a process which could take up to a decade. News of the exhibition would be kept a closely guarded secret until just days before it opened.

I was going to Tokyo.

* * *

As I prepared for what lay ahead, I began piecing together a timeline of the egg's improbable journey – from the depths of an Australian diamond mine to Japan's National Museum of Nature and Science. At my desk, surrounded by piles of books, battered catalogues and faded photographs, I traced its path alongside the milestones of my own life, slowly reclaiming

Dad's creation as part of our family's story. But there was still a significant missing chapter in the egg's story: the mysterious billionaire who had first bought the egg from Argyle.

Just then, a message from Tad blinked onto my screen, breaking the spell. I had been so deep in the past, I'd momentarily forgotten the present. I opened the email and gasped. There, in stark black and white, was the name of the elusive donor – the billionaire whose father had once bought Kutchinsky's egg and who had now donated it to the museum. The final missing chapter was falling into place.

Back in 2002, Argyle was approached by Uchihara, a prestigious Tokyo jeweller, whose story mirrored that of the House of Kutchinsky – it was an almost hundred-year-old family-run firm that had begun as a watch- and clockmaker. They were acting on behalf of their client, Kenichi Mabuchi, the head of one of Japan's wealthiest families whose fortune stemmed from producing small motors for consumer electronics; at that time, the company he co-owned with his brother controlled more than 50 per cent of the global market. The Chairman, as he was known, was an eccentric character and fearsome businessman, with a magpie-like fascination for sparkly objects.

In the early noughties, an ambitious salesman I'll refer to as Mr M, employed by the prestigious Takashimaya department store, set out to win the business of Chairman Mabuchi. He made regular visits to the Mabuchi family mansion in Matsudo, a quiet suburb of the capital, catering to the billionaire's every whim. Rails of designer clothes were delivered, along with lavish jewellery for his wife, while the Chairman himself requested expensive artworks, fine furnishings and a constant supply of his favourite rare tuna. Over time, the billionaire started asking Mr M to source ever more expensive, extraordinary items. Then in February 2002, the Chairman expressed his wish to own an incomparable piece of jewelled art. 'I don't want a ten-carat diamond, or even a fifty-carat diamond,' he said, smacking his lips. 'I want to own something that has a history.'

The first call Mr M made was to the Uchihara sales team, where the challenge was taken up by the owner's son, Ichiro Uchihara, an energetic man with strong eyebrows and a warm laugh. In his mid-thirties at the time, Ichiro contacted everyone he knew in the jewellery trade in Japan, to no avail. Then he reached out to all their foreign suppliers. Still nothing.

Pink diamonds were hugely popular in Japan, with the market fuelled by the relative proximity of the Argyle mine. But the connection wasn't made until during a routine meeting with the Australians, Mr Mabuchi's unusual request cropped up in conversation. I imagine the eyes of the Australian sales executives lighting up as they glimpsed an opportunity.

When Ichiro first heard of a giant jewelled egg, designed by a famous London jeweller, he was overjoyed. Finally, he had found something that might seduce the Chairman. But his elation was short-lived. 'It's not for sale,' Argyle told him, deploying the classic sales tactic of playing hard to get, while they checked the Chairman wasn't a member of the yakuza. But once Argyle had agreed to discuss a sale, Ichiro feared he was out of his depth. His family knew all about selling diamonds but dealing with a treasure on this scale, with all the costs and logistics involved, was a different challenge.

A glossy sales booklet in Japanese was hastily compiled and

KUTCHINSKY'S EGG

sent to Chairman Mabuchi, showcasing the egg's eye-popping statistics. Within a week, the Chairman's secretary confirmed his interest. He wanted to see the egg. Calculating the cost of transporting this multi-million-pound object 4,000 miles and storing it securely, Ichiro wondered if he was making a mistake.

'Just do it,' ruled his father, Keisuke, who, on the cusp of retirement, had decided that selling the egg would be his final achievement.

Kutchinsky's egg arrived in Tokyo in May 2002, its future still uncertain. It was whisked away to Brink's, a high-security facility in Ueno, a part of Tokyo famed for its museums and leafy park. But when Ichiro went to check the egg was in working order, he got a shock. Its big gold doors refused to open. Panicking, he called Argyle. The Chairman could request a viewing at any moment, he exclaimed, stressing the urgency of the situation. Argyle needed to send people to fix it, and fast. Two technicians were immediately dispatched from Australia and worked their magic. Finally, Kutchinsky's egg was ready.

A month passed, during which the Chairman continued to place orders for expensive items from Mr M, but the egg was never mentioned. As the huge cost of storing it at Brink's mounted, Ichiro again feared his gamble on the egg might end in disaster. Would Uchihara be the second family business to lose its painstakingly built century-old reputation to the egg?

Then a summons arrived from the Chairman. He wanted the egg to be brought to his guest house – a palatial Versailles-inspired annexe that looked out across the Japanese gardens bordering his home. Calling it a guest house does it a disservice. It had space to house twenty to thirty guests, with each assigned their own personal maid. Split between a European-style salon and a more traditional Japanese parlour, the decor was a riot of Renaissance kitsch. Gold was everywhere. The elegant furniture was gilt-edged, the doors were painted white and gold, gold-leaf light fittings twisted their way up the matching walls, a baby grand piano nestled in a corner framed by gold-fringed curtains and vast chandeliers twinkled overhead. It couldn't have been a more perfect fit for Kutchinsky's egg.

It was a warm and humid June day, when the armoured truck containing the egg pulled up outside the Mabuchi mansion. Awaiting its arrival were a top Uchihara salesman, Mr Fuji, and Mr M from Takashimaya. Their job was to install the egg on its pedestal and test the electronics so there were no unpleasant surprises. To their great relief, the doors slid open but as they inspected the doll's house-like interior, Mr Fuji let out a cry. The tiny, jewelled clock on the bookcase had stopped working. His heart racing, he telephoned his boss who was still at the office.

The battery must have run out, Ichiro said, sounding calmer than he felt. The only option was to run to the nearest shop, buy a tiny quartz battery and pray it fitted. Miraculously, Mr Fuji found one and raced back with minutes to spare. I picture him sweating, his fingers trembling, as he teased the clock out and slotted in the new battery. It worked! Disaster averted.

Shortly after, Ichiro arrived at the guest house, taking his place at the back alongside several Argyle representatives and members of the Mabuchi household. Perched on a narrow settee, the Chairman watched in silence, an inscrutable expression on his face, as the golden shell parted to reveal its wow factor: the sparkling pink library giving way to the cornflower blue hues of the portrait gallery. Then he smiled and politely dismissed them, expressing a desire to talk to his family. Ichiro returned to the office without an answer. The egg returned to Brink's, still in limbo.

A few weeks of nerve-wracking silence followed. Aware they were going up against one of Japan's most brilliant business minds, Uchihara and Argyle agreed an initial asking price of about 1.5 billion yen (about £8 million in 2002). But the message from the Chairman when it came was decisive: he wanted Kutchinsky's egg but would offer no more than 800 million yen. Take it or leave it. In 2002, that totalled about £4.3 million. When Ichiro heard the news, he turned pale. His firm had incurred huge costs bringing the egg to Japan. Once Argyle took their share, they would have made a loss. He shook his head. How did this happen? Should he refuse the offer, or should he take the hit?

It took Ichiro just five minutes to decide. Reasoning that it was 'more for the achievement rather than the making or losing of money', he said yes but neglected to share the final sale price with his father, who he feared might not take it in such good humour.

The deal was done. The final hurdle was the Chairman's request that a new display cabinet with bulletproof glass be built to show off his treasure. Ichiro and his staff scrambled to find the right person to make it at short notice. In the end, it cost the Chairman a further 2 million yen and was completed with days to spare.

While it was being built, a horrific tragedy befell the

THE FINDING

Mabuchi family. If you were superstitious, you might think the curse of Kutchinsky's egg had struck once again. In August 2002, a robbery took a deadly twist when the wife and daughter of the Chairman's younger brother, Takaichi, were brutally murdered in their home; thieves strangled Etsuko, sixty-six, and Yuka, forty, and made off with jewellery worth millions of yen and a pile of cash. To cover their tracks, they set the house on fire before fleeing the scene. It was several years before the men were finally caught and sentenced to death under Japanese law.

At first, it was believed the killers were acting out a deep personal grudge against the Mabuchi family. But it later transpired that their primary motive was robbery, with the brutal murders carried out to eliminate eyewitnesses. Although there was great media interest in the case, the family rarely spoke publicly of their grief, prizing privacy above all else. Despite this terrible tragedy, the sale of the egg still went ahead, although the delivery was delayed until 1 November 2002. It was a cool, cloudy day when the egg was once again driven over to the Mabuchi mansion in an armoured truck, almost six months after it had first arrived in Tokyo. After twelve years of false starts, it had finally found a home.

David Fardon and his team were standing by the phone in Western Australia when the news came that the delivery had been a success. 'The victory was when the money hit the account,' Fardon had told me, before I knew the identity of the buyer. 'I learned a long time ago: don't count your eggs until they're hatched, and in this case, incubated for quite a period.'

When the Chairman died in 2005, Kutchinsky's egg passed to his eldest son, Takashi Mabuchi and his wife, Reiko. It stayed in the guest house, which Takashi also inherited, and remained out of sight, while rumours swirled of its fate. Confident that few people knew of its existence, the Mabuchis stopped paying the astronomical insurance and instead designed an alarm system for the guest house which was turned on at night.

In 2013, I published an article in the *Sunday Times* about my father's egg and a rumour reached Reiko that Paul Kutchinsky's daughter wanted to buy back the egg. Although she soon realised that this was unfounded, this sparked an idea. Inheritance tax is exceptionally high in Japan, so the Chairman's extensive art collection had cost them dearly when he died. To avoid the same fate befalling their two children, Reiko set about scaling down their assets.

As one of the most expensive items, the egg was top of her list to rehouse. Aiming high, she phoned the British royal family. Might it be possible to return Kutchinsky's egg to its birthplace? For a family of the Mabuchi's wealth and connections, reaching out to royalty, while not an everyday occurrence, was within their grasp. And it wasn't a hard no. Reiko, who exudes a quiet determination, went back and forth with Buckingham Palace for about a year. But in the end the layers of protocol and the language barrier proved insurmountable, and she turned her attention elsewhere.

Around this time, Ichiro Uchihara was brought into the process once again to act as an agent. Finally, he saw a chance to recoup some of the money he had lost on the egg first time round. Deciding that discretion was the key to a successful sale, he eschewed publicity and kept it off the radar.

Over the next decade, a succession of wealthy Americans,

THE FINDING

Chinese, Arabs and Europeans visited the egg. While many marvelled at its craftsmanship and the wonder of its 'magical' mechanism, none were beguiled enough to buy it. The closest it came to being sold was to Princess Isabelle of Liechtenstein, a member of one of Europe's oldest royal families, whose private art collection is almost unrivalled. But the sale fell apart when the princess realised she would have to pay hefty customs duty because the egg was less than a hundred years old.

Around this time, the Mabuchis sold the land on which the guest house sat to a developer, who demolished it. Homeless once again, Kutchinsky's egg was transported across the road to Reiko and Takashi's house and locked away in a store room. At a loss, they left it to gather dust. Then came the Covid pandemic in 2020, and the subsequent travel ban, which extinguished any lingering hopes they might have harboured of selling it.

Then, one morning in June 2022, Reiko sat bolt upright in bed.

'I've got it!' she cried, rolling over to shake her husband awake. 'We must give the egg to the nation.' If they could not sell this extraordinary artefact, perhaps the time had come to let it go – not for profit but for posterity.

As fate would have it, Reiko's eureka moment coincided with the turning point in my own life, when redundancy led me to reignite my search for the egg, no matter what. In the end, I used my severance money to hire Kroll to bring me back into the egg's orbit.

Two paths, once parallel, had finally converged. And for the first time since that long-ago afternoon at the Victoria and Albert Museum, thirty-three years earlier, I was moving steadily toward Dad's creation.

*   *   *

I booked my flights to Tokyo and agreed on a date and time for the viewing at the National Museum of Nature and Science. Then, with just nine days to go before my flight, while I was at work I received a call from Tad that threw the whole trip into jeopardy. There was a problem. The museum staff believed they had evidence that I was a 'bad actor', posing as the creator's daughter to steal the egg. They were taking advice from the Japanese police. Unless I could definitively prove my identity, the meeting was cancelled.

Panicking, I offered to email over scans of my passport and birth certificate as soon as I got home that evening. That wouldn't be enough, I was told, those documents were too easily forgeable. At this stage it wasn't clear if anything would satisfy the museum, a terse-sounding Tad said. Concerned that his art world friend who gave us the lead was now compromised, he advised I cancel my flight and forget about seeing the egg this time.

'Shit,' I muttered under my breath. This couldn't be happening.

Numb, I sank back into my chair, eyes fixed on my phone. The only way out of this absurd mess was to figure out why the museum had suddenly got spooked. A bit of frantic emailing uncovered the cause: a contact working with the *other* Japanese researcher – unaware I had also employed Kroll – had heard a rumour about the egg's whereabouts and made an enquiry on my behalf.

THE FINDING

The problem was, the museum staff had no idea who this person was, or how they knew the egg's location, a detail that hadn't yet appeared in the media or on the museum's website. Panic set in. Though the museum housed tens of thousands of priceless natural artefacts, none had the same glittering allure to criminal networks as Kutchinsky's egg. Fearing a heist, they leapt to the wrong conclusion: someone impersonating me was trying to gain access to the museum while it was closed, with the intention of stealing the egg.

Several days slipped by as I struggled with how best to prove I was indeed Serena Kutchinsky. In desperation, I even phoned the British Embassy in Japan and explained my increasingly surreal predicament.

Originally, I was meant to attend the meeting accompanied only by a translator. But when I floated the idea of having someone from Kroll join me, the museum staff began to soften – slightly. Even so, it wasn't enough to fully put them at ease.

Following Tad's advice, I sent a letter confirming my identity on headed paper from one of my bosses at Sky News. This was rejected by the museum because they couldn't find the name of the editor who signed it on the website. Determined not to give up, I ran into our director's office, garbled out my problem and asked him if I could give him a letter to sign. Luckily, he agreed, and so I fired off a final email, and waited. My flight was due to leave in twenty-four hours.

I awoke the next morning at dawn, checked my email and leapt out of bed with a strangled yowl. The meeting at the museum was on. I hadn't dared to pack, just in case I jinxed myself, so several hours of frenzy ensued. Boarding the plane

KUTCHINSKY'S EGG

later that day, a glimmer of late October sunshine was breaking through the rain-streaked sky. I'd asked Mum and my sisters if they wanted to accompany me on the final stage of my quest, but they'd all declined. While I understood their reluctance to be reunited with an object that carried so much grief and loss, as so often happened when it concerned Dad, I was left alone.

I'd slept badly the night before, my mind tangled in a web of what-ifs. One question lingered above the rest: would the owners — the Mabuchis, as I now knew — be at the museum? In the scramble to prove my identity, I hadn't dared press the staff further on that point.

But as I sank back into my seat and closed my eyes, I found myself hoping they'd be there. I needed to understand what had drawn Chairman Mabuchi to Kutchinsky's egg — why he'd chosen to keep it. It felt like the missing piece in the story, the final chapter of Dad's legacy.

17

CITY OF GHOSTS

28–30 October 2023

A vague sense of dread had haunted me since my arrival in Tokyo. I'd waited for this moment for so long, what if I felt nothing when I finally saw the egg? I had landed two days before the meeting was scheduled, and eager for distraction, I immersed myself in the orderly chaos of the world's most populated city, wandering through streets filled with the colourful kitsch of Halloween. In the Japanese capital, this spooky celebration is a four-day carnival of street parties and late-night revelry. I'd been warned that staying in the love hotel-infested district of Shibuya would put me in the centre of the costumed crowds, which I welcomed. It felt right to be celebrating ghosts at the end of my hunt.

But there was an authoritarian twist to Halloween that year, with street signs ordering partygoers to stay away. The heavy police presence with officers shouting into megaphones added to my unease, although it did little to stop people swarming the streets at night. A deadly crush had occurred the previous year in Seoul, South Korea, where 150 people were killed while celebrating Halloween. Fearful that a similar disaster might occur on the famous Shibuya Crossing (a pulsating intersection across which thousands of people swarmed from all directions, neon signs flashing above their heads), the Tokyo authorities ordered a crackdown.

Feeling like a character in a video game, I wandered the crowded streets and narrow alleys, soaking up the city's distinct blend of tradition and hi-tech futurism, unable to shake the out-of-body feeling that had persisted since I boarded the express from Narita Airport into the city. I'd been so wrapped up in the 'will they, won't they' drama with the museum, I'd barely thought about Dad. What would it have been like to be here with him? I could imagine him joking about 'Kutchinsky and daughter taking Tokyo' and insisting I upgrade my bog-standard hotel, but aside from that my mind was blank.

At first, I tried to drink my way out of the fog. I got lost and wandered into a cosy izakaya, where I ordered a glass of expensive red wine. As costumed revellers streamed past the window dressed as everything from samurais to the Super Mario brothers, I made a silent toast to Dad, thanking him for this adventure. Tears trickled down my cheeks, but it was as if my jet-lagged emotions were out of sync. I went to two therapy sessions after Dad died but stopped because it was making me feel worse. Instead, I buried my sadness and focused on survival. And now, two decades later, I'd taken myself thousands of miles around the world to see an inanimate object that I'd convinced myself was the embodiment of him. The absurdity of it almost made me laugh.

The following evening, the night before my meeting at the museum, I went to see the city's shimmering sprawl from above to get a sense of its scale. Joining the long queue to ascend the world's tallest tower, the Tokyo Skytree, I nursed my hangover with a matcha tea ice cream, its earthy green swirls bold against the black sesame cone. The panoramic view from the observation deck was stomach-flipping; a galaxy of lights unfurled below, stretching endlessly into the inky blackness, while above my head, trippy cartoons played on loop. It was bonkers but I loved it. The old and the new clashing together, just like the influences that forged Kutchinsky's egg.

*   *   *

The big day dawned, beguilingly summer-like with sunshine and blue skies. I set off for the museum just before lunchtime, clamping my headphones over my ears to drown out the city's hubbub. That morning, I'd put on a black dress, which looked more expensive than it was, and black sandals. Aware that my outfit was slightly funereal, I added some bright coral lipstick and adorned myself with the few pieces of Kutchinsky jewellery I owned: a slim gold necklace with emerald beads, a vintage watch with a black leather strap and a bracelet of gold bears with diamond eyes that Dad made for a childhood birthday.

I still didn't know if the Mabuchis would be at the museum. I tried to brush it off, telling myself it would be enough to see Dad's creation up close, but I knew I'd be disappointed if I didn't catch a glimpse of the egg's most recent chapter. The story of a precious object begins with its creator but it moves on, capturing different moments in time and telling different tales. In Tokyo, Kutchinsky's egg became Mabuchi's egg. Did the Chairman see a bit of himself reflected back in it, just as Dad had all those years ago?

The Museum of Nature and Science is a dignified art-deco building nestled in Ueno Park. A mottled statue of a giant blue whale marked the museum's entrance, standing out against the autumnal blaze of the cherry and gingko trees that lined the park. The whale was suspended mid face-plant, kissing the cement walkway. The incongruity of it lifted my spirits. Dad would have appreciated the strangeness of his giant egg sharing a home with this majestic mammal. I had arranged to meet my entourage – Tad's colleague from Kroll's Tokyo office, Naoto, and my translator, Junko – outside so we could get acquainted and game-plan for any last-minute disruptions. It felt odd to be sharing this moment with strangers but I needed their help.

The museum was closed to the public on Mondays, so we would be the only people among its 25,000 artefacts and specimens. Ritsuro Miyawaki, the head gemologist, was waiting for us at a side entrance, a middle-aged man with greying hair and small, round spectacles. He was polite and friendly and made no mention of his previous suspicion that I was actually an international jewel thief. Instead, his earnest face creased into a smile. Mr and Mrs Mabuchi wanted to meet me, he said, and would be joining us shortly. I smiled back, fizzing with relief. Finally, I would have answers.

Our journey through a maze of deserted corridors took us past an exhibition on outer space, a fallen meteorite, a Second World War fighter plane and several life-size dinosaur skeletons. As we neared our destination, I got a shock. The petrified faces of a startling number of stuffed animals peered out from a vast glass cabinet, looking as if they might leap into life at any moment. Prowling tigers, majestic deer, antelopes with spiral horns, a pouncing cheetah and a polar bear with its fangs bared. Startled, I took an involuntary step backwards, hoping I hadn't caused offence to Mr Miyawaki, who was pointing proudly in the direction of the taxidermy herd.

Then we were off again, into a side room with a blue and grey checked carpet. A giant projector screen hung on the wall and a few metal chairs were strewn about. The space felt clinical and cold, like a doctor's waiting room, a far cry from the glamorous settings Dad's creation was previously thought worthy of, although this room was deemed the most secure space in the museum, partly due to its lack of windows. For a second, I considered turning and running away – fear and anticipation twisting in my stomach. Then I saw it.

Lit up inside its glass display cabinet, it resembled a golden spaceship about to launch. Suddenly, I felt like I was back in the V&A thirty-three years ago, when my burning desire to touch it got me in such trouble. Another memory flickered in my mind: Dad on *Wogan*, proudly demonstrating his creation and talking about his hopes of making future masterpieces. Not knowing that there would only ever be one Kutchinsky's egg.

Standing in front of it, I saw a reflection of my face warped and distended by the egg's golden curve. Kutchinsky's egg had become as much part of my identity as it was Dad's. A few weeks ago at a party, I heard a friend calling to her boyfriend across the dancefloor: 'Look Simon, I found the golden egg!' and had realised they meant me. Lost in thought, I almost didn't notice the Mabuchis arriving. Radiating grace and generosity, they swept into the room, shook my hand and put me instantly at ease. Reiko looked chic in a white dress with a string of large pearls, matching earrings and bright red lipstick. Her husband, Takashi, was also fashionably attired in an electric blue blazer, with a striped Mao shirt and grey trousers. They looked to be about the same age as my mother.

Advancing awkwardly towards the egg, I felt everyone's eyes on me. Mr Miyawaki darted ahead and started polishing it with his handkerchief like a proud parent. As he stepped back, he pressed the switch to power on the motor. I felt my heart racing. What if the mechanism failed in front of all these people?

As if by magic, the doors slid open and the interior rotated like a giant music box. It was faultless. I felt the ice in my heart melt. Folding my head and shoulders into the tardis-like cabinet, I marvelled at its celestial gleam, the perfect Barbie pink of its precious stones and the magnificence of the jewelled petals that carpeted its dome. Beneath this sparkling sprawl was our name, carved on its shell for posterity. As I ran my fingers over each letter, I thought of all the hands that had helped shape it, and all the different roles it had played over the years.

An object of excess. A totem of ambition and passion. A vanity project that spiralled out of control. The embodiment of Dad's flawed ego. A jagged line marking the end of my childhood.

For years, Kutchinsky's egg had been locked away, almost as if it had never existed. On the surface, its vanishing act brought peace, but beneath it my family's wounds had continued to fester. Unable to face being hurt again, Mum had poured all her affection into us three girls and refused to even talk about the egg for many years. 'I loved Paul and that was enough,' she would say. When I started looking for it, I had to battle through my family's opposition. There were bitter rows and screaming matches. I understood it was painful for them but I was determined that confronting the past would restore the egg as a source of pride, rubbing away the tarnish that had stained our memories.

Now, as I watched the mechanism working just as Dad always dreamed, I felt a rush of vindication.

'It's fixed,' I sputtered. Takashi Mabuchi grinned widely and thrust a small, barrel-shaped motor into my hand. Talking rapidly in Japanese, he explained that shortly after his father bought the egg, the doors again refused to open. So, Takashi, who was an expert engineer, took a big risk.

'My family had paid 800 million yen for it. If I destroyed it, it was my responsibility,' he said. 'That's why I had the guts to do it. I wouldn't have dared if it had belonged to someone else.'

Piece by piece, he had taken it apart. Sweeping his fingers across the shell, he had scrutinised every joint, searching for the central screw holding it together. As his fingers encircled the large 5-carat diamond on its summit, he'd gently twisted the stone's metal casing to see if his hunch was right and held his breath. There beneath it, sat a big brass screw. Bingo.

Replacing the motor had been easy. He'd bought a new one from a local electronics store for just 9,500 yen (about £50 in 2002). But as he placed it inside, he noticed a bigger problem. The doors were designed to rise up and slide back, meaning the top of the egg had to lift to make space, placing extra strain on the motor. Grabbing a blow torch, Takashi had soldered the egg's golden hinges and restructured it so that the doors opened in a single motion. 'The way it was designed, with the top and the bottom moving together was extremely advanced,' he explained, politely glossing over the fact that it never worked.

Smiling back at this beaming billionaire, I felt my anxieties slip away. The egg belonged here. The fact that those who bought it were among the few people in the world who possessed the skills and expertise to fix it, was a perfect coincidence.

'Have you heard of *goen*?' Reiko Mabuchi asked. I shook my head. It is a Japanese theory of karmic-like connection, she explained, where people are brought together to help each other, and sometimes, objects play a pivotal role in these connections. It's possible there is *'goen'* between us, she said warmly.

We talked for over an hour, sharing our stories, and took photographs with our arms around each other and the egg in the middle. I remember smiling so much my face ached. When the museum staff started to show signs of wanting to kick us out, the Mabuchis invited me to join them for drinks at the new Bulgari Hotel, a location with a suitable heritage. Part of the Italian jewellery house's portfolio, it sits atop a 45-storey sleek, modern skyscraper in a bustling business district. The lift doors opened and we filed out into an elegant rooftop bar with a large terrace offering cloud-brushing views across the city to Mount Fuji. Inside, the interiors fused the best of Italian and Japanese design, with sweeps of black granite, green-veined white marble and artful flower arrangements. It was in an entirely different league to my budget hotel in Shibuya, where the reception was festooned with plastic Halloween pumpkins, lopsided bats and ghosts on sticks.

This was the world of wealth and wonder that Dad had inhabited but always as the seller, never the buyer. Never quite one of them. He had hoped that creating a modern masterpiece would earn him the right to belong, but his desire to move from maker to maestro had proved his undoing.

The Mabuchis ordered champagne and a selection of Italian-inspired food. Making my excuses, I wandered out onto the terrace, fringed by potted lemon trees, to watch the sunset and be alone with my thoughts. The sun was also setting on my quest. In a few days, I would board a flight and leave Dad's legacy behind. The staff at the museum had made me promise to stay in touch, asking for my help in securing a guest spot for the egg at a British institution.

If this was the final scene of a movie, I would have made a few phone calls and, hey presto, the egg would be back where it started – on show at the Victoria and Albert Museum. Letting my imagination wander, I pictured the scene: Alex and I walking through the museum with our boys, who were fizzing with excitement, just as my sister and I did more then three decades before. As we enter the room, Mum and my sisters are there. Smartly dressed and smiling. Hesitantly pleased to see the egg once more.

But this was real life. They were all thousands of miles away and I hadn't even spoken to Mum since I landed. My own emotions were so on edge, talking to her risked creating further upset but I hoped she understood the reasons for my quest.

As the sun sunk behind Mount Fuji's gnarled silhouette, I felt a stab of sadness. Growing up, I'd often wished that Dad had never made the egg and that our lives could go back to how they were before. But I see now that would have been impossible. With or without the egg, the House of Kutchinsky's foundations were already shaky and my parents were pulling in different directions. In some ways the egg became a shimmering scapegoat for my family's misfortunes. But it is true that Dad never got over losing such a high-stakes gamble. He was at a particularly low ebb when he died, desperate to escape the image of himself as a failure. But it's given me peace to know that, despite everything, he still felt proud to be the egg's creator. That the creative achievement mattered most to him.

As the sky darkened, the Mabuchis bid me a polite farewell. Their white, chauffeur-driven car was waiting for them at the hotel entrance, ready to whisk them back to their mansion. For them, this was just another interlude in their gilded lives, whereas for me the fantasy ended here. Grateful for their time and generosity, I hugged them both, evoking a look of amused horror on Mr Mabuchi's face. Hugging is not common practice in Japan, especially among older generations, my translator explained. Luckily, they took it in good spirits. As their car sped away, I could hear the echo of their laughter.

Later that night, I found myself in Black Rose, a dimly lit BDSM-theme bar, nestled in Tokyo's backstreets. Hidden behind an unmarked black door, it was a hedonistic haven with crimson lighting, velvet-clad walls and the heady smell of incense wafting in the air. Bottles of expensive spirits lined the polished dark wood bar, behind which lurked a stage and several forbidding metal cages. This was a space where reality was briefly suspended.

Stepping inside, I took in the scene with hesitant curiosity – the seedy glamour was a jarring contrast to the polished restraint of the Bulgari Hotel. Before I met Alex, I'd dipped a toe into the BDSM world of pleasure and pain, and its charged theatrics still held a certain allure. Now, untethered from my search and far from home, I found myself craving a night of freedom and forgetfulness.

Beautiful, leather-clad women wearing corsets, ripped tights and stiletto heels stood behind the bar, pouring drinks and tossing their hair. At regular intervals, they leapt up onto the stage and gyrated, cracking leather whips above their head, their eyes glazed and expressions blank. It felt more sad than sexy, but the women assured me it was a slow night.

Settling into one of the high-backed leather chairs at the bar, I watched with voyeuristic curiosity as a dancer dripped hot wax onto the arm of an eager tourist. Was the pleasure of success worth the pain my egg hunt had caused others? I wondered.

Realising I couldn't put it off any longer, I sent a video of myself with the egg to the family WhatsApp group – then held my breath. How would they react? Envy? Anger? Indifference?

When a message from Mum came through almost instantly, it caught me off guard.

'I'm happy for you and glad the egg has found a good home.'

'OMG, wow. This is iconic,' Katrina chimed in.

'It's weird to see it. Well done,' Hollie added, her tone wistful. She was only three when it was displayed at the V&A and has no memory of it.

'Mission accomplished,' I typed back, wiping away a stray tear as discreetly as I could – just as a whip cracked in the distance and murmured voices swelled around me in low, reverent tones. Here, in this strange twilight world, there was no room for shame or regret.

I'd travelled thousands of miles to witness the fulfilment of Dad's dream: his masterpiece working perfectly in a museum, with plans for a permanent display. For so long it had seemed an impossible task, lingering in the background while I ticked off other life goals. But sitting in that bar in Tokyo, I finally understood why my father risked everything to make his giant gold egg, and the similarities between us that had brought me here.

Sipping my cocktail, I texted Alex: 'You were right.'

I'd called him that morning on my way to the museum, catching him in that hazy space between sleep and waking. 'Why am I doing this?' I'd wailed, gripped by a last-minute panic. Why couldn't I just leave it alone – be content with life as it was and let Kutchinsky's egg fade into the past?

Grumpy at being jolted awake, he didn't mince words.

'Serena, you're doing this because, like your father, you want the spotlight. You want to be on stage telling the egg's story. Your dad loved being on *Wogan*, loved seeing his name in the papers. He wanted to be a celebrity jeweller. That's why he made the world's biggest jewelled egg. And that same stubborn ambition – it's hardwired into you. You'll always shoot for the moon, whatever the cost. Now, can I go back to sleep?'

I'd brushed it off at the time, but now I could see the truth in what he said. He knows me better than anyone – my strengths, my weaknesses, my fatal flaw. He loves me fully, just as Mum once loved Dad.

In writing this book, I haven't tried to imitate my father's choices but to unpick them. Maybe I've stepped into the light he once occupied, but only to shine it backwards – to illuminate the shadows of a glittering past.

The House of Kutchinsky is gone. Paul Kutchinsky is gone. Many of the figures in this story have already turned to dust.

CITY OF GHOSTS

But the egg endures – a singular object that carries within it a profoundly human story.

The egg has moved on now, into a new chapter that no longer belongs to me and my family. And for the first time, we're free to begin one of our own – life, after the egg.

Notes

Chapter 2

1. G. Alroey, 'Out of the Shtetl: In the footsteps of Eastern European Jewish migrants to America, 1900–1914', *Leidschrift* 22 (2007), pp. 91–122.
2. N. Evans and A. Newman, 'Introduction: Jewish Migration to South Africa – The Records of the Poor Jews' Temporary Shelter, 1885–1914', in *Jewish Migration to South Africa*, ed. A. Newman, N. Evans, J. G. Smith and S. W. Issroff (Cape Town: Jewish Publications–South Africa, 2006), pp. 1–11.

Chapter 4

1. Stephen Dorril, *Blackshirt: Sir Oswald Mosley and British Fascism* (London: Viking, 2006), p. 455.

Chapter 6

1. Old Lawrentian Community. 'Old Lawrentians across the decades.' St Lawrence College. https://www.slcuk.com/alumni/ol-community/

Chapter 8

1. https://www.abc.net.au/news/2022-08-01/argyle-diamond-mine-legacy-barramundi-dreaming-sacred-site/101178684

Chapter 9

1. While she did work in Johnston's nightclubs, there is no suggestion that she featured in his glamour photography.

KUTCHINSKY'S EGG

2. In 1989, Argyle was an open pit mine, which is basically a large hole in the ground where workers dig to extract diamonds from deep within the Earth's crust. More important even than the A$430 million cost (£217 million in 1983), was the fact that it sat on a sacred Aboriginal site. Before the alluvial mine began in 1983, there were heated negotiations between Argyle and the land's traditional owners, which resulted in an agreement known as the Good Neighbour Agreement and the Good Neighbour Program in which there was a capital works element for work carried out in the first year and continuing grants for similar work in the future. By the 1990s it was becoming clear that the Good Neighbour Agreement and Program were not adequate to meet the aspirations of the local communities and this was resolved through more contemporary practices in agreement making, which resulted in 2005 in the signing of the Indigenous Land Use Agreement and the Argyle Participation Agreement.

Acknowledgements

I would like to thank my husband, Alex Allen, for his unwavering love and support. Without his faith in me, I would never have found the courage to write this book. To my sons, Caspian and Finlo, who will grow up knowing the story of Grandpa Paul and his golden egg – may it remind you always of where you come from and of the ties that bind our family together.

To my mother, Brenda, whose trust in sharing her secrets helped me uncover the truth of who my father was – and, in turn, who I am.

To my sisters, Katrina and Hollie – thank you for allowing me to tell our story.

To my agent, Toby Mundy, whose belief in me never wavered and whose conviction that the egg could be found kept me searching.

To my researcher, Laura Berry, for her skill and diligence in helping illuminate even the darkest corners of my family's past.

To my dear friends, who endured a decade of talk about 'the book' with grace and good humour and who carried me through the writing of it with laughter, love and endless patience.

To Fran, who is no longer with us, but whose words of faith and kindness remain a guiding light.

To my writing group, for your generosity, wisdom and encouragement.

And to my father – thank you for leaving me such an extraordinary story. Like you, it is truly unique.